THE OCCULT

The realm of the unknown has exercised an eternal fascination and challenge for mankind. Traditional science has sought to fathom the mysteries of the universe one way. A far different path has been chosen by the practitioners of the occult.

This book describes occultism in every aspect: wizards and philosophers whose names even today cast a powerful spell, the great alchemists and their search for the Philosopher's Stone, the signs and symbols of the Kabala, consultation of the stars, the occultism of the Far East. The author reveals all the strange paths of occultism, showing how they converge into a master pattern of search and discovery. Here, indeed, as in no other book, are the secrets of the hidden world.

ABOUT THE AUTHOR: JULIEN TONDRIAU, who died in a tragic accident on Mont Blanc in 1966, was a doctor of philosophy and letters, with degrees in philology and Oriental history. His many-faceted life included posts with the French government and the United Nations and explorations in many parts of the world, along with extensive writings in the fields of Orientalism and the occult.

The Occult

Secrets of the hidden world

A PYRAMID SPECIAL

Julien Tondriau

DOCTOR OF LETTERS

LICENTIATE IN ORIENTALISM

PREFACE

To write a systematic work on such a subject as occultism is admittedly something of an undertaking. For one thing, the term 'occultism'—or, more pretentiously, 'occult sciences'—is usually fairly loosely applied, to mean anything from the conjuror's hat-trick to the dark ceremonies of the witches' sabbat. So that one must at the outset cull through a confusion of quite diverse studies and practices all associated in popular tradition with occultism.

Occult belief comprises traditions both of immense antiquity and great complexity in which it is nearly impossible to find any degree of uniformity and consistency, and the followers of occultism are themselves notoriously given to mystification so that their own accounts of any subject are full of strange pseudo-scientific jargon and merely add to the confusion.

What, then, is occultism?

In spite of all the difficulties the authors have here tried to bring some order out of the prevailing chaos.

Their study begins with a history of occultism, dealing firstly with its more traditional forms; secondly, with rituals and beliefs derived from these. The third section treats paranormal powers like telepathy and telekinesis. But as an invaluable reference the student of occultism will undoubtedly find the two alphabetical sections most useful: the first (Great Figures of Occultism) providing biographies of people prominent in the history of occultism, and the Dictionary itself giving detailed definitions of a multitude of terms, and forming a comprehensive and fascinating guide to all aspects of this strange and secret world.

The Editor

TABLE OF CONTENTS

INTRODUCTION

Whatever is mysterious, strange or apparently inexplicable has fascinated man since the beginning of time.

Primitive Man, observing with awe the movement of the sun and moon, the changing seasons, and the cycle of human life, wondered what hidden power governed the universe and his own destiny. So the study of all that is dark and mysterious, occultism was born thousands of years ago. Not only is it interesting because of the mystery that surrounds it. As well, much can be learned from its history, beliefs and rites of the obscure regions of the human mind and personality. Yet, when we examine occultism in the light of contemporary reason, there is much that remains obscure, inexplicable, and inaccessible to science.

Some of the more aberrant fields of occultism, of course, have scarcely more than a clinical interest. In Satanism, for example, it seems that the desire for identification with elemental forces is such that the individual ultimately degrades his own human worth.

But behind all occultism there lies an ardent thirst for knowledge. It is revealed in the Cabala and in alchemy. The alchemist seeks to convert base metals into gold. The student of witchcraft searches for the secret of flight or metamorphosis. The sorcerer wishes to learn how he may recruit the powers of invisible supernatural beings.

The purpose of this book is to examine and explain these practices and beliefs, to lay bare the occult, the hidden. It is not only a scholarly and comprehensive guide, but also a completely impartial one. The author makes intelligible the unintelligible through his wide knowledge and open-minded approach; he neither affirms nor rejects anything without adequate and satisfying proof.

TRADITIONAL FORMS OF OCCULTISM

MAGIC PAST AND PRESENT

It is the dawn of time: a shaggy man, covered in the skins of wild beasts, puts the finishing touches to his representation of a bison on a wall of rock. There is a strange light in the man's eyes; he finishes his work by drawing an arrow penetrating the beast. For, obscurely, he feels that this arrow must secure the success of the hunt on which the subsistence of his tribe depends. In his act, Magic is born.

And a scene from the present day: A large fair in an important town. Before a caravan, oddly decorated with cabalistic signs, sits a surly woman. Does her gloom spring from the fact that she knows what the future holds? For she does know, as a flamboyant sign proclaims. A professional fortune-teller who lives by exploiting human anxiety and credulity, she is ready to disclose the future to anybody for a price. And if this seems a trivial example of magic—that most ancient and mysterious of arts—it serves to remind us of the universal and timeless fascination of the occult in all its forms.

The Mind of the Magician

When does mere superstition end and magic begin? What attitudes of mind does occultism foster? Do its devotees see life differently from ordinary people? Why do such people turn to occult practices?

The answer to these questions will help us come to grips with the spirit of magic, and to understand its history.

Broadly, the search for the occult is the search for power; it is a rejection of the normally accepted limitations of human life, of the laws of man and of nature. The magician is confident that he can circumvent the natural order and impose his will upon it; he believes in the infallibility of his magic formulae and his complex rites; he thinks he can mysteriously influence events, bringing good to his friends and harm to his enemies.

If his magic takes account of good, and works for virtue, it is termed 'white'; it is black magic if it sides with the devil and solicits his help.

Clearly, the variety of occult beliefs and practices will be limited only by the imagination of their authors; in fact, a surprising unity of conception and similarity of procedure is observable in all manifestations of occultism no matter how far they are separated by time or place. One is tempted to postulate a single body of knowledge passed from one people to another through the ages and across continents; but this would be to over-simplify the case. It is important to examine each phenomenon in both time and context.

Primitive Magic

It is probable, and the examination of rock paintings and prehistoric objects reinforces this hypothesis, that prehistoric man set great store on magic. Threatened on all sides, in his fight for survival he sought material and supernatural protection. Was it his magic or his watchfulness and agility which assured his success in hunting? To the superstitious mind, magic must be all-powerful: if the magical act is ineffective, it is because the formulae have been badly pronounced, the rites badly executed, or hostile counter-magic has intervened. The man of knowledge thus triumphs over the man who is merely strong, and true power is in the hands of the Grand Sorcerer.

Broadly, we may assume that the same comments apply to primitive peoples today. Their magic also aims at particular objects and acknowledges specific forces; diffused forces (for example, *mana, orenda*) or spirit-entities (*Great Manitou*), both personal and impersonal, which the magician will subdue and use.

For example, here is the ritual invocation of a sorcerer of Gabon:

> Oh! you, who commands with strength, you the Spirit of virile energy,
> You can do all, and without you I can do nothing, I can do nothing,
> I who am consecrated to you, I who am sworn to you, O Spirit,

From you I get my strength, my power, You have given
  me the gift.
Spirit of strength, it is to you I call!
You must obey, I have given you what you ask, O Spirit;
The sacrifice was offered, sacrifice offered in the forest;
Spirit, I am yours, you are mine, come!

*Hand prints on the walls of the cave of Castillo in Spain, a magic
symbol to assert man's domination over animals.*

If it is the *mana* that confers efficacy on the formulae or
the rite, if it is a dynamic impersonal energy, this is personalized
in the animal totem which watches over each tribe. The totem
itself is protected from the uninitiated by taboos or prohibitions
of all kinds, both laical and religious. Provided with this formid-
able power, the sorcerer, if he is skilful, can achieve the highest
status.

The Ancient East

The beginning of the historical era, from 3,000 B.C., was a golden age of magic in Egypt and Chaldea.

In Mesopotamia a Sumerian religion flourished, and with it came Chaldean magic, enhanced by astrology. Thus, it is difficult to separate this magic from the naturistic Sumerian religion and the semitic astral religion. Part of this network of belief is as follows:

Before the 'Seven', the traditional group of demons led by Nergal, the king of Hades, it was necessary to invoke the great gods, especially Ea and his son Marduk, along with the exalted powers Lamassu and Sheda.

But to confront these powers required a complex ceremonial and a highly specialised officiating personnel: the magician, the *ashipu* or high priest, helped by an incantor, prophets and a medicine man. The gods thus invoked competed for him. Once success was obtained, a quantity of amulets and charms saved the client from a further return of scourges.

Nothing is expressly promised: everything depends on the gods. The texts do not reveal anything of the wonders subsequently attributed to Babylonian magic (metamorphoses, resurrections, invisibility).

Two domains are privileged: medicine (illness is a demon which magic drives from the body of man) and astrology, which enjoyed immense prestige in the ancient world, its mystery magnified by an unintelligible vocabulary.

In Egypt, magic was just as much a part of official religious ceremonial, but had fewer exalted powers and demons. There was no specialized magician, and it was the priest who invoked and evoked at his pleasure. The border between the divine and the human was not clearly defined and there was often little difference between evocation and threat. Since the Name was everything, it was also a means of pressure. If the gods wanted a cult, they assisted their faithful.

The Pharaoh was 'the master of magic charms' and he had his magician-priests (we recall the episode of their struggle against Moses and the serpent). The temple builders themselves were not averse to trickery.

But Babylonian prestige was to collapse; Egyptian magic was

to be democratized. The Hebrews were to inherit and to exploit it.

However, the Jewish religion, a unique exception in antiquity, did not accept magic. To cite Exodus 22:18, 'Thou shalt not suffer a witch to live', or Leviticus 19:31, the Bible condemns magical practices, considering them pernicious. Some traces of magic, however, appear in primitive Judaism: the bronze serpent fetish against bites; the sacred *'urim'* and *'tummim'*, used for the divination of God, in the breastplate of the Ephod-oracle; the rite of the scapegoat charged with all the sins of Israel; the predictions of prophets based on the trajectory of arrows; the magical capture of Ai in the Book of Joshua; Saul consulting the prophetess of Endor on the invasion of the Philistines, and Manasseh establishing necromancers.

The famed Cabala was particularly important. It presented God engendering the universe by the Word, and was to develop a prodigious magic in the Middle Ages.

(1) *See* page 52, the Cabala and the Golem.

Greece and Rome

In the classical world, the religion of the Pantheon was contaminated by magic. The mysteries themselves were, for most of the Greeks, acts of magic. For example, there were those of Eleusis, strictly forbidden to the uninitiated, or those of Orphism. The people considered Orpheus a Thracian sorcerer, founder of the cult of the Triple Hecate, guardian saint of the sorcerers. Thessaly was the favorite land of the magicians.

Foreign influences were added to the magic of the primitive natives. These were rich in sorcerers (Telchines, Corybantes, Couretes), and in enchantresses (Circe in the *Odyssey*, Medea in *The Conquest of the Golden Fleece*), so that Greece was Orientalized as much as it Hellenized the Orient.

However, a new and important element occurred in the classical age: the spirit of enlightenment. The Phoebus Apollo sparked off the critical Greek mind. Long before Descartes, Greece established methodical questioning, leading to scepticism. Since the magical ceremonies described by Homer to the Witches of Theocritus or the performances of Apollonius of Tyana, the path worn by magic is long, interspersed with brilliant success (Pythagorism, great oracles) but also with virulent attacks, notably on the part of philosophers.

In Rome the situation was different. The Roman believed in the existence of diverse forces, the *numina*. His realism pushed him further away from magic, and from 451 B.C. the law of the Twelve Tables, the first compilation of Roman law, forbade magic formulas and charms. However, the great historical upheavals and the Greek and Oriental influences increased sorcery and divination. Cybele, Bellona, Sabazios and Anahita were brought from Asia Minor; Sarapis from Egypt; Dea Syria, Baal, and Chaldean eschatology from Syria; Zoroastrianism, Mithraism, the Egyptian and the Asiatic Bacchus from Persia. *The Golden Ass of Apuleius* and many writings of Lucian have become famous in describing these, despite the attitude of the authorities.

Christianity

There was to be a long struggle between Christianity and magic after an early compromise. The third and fourth centuries abounded in the supernatural. The neo-Platonists proposed to distinguish theurgy (or white magic) from goety (or satanic magic). Oriental demonology spread. Soon the struggle became inflexible: paganism and magic were confused or united. Driven out, magic sought refuge with the Jews and Arabs and survived only under cover.

Middle Ages and the Renaissance

Arabian literature on magic, not shackled by the Koran, developed strongly. It also distinguished white magic (that of angels) from satanic magic (that of *djinns* or *genies*). It penetrated the West through Spain—where Toledo, reconquered in 1085, was its principal center—and through the Crusades. Endowed with a remarkable occult literature, even in the Apocrypha, crowned by the success of their Cabala, the Jews were soon to be considered great masters in magic.

In the West, the Church, with some trouble, tried to replace the magic arsenal with blessed objects and minor concessions. But it vigorously fought the occultists who, in return, parodied its rites and invoked the devil. The result was a great wave of sorcery, of witch's sabbats, manifestations of the devil, pacts, sacrileges, pyres and collective madness. This was followed by a tragic repression, these events prevailing from the 13th to the 18th century.

Far thinking people became deeply interested in 'natural magic', a purified occultism. Michael Scot, Arnaud de Villeneuve, Roger Bacon, Albert the Great (master of St. Thomas Aquinas, who has been falsely credited with two treatises on magic dating in fact from the 18th century) studied astrology and alchemy in the 13th century. In the 16th century, they were succeeded by minds equally questioning but clearly more disquieting: Abbot Tritheim de Wurtzburg, Cornelius Agrippa de Nettesheim, Dr. Johann Faust (made famous by Goethe), and Aureolus Theophrastus Bombastus Paracelsus, who is considered by some as the forerunner of medicine and 'animal magnetism'.

Modern Times

Sorcerers were condemned to death up until the 17th century. Capital punishment for sorcery, for instance, was only abolished in France in 1731.

In the 18th century, rationalism seemed to sweep out occultism but this was only an illusion. Montesquieu's and Voltaire's ironical attitude was in vain. The supernatural was too deeply anchored in the human mind. Freemasonry secretly restored magical rites. In France, for example, the book Le Grand Albert became very popular, Paris abounded in secret societies, and magic became commonplace in the homes of French noblemen such as the Duke of Chartres.

Frederic Antoine Mesmer cured by the magnetism in his 'healing tub'; the truculent Joseph Balsamo, better known as Count Cagliostro, astounded and scandalized Europe; the Count of St. Germain, 'the man who could not die', amazed Europe, only to disappear mysteriously; Emmanuel Swedenborg invented Spiritualism, which was taken up by the Rose-Cross Martins of Pasqually; Claude de Saint Martin, the 'unknown philosopher' of Lyon, created Martinism.

Threatened by progress and always condemned by the Church, magic continued to exist. Its disciples tried to regild its heraldry as it entered its 'scientific phase'. Spiritualism, taken up again in 1847 by the Fox family in the United States, had an over-whelming success; Allan Kardec codified it in France. Hypnotism was studied by Charcot, and later by Freud, at the Salpetriere clinic.

Later came the 'metaphysical' vogue with the mediums (reduced in value following infra-red and photography and Robert Amadou's book *The Great Mediums*), the fakirs, the clairvoyants who collect millions every year, the 'infallible' telepathics, and all the manifestations of sensational magic.

Who wrote that occultism and magic are dead? They will endure as long as man has a taste for the supernatural, or a naive credulity.

Magic and the Paranormal

Where do we find the border between magic and the para-normal? The problem has been written about a great deal, and reasonable hypotheses have been advanced.

We will briefly consider some of these positions. The 'intellec-tualist' thesis states that science and its lesser sister, magic, result from the disinterested desire which tests man's knowledge and understanding. It judges primitive societies according to our own, but is this not to attribute to primitives desires that they do not have?

More realistically, the biological or pragmatist thesis believes that it was to satisfy his own immediate needs that primitive man discovered and utilized magic, then science. The human intelligence is at first directed to action, not to speculation.

For the sociological school, religion engendered magic, then science. Count Augustus took up this evolutionary view through the 'law of the three states'. First of all, behind the natural phenomena, man had pictured a will analogous to his own, and had rendered homage to this force through religion. Then, hoping to influence it, he conceived formulas and rituals. Magic no longer implored but instead commanded. Lastly came science which, through knowledge of the laws of nature, disproved the foundations on which magic was based.

This last hypothesis is perhaps valid, although it can be opposed by others just as plausible. For example, that of the English ethnologist, Sir James Frazer, who in his twelve volumes

The mandragora, a magical plant used from antiquity in the preparation of love potions.

of *The Golden Bough* asserts that religion comes from magic rather than precedes it. Out of primitive fear a methodical piety emerged. Another theory is that of Bergson, who in *Les deux sources de la morale et de la religion* declares that religion, science and magic are not derived one from the other, but have always co-existed as forms, superior and inferior, of a like tendency of the human mind. He adds that magic was the biggest obstacle to the development of true science.

It would be pointless in the framework of this book to resume the argument, since the frontiers of religion, magic and science are always changing, depending on the age, the country and the regime. All that can be said is that the great periods of faith have seen a joint expansion of authentic religious belief and of streams of magic. Is it surprising that the human mind still contains irrational elements?

Above all, in each difficult moment in his history, man has revived what was previously rejected. For, when man's future is uncertain or threatening, the human mind seeks its light where and how it can.

FROM SHAMANISM TO SORCERY

The Great Primitive Sorcerer

Since the beginning of the century, ethnology has given the names shaman, medicine man, sorcerer, even magician to those endowed with magico-religious powers, based on *ecstasy*, which confer on them an essential role in so-called primitive societies.

There is Siberian, Indonesian, Oceanic, North and South American shamanism. In spite of this geographical diversity, their characteristics are so constant that they were able to be integrated in the study of certain religions of evolved peoples. The existence of Chinese, Indian, Iranian and Germanic shamanism indicates the assembly of primitive and magical elements existing in the folklore and religions of these peoples.

We could perhaps say that, strictly speaking, shamanism is above all a phenomenon of Central Asia, and that it may be defined as a 'technique of ecstasy', endowed with miraculous powers.

This technique of ecstasy implies trance, but not possession. If the shaman in his ecstasy communicates with the spirits of nature or with the dead, it is to impose on them his views and to utilize them, not to become through possession, their docile instrument.

This is obviously not within reach of all. The shaman is a chosen one. He is not only a magician, but also a mystic, priest and poet, responsible for the souls and the religious life of the community. His vocation arises in different ways: by heredity in the female line with the Voguls; by masculine heredity and recognition of the Spirits among the Ostyaks and the Siberian Samoyeds; or, elsewhere, by revelation in a dream from a deceased shaman or by gift from the gods.

Like our mediums, the shaman is often affected by morbid states which Ohlmarks qualified as 'Arctic hysteria'. However, the shaman is always master of his trance, so that he is not to be confused with the epileptic.

Powers of the Shaman

The experience of the shaman is rich in ecstasies, illnesses and dreams, either from Heaven or provoked. Chosen, and having undergone his initiation-illness (suffering, symbolic death and resurrection), the shaman becomes the great master of the ecstatic trance. This ecstasy enables him (1) to discern the souls of mortals, to follow them when leaving their bodies (sleep or death) and to restore them eventually to this body; (2) to descend to Hades to redeem the broken or ailing souls and to rescue them from the demons; and (3) to go up to Heaven and converse with the gods. Briefly, it frees him from the conditions of space and time. It accords him amazing powers: levitation, flying in the air, invisibility, mastery of fire, etc. Healer and conductor of souls, the shaman tames the elements, understands the secret language of the gods and the demons, takes on animal forms at will, renders himself invisible at his inclination, is master of heat and, producing for himself a 'magical sedation', ignores cold and braves injury. As a healer, he practises in this world and in the other.

A first stage of shamanistic healing consists of a 'call to the soul'. With the Bouriates from the region of Ala; for example, the shaman sits on a rug near the patient, surrounded by several objects, among which is an arrow: from its point a thread of red silk leads to a birch-tree erected outside in the yard. It is through this thread that the soul of the patient is thought to return to its body; for this reason, the door is always kept open.

If the patient's soul refuses to come back, the shaman proceeds with his quest and finishes by descending to the Realm of the Dead to bring it back (on this subject see *Shamanism*, by Mercia Eliade).

The Tibetan Buddhists also set about counselling the deceased in the beyond. Here is a text of instructions to the dead, an extract from the Tibetan *Book of the Dead (Bardo Thodol)*:

The bodies of the largest of the Peaceful and the Wrathful deities are equal (in vastness) to the limits of the heavens; the intermediate, as big as Mt. Meru; the smallest, equal to eighteen bodies such as thine own body, set one upon the other, will come to refill the systems of the world. They will come, biting their lower lips, their eyes glazed, their hair knotted at the top of their head, large bellies, narrow of stature, holding a plank of inscriptions, crying 'kill', licking a human skull, drinking blood, snatching heads from their bodies, snatching hearts. Thus will they come, refilling the world.

O, noble born, when such things are manifested, be not terrified, be not awed; the body you now possess being a mental body, were it to be struck, cut into pieces, it could not die. Because your body is in reality of the nature of the void, thou must not be afraid. The bodies of the deities are also emanations, radiations of thine intellect; they are not constituted of matter; the void cannot hurt the void. Beyond the emanations of thine own intellectual faculties, the Peaceful, the Angry, the Drinkers of blood, those with different heads, the radiance of the rainbow, the terrifying forms do not really exist. There is no doubt of this. Bearing this in mind, all fear and terror are dispelled.

It is impossible to verify scientifically or even to estimate the results which the shamans attained in primitive societies.

At best, we can imagine that they inspired originally certain techniques of yoga—those which allow such mastery of oneself, physically and mentally, that the results can appear, as it were, 'magical'.

In addition, shamanism has been at the source of some famed feats of Arab and Hindu fakirism: the famous Hindu cord or 'rope-trick', the ladder of sabers, the Tibetan suspension (throat on a saber), rigidity on blades, the mango trick or the miraculous growth of a mango-tree seed, etc. The fakirs testify to the decline of modern shamans. One still thinks of their fabulous powers, but one is no longer afforded a demonstration.

Western Sorcery

We admit that besides the amazing powers attributed to the shaman, those of our Western sorcerer appear very ordinary.

In fact, sorcery cannot even, like magic, lay claim to the

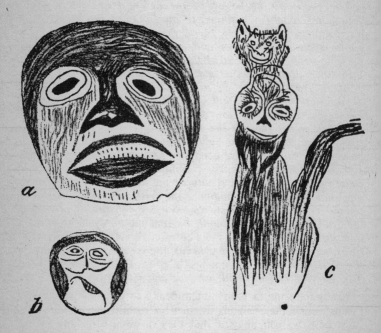

a and *b*: Siberian spirits with the power to provoke epilepsy; *c*: Spirit
transformed by a Shaman's gaze.

name of science. It is only the lesser, corrupted sister of magic, as fakirism is the aberrant brother of yoga. What is worse, it was for centuries a scourge.

The magician wants to be master, commanding the forces of evil. The sorcerer remains an apprentice. He cannot master the forces which he lets loose.

Besides which, where the magician prefers the town to cultivate a new heresy, the sorcerer lives in the village and has to perpetuate only a pagan or Druidic cult that he has adopted for better or for worse. Limited and ignorant, the sorcerer, as Jean Palou noted, is a child of misery, and is more often persecuted than effective.

Sorcery seems to have two sources. Firstly, it was a masked revolt against religion. Paganism at the point of decline is perpetuated in sorcery, free to take the place of Pan, Dionysus, Bacchus, the satyrs and the fauns, by the devil and his imps. Raillery and parody are often the unique vengeance of the weak or the vanquished. To parody Christianity therefore constitutes the revenge of the dethroned pagan gods. The parody is usually mediocre because the performers are mediocre.

A second source appears to be the wish to caricature the social order.

Briefly, then, sorcery is a feeble revolt against the spiritual and the temporal.

Brief History of Sorcery

Sorcery is typically feminine, and there are many more sorceresses than sorcerers. This has always been the case. The most faithful of the primitive cult of Dionysus were women, the nocturnal dancing Bacchantes covered in the skin of cows. On the other hand, magic-science numbers only men as its performers.

In 589 A.D. the term sorcerer appeared for the first time. Soon the sorcerers and sorceresses displayed their profound characteristics: paganism in its earliest stage, ignorance, devil worship, and hostility to established order. Each time a scourge descended on society, sorcery spread. It has often been falsely presumed that the Middle Ages was the privileged age of sorcery. In reality, however, sorcery was relatively rare in Europe until the 13th century.

In the 5th century the French invaders repressed sorcery by the Salic Law. The Code of the Visigoths, in Spain, punished by whipping and slavery 'the malevolent and the agitators, along with those who invoked the demons and troubled the spirits of men'. The Church (Councils of Tours in 567 and of Berghampstead in 697) likened paganism to sorcery, but punished in moderation.

The Merovingian period, fertile in supernatural prodigies which were inflated by the annalists, did not show the intolerance of the Carolingians towards sorcery. However, the capitularies of Charlemagne reduced sorcerers to a level whereby they were regarded as village idiots.

The Church, on the other hand, did not underestimate their influence and in 829 the Council of Paris called on the help of Louis the Debonair to punish sorcerers.

The real repression came only with the Inquisition which was established in 1220. It is important to note that although it defined magic and sorcery, the Inquisition reserved punishment only for heretics; in other words, a sorcerer who did not worship the devil, and thus deny God, was answerable to secular justice alone. Unfortunately for the sorcerers, this distinction was not maintained for long, and the ecclesiastical and secular authorities soon agreed to fight the common enemy.

Two tragic affairs were to follow: the trials of the Templars (1325) and of Joan of Arc (1431), in which magic and sorcery were but pretexts furnished for Phillipe and the English. The horrific story of Gilles de Rais, Marshal of France, hung for devil-worship in 1440, inspired an epidemic of sorcery and the joint repression which already had prevailed against the Gazarians or Vaudois, disciples of the heretical Peter Waldo, in the Upper-Alps of France.

The Renaissance saw lawsuits, tortures, and stake-burnings multiplied. The author of the famous *Demonolatrie,* Nicolas Remy (1530-1612) served on the Lorraine tribunal, and was responsible for the execution of some three thousand sorcerers and witches. He was imitated by Henri Boguet in the Jura and De Lancre in the Basque Country. Spain, Italy, England, and especially Germany, also had their sorcery crises and anti-witchcraft drives.

The 17th century, supposedly the 'age of reason', hardly restored calm. On the contrary, together with the 16th century, it holds the record for violence and repression. The devil invaded the convents; profane sorcery was common, as the affair of Meautis in Normandy (1661-1672) and the black magic of the shepherd Hocque (1687-1691) attest.

America also had its executions, in 1645 and in 1692, with the trials of the Salem witches.

In the 18th century 'possession' continued and sorcery became a pastime for some of the nobility, but after the Revolution, people ceased to pursue sorcery. The sorcerer lost his occult prestige, and was regarded as no more than a swindler. The process continued in the 19th century, when the Church proceeded with more circumspection than had the Inquisition. The sorcerer now lost his martyr's halo, and the devil was left to manifest himself in haunted houses.

Sorcerers have not vanished completely. The practice of spells continues as, for example, in the south of Italy, where the village of Castelmezzano became sadly famous on this account, and in the modern interest in sorcery in the United States.

However, sorcerers nowadays are very rare and their powers are recognized as being feeble.

NUMEROLOGY, ASTROLOGY, GEOMANCY

If the number was invented by the human mind to express quantity precisely, it was very soon charged with an occult power, with symbolic and even metaphysical significance. It is thus that the numbers 3, 7, 9, and 13, to name only the most important, have become mysterious symbols.

Numerology has behind it a long and strange history.

Secret Value of Numbers

The 'secret value' of a number is the total sum of the figures which constitute the number. The figures are considered as elementary units and no account of their order is taken. The secret value will be lucky or unlucky according to the total obtained.

For example, 36 is divided into three large units of ten each and six small units. That is a total of nine units. Nine is therefore the secret value of 36 and nine is reputedly lucky. Several cabalists developed this method, which is rather rudimentary, to probe the future. It allowed them to establish sufficiently unforeseen relations between two numbers or between certain numbers and particular letters of the alphabet. Thus, by giving a number to each letter of the Hebrew alphabet, they obtained a series of numbers, 1 to 22, of which the total is 253. The secret value of 253 (2+5+3) is 10, which is the basis of Hebrew numeration.

This is very simple compared to the exploitation of numbers and their projection in the sky in astrology.

The Zodiac and its Twelve Signs

Gross ignorance, absurd prognostications and ridiculous advice have characterized astrology where charlatans and tricksters have exploited it for their own ends. However, the disreputable practices of these people in fleecing the credulous and gullible should not be allowed to discredit astrology, which has its many honest and sincere devotees.

Our ancestors noticed a relationship between the stars and human beings. Nobody would deny, for example, the influence of the moon on the tides, on menstruation, and on the behavior of many of the insane.

But how far, within reason, should and does this relationship go? Astrology was, and still is, based on a geocentric system (the Earth is the center of the Universe) which has been outdated since Galileo, and the ancients knew only the sun, moon, and five planets. They were ignorant of Uranus, Neptune, and Pluto, which have since been 're-adjusted' by contemporary astrology.

Seen from Earth, the celestial bodies seem to travel through the sky on a circular route which is called the Zodiac. This ideal circle, divided into twelve equal parts, gives the twelve zodiacal signs which succeed each other in precise order (see table next page) There is, however, some dispute on the exact dates—one or two days—and some annual variations are recognized.

TWELVE SIGNS OF THE ZODIAC

Natural Order	Sign of	Longitudes	Dates	Ruling Planet	Seasons	Weather	Character
ARIES	Fire	0°- 30°	21 Mar.-20 Apr.	Mars	Spring	Warm-humid	Cardinal +
TAURUS	Earth	30°- 60°	21 Apr.-20 May	Venus	Spring	Warm-humid	Fixed —
GEMINI	Air	60°- 90°	21 May-21 June	Mercury	Spring	Warm-humid	Common +
CANCER	Water	90°-120°	22 June-22 July	Moon	Summer	Warm-dry	Cardinal —
LEO	Fire	120°-150°	23 July-22 Aug.	Sun	Summer	Warm-dry	Fixed +
VIRGO	Earth	150°-180°	23 Aug.-22 Sept.	Mercury	Summer	Warm-dry	Common —
LIBRA	Air	180°-210°	23 Sept.-22 Oct.	Venus	Autumn	Cold-dry	Cardinal +
SCORPIO	Water	210°-240°	23 Oct.-21 Nov.	Mars	Autumn	Cold-dry	Fixed —
SAGITTARIUS	Fire	240°-270°	22 Nov.-20 Dec.	Jupiter	Autumn	Cold-dry	Common +
CAPRICORN	Earth	270°-300°	21 Dec.-19 Jan.	Saturn	Winter	Cold-humid	Cardinal —
AQUARIUS	Air	300°-330°	20 Jan.-18 Feb.	Uranus	Winter	Cold-humid	Fixed +
PISCES	Water	330°-360°	19 Feb.-20 Mar.	Neptune	Winter	Cold-humid	Common —

Note: The signs + and — in the final column signify 'positive' and 'negative' respectively. The words 'Typology' and 'Zodiac' in the dictionary are accompanied by detailed tables of planetary typology and zodiacal affinities.

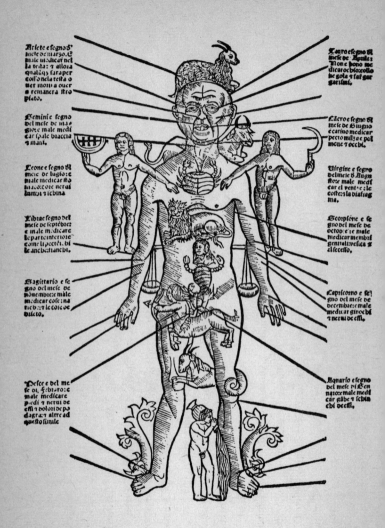

Affinities of the signs of the Zodiac with the human body.

Compass card attributed to Pius IV, and believed to give information
about future pontiffs.

The Zodiac is the celestial trail where the movement of our stars takes place at different speeds. The divisions each correspond to thirty degrees of longitude counted on the ecliptic. Some astrologers again subdivide each sign into three parts: first, second and last, each of about ten days' duration, but the effectiveness of this method is a matter of dispute.

To say of someone that he is born under this or that sign signifies that, on the day of his birth, the sun occupied a zodiacal position between the first and last degree of the sign in question. To be born under the sign of Leo, for instance, signifies that birth occurred between July 23 and August 22.

The ephemeris, or table of planetary positions, allows astrology to determine at what point of the Zodiac was or will be found the sun and other celesial bodies at a particular time on a certain date. To make his reading, the astrologer calculates from the place and hour of birth the position of the planets in relation to that place and time, and draws a chart of the sky at the moment of birth.

However, another factor comes into this. The rotation of the Earth constitutes a wheel of fortune which, in the course of its journey, brings forward successively the twelve signs of the Zodiac. The corresponding point at the place and time of birth is called the ascendant; the sign of the Zodiac which is found there is called the ascendant sign, and the sign of the month of birth is named the solar sign. The twelve signs of the Zodiac are placed in relation with the four elements (air, water, fire, earth), the four body fluids (blood, bile, black bile, phlegm), and with the character, colors, metals, minerals, plants, parts of the body, planets and human types (see table of affinities, page 255). Each is either active or passive, positive or negative, paternal or maternal. Every sign is associated with a planet, called 'ruling', with which it is in 'harmony'.

The Houses

Dividing the sky into two planes, horizon and meridian, one obtains four phases for the passage of the sun each day: at midnight, the lower meridian; in the forenoon, rising at the Eastern horizon (ascendant); at midday, upper meridian (M.C. or Médium Coeli); in the evening, setting on the Western horizon (descendant).

By dividing each quarter into three equal parts, one obtains twelve divisions or Houses, which are put on a parallel with the twelve signs of the Zodiac. They are: I, IV, VII, X or Angles,, which are very fortunate; II, V, VIII, XI or Succedants, which are rather lucky, except VIII; and III, VI, IX and XII or Cadents which are unfortunate, especially VI and XII. There is also a terrestrial Zodiac putting into affinity Aries—House I, Taurus—House II, etc.

The Meanings of the Twelve are:

House   I: The individual personality, fundamental tendencies; constitution, temperament.

        II: Acquisitions, fortunes; business.

      III: Exchanges with others, education, moves, correspondence.

     IV: Security, home, property, heirs.

      V: Leisure, children, loved ones; speculations, luck.

     VI: Work and general well-being, health; called the hospital of the Zodiac.

   VII: Complementary and adverse world; marriage, friendships, associations and hostilities; public life.

  VIII: Death and inheritance, changes; subconscious, injury.

    IX: Spiritual life and long trips; dreams.

     X: Friends, loyalty, ambition.

    XI: Compliments and patronage, hopes.

   XII: Tests and checks, repressions and illnesses, hidden enemies, the unexpected.

Planets, Aspects and Configuration

The planets move simultaneously across the signs of the Zodiac and across the Houses, increasing or diminishing their influence. Each planet, however, possesses its own tendency, which corresponds with a global function of man, and this has led to the establishment of planetary types. There is a table in the dictionary at the end of this volume which sums up this typology.

Each person is free to accept or reject the theories we have

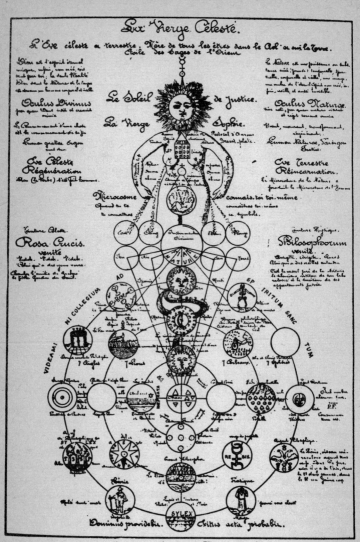

Astrological diagram of creation.

briefly summarized. In any case, it is necessary to reject the obvious absurdities, such as ready-made horoscopes, infallible means of winning a lottery, and the total influence of good and bad signs.

Main Stages of Astrology

1. The oldest Chaldean tablets tracing astrology date from Sargon I the Ancient, of Agade (about 700 B.C.).

2. Some Chinese astrological predictions, political and cyclic, reproduce those of a collection of Assurbanipal.

3. About 250 B.C., Greeks, aided by the Babylonians, made astral predictions, which until then had been collective, to each individual. The theories of Aristotle (384-322) contributed to these trends; the astronomers Eudoxus (4th century B.C.) and Carnead (2nd century B.C.) combatted them. The affinities between the stars, minerals and vegetables were probably established in the 2nd century B.C.

4. The Alexandrian, Ptolemy, who died 150 A.D., codified astrology. His *Almageste* remained for fourteen centuries the bible of astronomy, and his *Tetrabiblos* for astrology.

5. Frequented at first by slaves, the astrologers who prevailed in the Roman world were driven out in 139 B.C., but soon returned. Cato and Cicero attacked them, and Augustus, Domitian and Hadrian expelled them, but their success was unimpaired.

6. Astrology fell from favor for five centuries after the fall of Rome. Between A.D. 800 and 1100, the Arabs associated astrology with alchemy and medicine, and introduced it to the West in the 11th and 12th centuries. Alcabitius, Albumasar and Hali were the most famous authors.

7. The letters of a mysterious Jean de Toledo were published first in the Germanic countries in 1179, and predicted a cosmic catastrophe for September 1186. This caused great fear and terror, but equally vain were ten other false predictions in 1230 and 1487. Johann Stoffler falsely predicted annihilation by deluge in February, 1524.

8. Astrology reached its zenith in the 16th century, when each prince wanted his own astrologer. Come Ruggieri and

Table of Zodiacal signs drawn up by the Persain poet Omar Khayyam.

Ogier Ferrier were astrologers for Catherine de Medici, and Morin de Villefranche for Anne of Austria.

9. The *Centuries* of Michel de Notre-Dame, called Nostradamus (1503-1568) were published at Lyon in 1555.

An Italian colleague, Jerome Cardan (1501-1576), also became famous. He had the great merit of recognizing his own errors and of questioning the horoscopes after a check (death of the young Edward VI).

10. The heliocentric system and modern astronomic telescopes dealt a severe blow to astrology, but the astronomers believed in its death too soon. Laplace, for example, declared: 'The knowledge of the true system of the world has destroyed it forever'. However, because of the Rodolphine Tables, the astrologers from the 17th century were able to continue their predictions . . . without further observing the sky.

11. Today there are in the United States about twenty astrological magazines, all equally prosperous.

Despite the suspicion that astrology rightly inspires, who can boast of never having paid attention to the horoscopes 'prefabricated' in the newspapers?

It should be pointed out that the Zodiac has its place among the great universal myths. Occultists affirm that today we are at the end of an era of two thousand years, that of Pisces (which anyone easily identifies with Christianity, seen in the symbolism of the 'ichthus', or fish), and entering a new era, that of Aquarius.

Geomancy

Geomancy was often mentioned in *The Tales of the Thousand and One Nights,* which shows that the Arabs had recognized it for a long time. In Greek, *ge* means earth and *manteia* divination. Divination by the earth is practised in several ways.

The diviner throws some small stones on the ground, or else, with his finger or a stick, traces on the sand, or on the earth, a number of dots which he then counts and groups in figures. He can still, as at the present in Islam, convert these by tracing on paper a series of dots according to the following technique: when the question has been asked, the geomancer concentrates on it and lets his hand run and trace on the paper sixteen horizontal lines of dots. He then counts the dots of each line and notes the respective totals.

Each group of four lines produces a geomantic figure, the sixteen names of which are:

Acquisitio — Albus — Amissio — Caput Draconis — Cauda Draconis — Carcer — Conjunctio — Fortuna Major — Fortuna Minor — Laetitia — Populus — Puella — Puer — Rubeus — Tristitia — Via.

Following a procedure too complex to be detailed here, the geomancer divides these figures according to the following Table of Cases:

VIII Daughter	VII Daughter	VI Daughter	V Daughter	IV Mother	III Mother	II Mother	I Mother
XII NIECE		XI NIECE		X NIECE		IX NIECE	
XIV LEFT WITNESS				XIII RIGHT WITNESS			
ASSISTANT JUDGE (optional)		JUDGE					

Each Case is called a House. The value or equation which follows allows a reply to the questions asked.

    I: Concerns the questioner, the beginning of the enterprise.
   II: Benefits and gains.
  III: Family of the consultant; realizations; short journeys and writings.
  IV: Patrimony and paternal heredity.
   V: Children; joys; loves.
  VI: Misfortune; illness.
 VII: Marriage partner; associates and enemies; contracts, lawsuits.
VIII: Serious illness; death.
  IX: Spiritual, religious life; long trips.
   X: Profession; maternal heredity; long trips.

XI: Friends.
XII: Sorrow; corruption; hidden enemies.
XIII: Past and private life.
XIV: Future and social life.
XV: The entire subject; reply to the question asked.

The first twelve houses are said to be very close to those of astrology. They also carry indications of the future.

Geomancy is also used as an aid to clairvoyance.

DIVINATIONS, PROPHECIES AND GREAT ORACLES

When the Greek god Apollo slew the enormous serpent Python who had devastated the land of Delphi, he had to replace one of the talents of the monster. For the serpent, son of the Earth, had the gift of clairvoyance. Apollo therefore instituted at Delphi a priestess who, borrowing the name of the slain serpent, became Pythia, a priestess destined to play an important religious and political role in the history of Greece.

The wisest of the gods thus showed the ties between religion and divination. Certainly, the latter maintains some close connections with magic; the same person often practises them both.

However, the objectives of magic and of divination are clearly opposed.

Aiming to modify the natural laws and the course of events, thus turning toward the future, magic is essentially active.

On the other hand, divination, turned towards the past, present or future, seeks to know and foresee, but not to modify. It is contemplative, rather passive, and its attitude is religious.

From the Ancient Orient to Western Man

In the Orient divination dates back to the earliest times. If the Chinese observed the sky, they also practised diverse mancies or divinations, of which one was based on the study of the feet (podomancy), another on the examination of the scales of a tortoise.

India had neither an assembly of augurs nor organized oracles. Rich in magical arts, it utilized in divination only rather primitive techniques, which Victor Henry analyzes in his book *Magic in Ancient India*: the cooking of rice, a twig of green wood thrown on a fire, counting a heap of grass blades, the trajectory of an arrow, the fall of an object balanced on the head, dice, etc. The Indian used all these procedures to gain knowledge of his posterity, and to foresee the time or end of a battle, and to find a lost object.

The three volumes of Lexa's *Magic in Ancient Egypt* have illuminated to some extent the mystery surrounding the magical papyrus. We learn that the priest, after summoning the gods, used an adolescent medium, eyes closed, before a lighted lamp.

For Greece and Rome, the work in four volumes of Bouche-Leclercq, *Divination in Antiquity*, published as long ago as 1882, remains a classic, as does the *Psyche* of Rhodes.

In addition to the celebrated oracle of Delphi, where Pythia, in a trance state, let Apollo speak through her mouth[1], the Greeks also consulted the Apollo of Claros, Branchides of Miletus at Didymean, in Asia Minor, and the Zeus of Dodona, in Epirus, which was manifested in the leaves of oak trees or the brass of basins. The Greeks were also familiar with divination by dreams (to quote Homer in the first part of the *Iliad*, 'for the dream comes from Zeus'); that practised by the priest 'Oneiropolos', which indicated a means of healing at the sanctuary of Asklepios at Epidaurus; and that by evocation of the dead (necromancy), to which Ulysses referred in the *Odyssey*, X, and which was made the object of a small treatise by Lucian.

The Greek world examined also the most famous of the Egyptian oracles, that of Ammon-Zeus, the god of the Sands, in the Libyan oasis of Siwa. The procedure here was original: guided by the grand-priest, a sacred barge led the idol (head of a ram in gold, chest of a man covered in emeralds, a phallus jutting from the navel), the oscillation of which was then interpreted. A procession was used also at Heliopolis and at Hierapolis, in Syria.

The Romans took the basis of their divination from the Etruscans. Aruspex, or the examination of entrails, as well as the study of the flight of birds, were favored. Augural science,

[1] It is interesting to recall that Pythia sometimes prophesied with the help of dice. This divination reappeared in the Middle Ages but was still influenced by the cards.

exercised by the aruspices and augurs, was a dogma of state, but it did not prevent Cicero from noting that two augurs could not look at each other without laughing. However, if certain emperors, such as Augustus, Claudius, Vitellius and Vespasian, banished diviners and witches, it was not from hatred of divination, but to combat unfair competition with official institutions.

In *Memorable Actions and Words,* the work of the Romans, Valerius Maximus, there is a catalog of auspices, omens, wonders, dreams and ancient miracles.

When Christianity replaced the Alexandrian gods and Mithraism it combated divination, since to triumphant religion, divination meant magic and the diviner, like the magician and sorcerer, was suspect of commerce with the devil. In A.D. 775, Charlemagne condemned 'astrology, augurs, predictions of the future, and the interpretation of dreams'. Astrology alone succeeded, at least to some extent, in escaping persecution until the 17th century.

In 1691 the last diviner was executed. Then followed an extraordinary triumph for divination: Cagliostro overwhelmed Europe and Mademoiselle Lenormand read the future for all Paris. The Revolution only temporarily arrested the movement.

Magicians, fortune-tellers, diviners, reappeared even in the 20th century, although today swindlers and charlatans exploit occultism.

The 'Book of Changes'

We noted at the beginning of this chapter the differences between magic and divination.

Let us say now that occultists have a tendency to affirm that the diviner predicts without divine intervention, which was necessary to the prophets and the ancient oracles.

We must also define the essential characteristics of divination and of its different forms, the mancies. These constitute a group of rites of magical appearance, ranging from the use of formulae to possession by a god, demon or spirit, or of techniques established on a rational basis, such as examination of the sky, study of the hand, etc.

Unfortunately, pseudo-relations of cause and effect were established.

ZAPHKIEL. ל אי פ פ צ׳

ה י כ ל ק ידשים אל.

PALAIS DU SAINT DES SAINTS.

ה ש מ ל י ב

ESPRIT DE SAGESSE.

א ב ג י ה

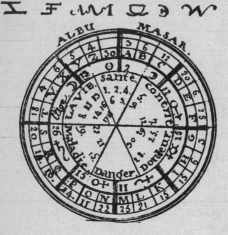

ARATRON

SATVRNE ♄ 8

ע ר ב ו י ה ה

CASSIEL

אית. PLOMB

Hebrew planetary wheel indicating health, fortune and death.

The practitioner was believed to be gifted with the faculty of clairvoyance, either naturally or by external intervention, with help of an excitant (music, dance, and drugs are the most common), or with a 'support' or object which made his task easier.

The most famous method, however, and the most valuable in psychological and metaphysical extensions, is based on the *I Ching* or *Book of Changes,* which, besides being a book of divination, is a fundamental work of Chinese philosophy.

According to legend, the Emperor Fou-Hi was walking on the bank of the Yellow River one day when a dragon emerged from the water and came towards him. On its back a saddle carried an octagonal diagram: eight conjectural signs each arranged in trigrams, the *Bat-Quaï* or *Pa-Koi*, appeared there. Not doubting that this was a precious celestial message, the emperor copied them as the arrangement of scales of the dragon, thirty black and square, twenty-five white and round.

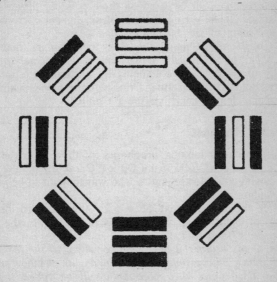

The combinations of the eight signs have been grouped in a diagram named *Ha-Do* (see above), meaning diagram discovered on the banks of the river. This diagram usually precedes the *Book of Changes*, along with an analogous diagram, the *Lac-Thu* ('writing discovered on the bank of the River Lac', flowing from the Yellow River), revealed to Emperor Yu the Great, this time by means of a tortoise. Fou-Hi interpreted the revelation in sixty-four symbols of six lines in place of three. This was the first *Book of Changes*. It was completed later and even seriously altered by Wen-Wang, of the Chou dynasty, to allow diviners better use of it.

The ancient *I Ching* was thus presented as a collection of sixty-four hexagrams constituted by the grouping, which is different each time, of two complementary principles, the *Yang* and the *Yin* (masculine and feminine). Each hexagram has a name and is accompanied by a brief text (*T'ouan*), which explains it. A second text (*Yao*) completes the first and interprets each figure.

The examination of the hexagram to give the reply to the question asked is done by drawing three coins or fifty wandlike stalks several times, giving a series of six figures corresponding to the six parts of the hexagram.

The Chinese have made the *Book of Changes* their most sacred book. The obscurity of the text in its original form has given rise to a number of commentaries and interpretations. The great psychologist, C. G. Jung, is one of the few non-sinologist Europeans to lean heavily on the *I Ching*.

Saint Odile, Prophet

Among the most famous 'prophesies' of the end of the world are those of Saint Malachi, Saint Odile d'Orval, the monks Adson and Hermann, and Nostradamus, who was thought to be inspired by the demon Bael.

Here is the integral text of one of the most curious, the prophecy of Saint Odile, which seems to date from the beginning of the 17th century:

Listen, O my brother! I have seen the terror of the forests and the mountains. The peoples were chilled with the horror of it. The time has come when Germania will be called the most belligerent nation of earth. The period has arrived when from its midst will appear the terrible soldier who will undertake a world war, and whom the people in arms will call the Anti-

Christ, the one who will be reviled by the mothers crying for their children like Rachel and not wanting to be consoled. Twenty different peoples will fight in this war. The conqueror will set out from the Danube. The war he will undertake will be the most horrifying that humans have ever endured. The arms will be flamboyant and the helmets of the soldiers will be covered with points and will emit flashes, while their hands will brandish flaming torches. He will win victories on the ground, in the sea and in the air, for one will see soldiers winged in unimaginable raids raised into the firmament as if seizing the stars in order to hurl them on the towns and to light up great conflagrations. The nations will be astonished and will cry out: 'Whence comes this nightmare?'

The earth will be turned upside down by the shock of combat. Flowers will be corroded with blood and even the sea monsters will flee terrified to the depths of the oceans. Future generations will be amazed that the other side had been unable to halt the advance of these victorious soldiers. Torrents of human blood will flow around the mountain. This will be the last battle. However, the conqueror will reach the peak of his triumphs around the middle of the sixth month of the second year of hostilities. This will be the end of the first period of so-called bloody victories. He will believe that he can dictate his own terms.

The second part will be half as long as the first. It will be called the period of domination. It will be full of strange things which will make the people tremble with fear. Around the middle of this time, the subjected people will call: Peace! Peace! But there will be no peace. It will not be the end, but the beginning of the end when the conflict will be abandoned in the City of cities. At this time many of his own will want to abuse him. It will cause prodigious things in the East.

The third period will be of short duration. It will be called a period of invasion, for through a just turn of events the country of the conqueror will be invaded on all sides. The armies will be decimated by great hardship and all will say: 'The finger of God is there!' The people will think that the end is near. The scepter will change hands and the mothers will rejoice. All the deprived people will recover what they had lost and more. The region of Lutece will be spared for the sake of its blessed mountains and its devoted women. However, all will have *believed in its loss. But the people will go to the mountain and will offer thanks to the Lord. For men will have seen such abominations in this war that generations will never wish for it again. However, misfortune will still afflict those who will not fear the Anti-Christ, for He will stir up new murders.*

But the era of peace under the sword will come and one will see the two corners of the moon meet at the cross. For in these times terrified men will adore God in truth. And the sun will shine with an unaccustomed brilliance.

FROM HERMETISM TO ALCHEMY

Alchemy was primarily an attempt to transform all metals into gold with the aid of the philosopher's stone. This transformation is actually possible, thanks to thermo-nuclear chemistry, but the gold thus obtained would be dearer than normal gold. Would our era thus be the age of gold or of alchemy? Perhaps alchemy is not quite what it is generally thought to be.

The Orient

Legend claims that the Chinese practised alchemy from 4500 B.C. History assures that about 500 B.C. Taoism, the doctrine of Lao-Tzu, sought the philosopher's stone and the elixir of long life with the edifying aim of taking beings to their highest degree of perfection.

In India, exchanges of 'power' took place between alchemists, yogis and fakirs. Long before Arab influence, Buddhist literature mentioned alchemical procedures and, from the 2nd century A.D., the 'essence *hataka* capable of transforming bronze into pure gold'. The illustrious philosopher Nagarjuna mentioned in his Treatise, *The Great Virtue of Wisdom,* four means of transmutation of metals, among them yogic concentration, which is confirmed by the Tibetan treatise concerning the eighty-four magicians.

Briefly, the elixir of long life, the conservation of bodies and the 'preparation of gold' have a rich past among the Chinese, Hindus and Tibetans.

Alexandria, Byzantium, the Arabs

Western alchemy originated in Alexandria. It adopted a strange mixture of Chaldean, Jewish, Egyptian and Greek practices and theories. The 'sacred art' had an astonishing success from the end of the 3rd to the beginning of the 5th century. Its exalted mysticism made use of works attributed to the gods, famous sages and illustrious sovereigns. Its main representatives were

Allegory showing the alchemist ready to break 'the primordial egg' in order to gain knowledge.

Zozime, Synesius, and Olympiodore, as well as Maria the Jewess, who invented the *kerotakis*, the sealed vase of the alchemist which went under the name of *bain-marie*. Through the philosopher's stone, this alchemy claimed to change metals into gold or silver; through the panacea, it was said to cure all ills, prolong human life, and to secure the perfect happiness of the adept.

While the Emperor Heraclius supported it, alchemy was more or less persecuted in Byzantium. It was through the Arabs that it reached the Christian West. The words alchemy, alembic, alcohol, and elixir are derived from Arab words.

Prince Chalid ibn Yazid is believed to have learnt alchemy in Egypt, in the first half of the 7th century. His successors worked wonders: Gebeb (about 720-800) discovered aqua regia, sulfuric acid, nitric acid; Al Razi (died around 930) developed medical alchemy; Avicenna (980-1036) was a geologist and Al Gazali (died in 1110) extolled an alchemy of bliss, uniquely spiritual.

Hermetism

By way of Spain and the Crusades alchemy filtered through to the Christian world, where it became fashionable towards the middle of the twelfth century.

From this time onwards there appeared a series of alchemical writings attributed to Hermes Trismegistus, the 'Thrice Greatest', who was identified with the Egyptian-Greek god of magic, Thoth.

The most famous of these works is *Tabula Smaragdina* or *Emerald Table*, which has drawn much comment since the Middle Ages and which is hermetically perfect. It was claimed to have been engraved on an emerald by the god Hermes-Mercury and discovered by Alexander of Macedonia in the Great Pyramid. In reality, it is perhaps the Latin translation of an Arab text of the 10th century, the latter itself being a translation of an original Greek treatise dating from the 4th century. Here is an English translation:

It is true, without lie and very variable.

The low is as the high and the high is as the low, in order to make miracles of a single thing.

And as all things have been and have come from one, thus all things are born in this unique thing by adaptation.

The sun is the father, the moon the mother, the wind carried in its belly, the earth is its nurse, the father of all, the Theleme of the whole world is here, its strength is entire if it is converted into earth.

You will separate the earth from the fire, the fire from the thick, gently, with great industry. It goes from the earth to the sky and once more it descends to earth, and it receives strength from the superior and the inferior. You will have, by this means, all the glory of the world and all the darkness will go from you.

It is the force of forces, for it will conquer all that is subtle and will penetrate all solids.

In this way the world was created.

From this will be and will come innumerable adaptations the means of which is here.

This is why I have been called Hermes Trismegistus, having the three parts of the philosophy of the world.

What I have said of the operation of the sun is accomplished and perfected.

History

Western alchemy developed in the 13th century. It was represented by such illustrious followers as Albert the Great (1193-1280), Roger Bacon (1214-1294), Doctor Arnaud de Villeneuve (1235-1312), who orientated it towards spiritual philosophy, and a disciple, Raymond Lully, the 'illuminated Doctor' (1235-1316). It remained orthodox.

On the other hand, anti-Christian tendencies appeared with the increase of written works in the 14th century. However, Nicolas Flamel (1330-1418), with the help of his wife Pernelle, was proclaimed first master of the recognized Royal Art of divine inspiration. It was he who composed this admirable prayer:

God Almighty, Father of light, from whom come all goods and perfect gifts, I implore your infinite mercy; let me know your eternal wisdom, that which surrounds you, which has created and made, which guides and conserves all. Deign to send it to me from the heavens, your sanctuary, and from the throne of your glory, so that it may be and work in me; for it is the master of all the celestial and occult arts, which dominates the science and intelligence of all; see that it accompanies me in all my work; that through its spirit I have true intelligence; that I proceed infallibly in the noble art to which I am dedicated, in the search for the miraculous stone of sages which you have

*hidden in the world; but which you at least are accustomed to
uncover for your chosen ones; that this great work which I
have to do here below, I commence, I pursue it and I complete
it successfully; that, content, I rejoice forever. I ask you through
Jesus Christ, for the celestial stone, cornerstone, miraculous,
and founded in all eternity, which commands and reigns with
you, etc.*

In the 15th century alchemy evolved in secret mystical
doctrine, more and more opposed to the church. Basil Valentin d'Erfurt commended the divining rod for discovering subterranean metals.

During the Renaissance alchemy came closer to the Cabala
and magic with Englishman John Dee (1527-1608), German
Abbe Johann Tritheim (1462-1516), Theophrast Bombast von
Hohenheim, called Paracelsus (1493-1541), both theosophist
and chemist.

At the beginning of the 17th century all forms of alchemy
flourished. Emperor Rudolph II (1562-1612) had his gathering
of alchemists. Belgian doctor Jean-Baptiste van Helmont (1577-
1664) reconciled hermetism and medical practice. The Brothers
of the Rose-Cross or Rosicrucians developed their secret lodges,

An alchemist's laboratory.

The 'Great All', from a 17th century German alchemical representation.

especially in Germany, seeking universal knowledge. Among them were the German Johann-Valentin Andreae (1586-1654) and the English doctor Robert Fludd (1574-1637). The 'inspired bootmaker', Jacob Boehme (1575-1624), borrowed much from them. Descartes dealt a strong blow to alchemy. Stahl (1660-1734), with the theory of 'phlogiston' (principle of inflammability formerly supposed to exist in combustible bodies), attempted in vain to save it. Chemistry absorbed it and the theories of Lavoisier consecrated the final rupture between adepts and chemists. Count Saint-Germain and Cagliostro served only to discredit alchemy further.

Modern Tendencies

Alchemy has nevertheless survived. Today, its followers can be divided into three types:

1. Those who perpetuate the tradition of the Middle Ages and the Renaissance. The authors who are disguised under the pseudonyms of Jacob and Auriger belonged to this category.

2. The 'scientists' who, while endeavoring to prove scientifically the possibility of metallic transmutations, realize in some degree a 'hyperchemistry', as, for example, the Frenchmen Delobel or Jollivet-Castellot.

3. The 'mystics' for whom alchemical practice is especially an analogous and symbolic operation with a view to the transformation of being. The larger number of them are masonic writers. It is well-known that a similarity exists between numerous alchemical emblems and those of freemasonry.

The Doctrine

In all alchemical writings there is a desire for esoterism. Only he who is deserving can attempt the Great Work. So the Chemical Nuptials of Christian Rosenkreutz commenced with the following text:

Today, today, today,
Are the nuptials of the king;
If you were born to take part
Chosen by God for the joy,
Go towards the mountain

Which has three temples.
See the events.
Take care of yourself.
Examine yourself.
If you are not purified assiduously,
The nuptials will take pity on you.
Misfortune to whoever lingers there.
Let he who is too light abstain.

So as not to be understood by the uninitiated, who could be harmed by its excessive use, the doctrine uses a vocabulary reserved for initiates and its symbolism is often very complex: for example, square = the four elements; Pelican or Christ = the philosopher's stone; sword = fire; hermaphrodite = sulfur and mercury united; Mars = iron; Neptune = water; Saturn = lead, etc.

The alchemical theories are based on (1) the unity of matter; (2) that sulfur is active, mercury passive, and salt or arsenic unified; and (3) the seven metals: gold—Sun; silver—Moon (both perfect) and the imperfects, quicksilver or mercury; lead—Saturn; tin—Jupiter; iron—Mars; copper—Venus.

The Practice

The first operation of the alchemist consisted of accomplishing the Lunar Tree (Small Work or Small Magistery); in other words, to make the white stone which changed imperfect metals into silver.

Next to be accomplished was the Solar Tree (Great Work or Great Magistery), which produced the red philosopher's stone, changing metals into gold. The primitive mixture was made in the philosophical egg, or Chicken Home, a hermetically sealed vase, and underwent a slow and complicated cooking process at four degrees in the athanor, a type of reverbatory furnace.

The mixture became black (state of putrefaction), then white (state of resurrection or argyropea), then finally red (rubification symbolized by the pelican, the phoenix or a young crowned king).

The philosopher's stone could be used as a solid (part could be projected to be made into gold, whence the name of powder

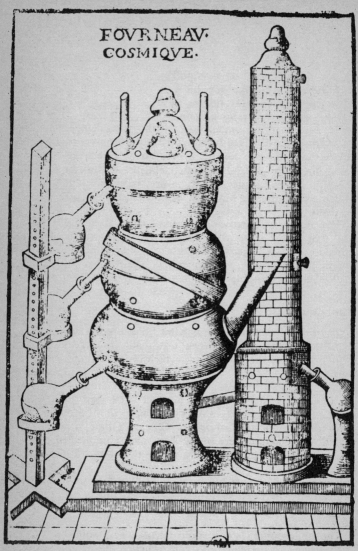

The athanor or cosmic furnace.

of projection) or liquid (potable gold; it was then dissolved in mercurial water, making it possible to speak of a universal solvent).

To these healing properties (panacea), were joined those of longevity (elixir of long life), but not immortality; an accident is always possible! Subsequently, it could render one invisible, make it possible to be diplaced in space, know the ultimate answer to everything, and converse with the celestial powers. Here is one of the numerous recipes for the elixir of long life, an extract from the *Admirables secrets du Petit-Albert,* a grimoire falsely attributed to Alfred the Great.

Take eight pounds of mercurial essence; two pounds of essence of barage, stems and leaves; twelve pounds of honey from Narbonne or another, the best in the country; bring it all to the boil, simmering in order to scour it, pass it through a filtering bag and clarify it. Put it aside to infuse for twenty four hours, four ounces of gentian root, cut into slices in three chopins of white wine, on warm ashes, stirring from time to time; put this wine in linen without expressing it; strain in the essence with the honey, bringing it all gently to the boil and cook to the consistency of syrup; cool in a glazed earthenware basin, then pour into bottles, which you will keep in a warm place. Take a spoonful every morning. This syrup prolongs life, restores health after all kinds of illnesses, even gout, and dispels flatulence. When only a small part of the lungs work and the rest is damaged, it supports the good and repairs the bad; it will cure pains in the stomach, sciatica, vertigo, migraine, and generally internal pains.

Some alchemists also believed in the possibility of artificially creating human life: the homunculus which was specially made popular in *De Natura Rerum* of Paracelsus.

Mystics

One finds in alchemy whatever one wishes to find. For the mystics, the Great Work or *Ars Magna* was firstly a symbolic act: to seek the stone was to regenerate the mind, to be reborn, to purify the soul, to attempt to be a superman.

To each, therefore, according to his means. Nevertheless, it would be unjust to confuse the uninitiated, who aspired only to material goods, with the sincere initiate, who, through the transformation of matter, applied alchemical symbolism to spiritual operations for the sake of knowledge and morality. The alchemist thus becomes the purification of being, which is essential if man wishes to gain supreme knowledge.

THE CABALA AND THE GOLEM

The Cabala is typically Jewish. It is false to claim that it originated in India or to compare it with a certain cult of Cybele.

To say, as do the Reinach brothers, that it is an 'aberration' or a 'poison of Judaism' is also false.

Cabala is derived from the Jewish and means 'to be in the presence of, or to meet with'. The Cabala is, in fact, the oral Law which Moses received on Mt. Sinai, at the same time as the tablets of the written Law (Tora). Briefly, it is the divine message transmitted according to the best Oriental methods, from master to disciple, from 'mouth to ear'.

With all the uncertainty of spoken messages, it continued to expand along with the Talmud until codified about the 5th century A.D. This work was exoteric, destined for the public, while the Cabala (the word became vulgarized in the 12th century) remained in the esoteric tradition. It is the divine wisdom manifesting itself in successive revelations to Adam, to Moses, who communicated it in their turn to men of the Grand Synagogue. They at last revealed it to members of the Cabalistic chain, spiritual masters and disciples from the elite of the diaspora.

Rabbi Simeon and Creation

The edifying life of Rabbi Simeon Bar Yochai in the 2nd century A.D. brought the tradition closer to the supernatural. Rabbi Simeon led a saintly life. Great defender of the unselfish prayer, he was exiled for twelve years with his son in an isolated cave, and through too much study and too little rest, died at Meron, a small village in Upper Galilee. A holy lamp shone with amazing brilliance during his death struggles, and when his body was being carried out of the house it was raised in the air, preceded by a column of fire! A thousand years passed without the lamp being extinguished.

Through the medium of the *Book of the Formation* or *Sepher Yetsira*, written between the 5th and 7th centuries, the Cabala studied the ancient literary doctrine of the origin of the world.

God created the universe, with the help of three superior beings called Sepharim (*Sephar*, the letter figure; *Sipour*, the oral letter-expression; *Sepher*, the written letter-expression). The ten divine attributes, named the *Sephiroth belima* (1. Sovereignty; 2. Wisdom; 3. Intelligence; 4. Mercy; 5. Rigor; 6. Beauty; 7. Triumph; 8. Glory; 9. Foundation; 10. Royalty) represented in the Sephirothic Tree, and the 22 letters of the sacred alphabet (three pure, seven intensified and twelve simple) enabled this creation: God engraved the letters and this was the model of the universe.

From this alphabetical-numerical creation arises the Cabala, which comprises three parts—the *gematria* (science of the combination of the numerical value of letters), the *notarique* and the *themura*.

The Three Centers of the Middle Ages

While for the Jews the 13th century was marked by several persecutions, it also had three active centers of Judaism: in Arabized Spain (the Jewish community was called Sepharad), in the Rhineland (persecuted, it was called Ashkenaz), and in Provence (the dynasty of the Tibbonides, it was known as 'pre-Renaissance').

The creation of the Cabala in the strict sense goes back to Ezra Ben Solomon of Gerona (1160-1238). For the first time, the secret messages 'from mouth to ear' were committed to Ezra Ben Solomon de Gerone (1160-1238). For the first time, the secret messages 'from mouth to ear' were committed to writing. From 1290, the prophet Abraham Ben Samuel Aboulafia was prominent in this field. It was he who worked extensively on the combinations of letters and figures of the *gematria*. This system of combinations or *tserouf* could be unlimited and lent itself to the most frenzied interpretations. For its creator it was a kind of numerical musical composition, a technique of meditation or ecstasy aimed at 'undoing the knots', freeing the divine in man. Scholem justly named it 'Jewish yoga'.

Towards 1280, the first manuscript copies of a book which was to be an enormous success for several centuries appeared. It was the *Zohar*. A summary of Jewish mystical life, it was seen by occultists as a secret interpretation of the scriptures.

In order to know God and to be united with him, the Jewish man must seek true faith. This Jewish theosophy in cabalistic study postulates prayer and love. God, the mystery of the mysteries, is infinite or of Himself. He is manifested in the Eternal (*Elohim*) through the ten *Sephiroth* or divine attributes mentioned previously (three superior, seven inferior). A symbolic complex is elaborated apropos of God, his manifestations, the 'Adam Kadmon' model of man, and the triple soul. It is necessary to 'realize the living union', the unity or *yichoud*.

The essential is to restore the order destroyed by sin: this is the *tikkoun*.

Christian Cabala and Misunderstanding

From 1391 Spain persecuted the Jews. Other waves of persecution, with autos-da-fe, followed in 1481 and 1492. In exile, the new Cabala aimed no longer at the secret, but at spiritual pre-eminence; it had both a religious and social role, and this was eventually to be the cause of its decadence. The Zohar took precedence over the Talmud.

Continually hunted, the Jews sought refuge in the empire of the Sultan Bajazet and in central Italy. In Rome, Cremona, Mantua, Padua, and Florence the Cabala had an unforeseen success. The humanists became interested in it. From 1553, it was persecuted again, but by then it had influenced some famous occultists of whom Pic de la Mirandole (1463-1494), Cornelius Agrippa (1486-1535), Paracelsus (1493-1541) and, especially, Robert Fludd (1574-1637) all became suspect in the eyes of the Church.

The public immediately concluded that the Cabala, sorcery and sin were synonymous. This did not stop them, however, from seeking cabalistic amulets as a means of protection or healing. La Galigai and Marie de Medici had the same two healers, Philotee Montalto and Philippe d'Aquin, who used amulets assiduously.

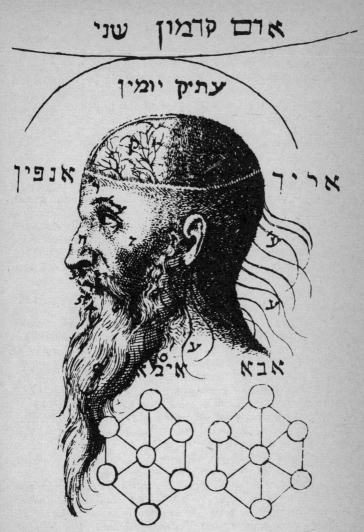

The 'Great Face,' or hidden face of the God of creation, represented by the Christian Cabalist Knorr de Rosenroth.

It required only the *Keys of Solomon* and other magical miscellanies to transform the pure tradition of Rabbi Simeon to occult science. Its renown was such that all occultists from the 7th century to this day have studied the Cabala. The original spiritual message, however, is quite forgotten and the Hebrew vocabulary was debased. (Shechina, feminine name of the divinity, became the Christian name of fortune-tellers at village fairs!)

Lurianism and Chassidism

At this time the Jewish community of Palestine was the only one to follow the genuine mystic Cabala, in the vineyard of Safed, in Upper Galilee. At the end of the 16th century, with Isaac Luria (1534-1572 or 1574) came the ascetic practices which, after the degradation of the doctrine, led to its deterioration. The Companions, a society founded under the direction of the philosopher Rabbi Moses Cordovero (1522-1570) struggled vainly to preserve the mystic Sepharad. Cordovero thus described the moral preoccupations of the new sect:

Not to let one's thoughts distract one from the words of the Tora and sacred things, that lead to the Shechina. Not to succumb to anger. Not to say anything bad about any creature, not even an animal. Not to curse beings but to bless them, even in the midst of hostility. Not to swear, even on the truth. Not to have any part of the four individuals rejected from the Shechina: the liar, the hypocrite, the arrogant one and the slanderer. Not to frequent banquets, except for a religious occasion. To share the joys and pains of the Companions. To be generous towards one's fellow creatures even if they transgress the laws. To meet with one of the Companions for one or two hours a day to discuss mystic thoughts. To review with one of the Companions each Friday all the actions accomplished during the week in order to be purified, awaiting the favor of the Sabbath Queen. To say Grace in a clear voice separating the words and letters in such a way that the children themselves can repeat them at the table. To confess one's sins before each meal and before going to bed. To speak exclusively in Hebrew with the Companions and on Sabbath days with everyone.

The 'Lion' Luria, first founder of an intellectual kibbutz,

which nevertheless was to fail, preached saintliness to his disciples, 'the lion cubs'. At the death of Isaac Luria, the ascetic methods deteriorated and magical practices multiplied. Lurianism engendered heresies, the main one of which, in 1665, was due to Sabbatai Zwi (1626-1676).

A large popular pietist movement, Chassidism, was launched by Rabbi Israel Ben Eliezer (around 1700-1760). Hawker of amulets, the Master popularized the Cabala, which spread among the Jews of Poland and Russia.

The Talmud and Magic (2nd-6th Centuries)

It is well known that the holy book of the Jews is the Talmud. In reality, there are two Talmuds: that of Jerusalem (in which the Mishna, the law of the Jewish Doctors, was formed towards the end of the 2nd century and completed about 380 at Tiberias), and that of Babylon (drawn up by Rabbi Aschi at the beginning of the 6th century).

The four centuries between were rich in magic. The Bible spoke vainly against occultism, noting that there were many demons to combat (Schedim, Mazzikim, Lilim, Ruchoth). It was the same with divinations: by trees (Judges; 9, 8), by the drinking cup (Genesis; 44, 5), by arrows (IV Kings; 13, 15), by animal liver (Ezekiel; 21, 21), by knots (Ezekiel; 13, 18), by the teraphim or divining statues (Hosea; 3-4), and, lastly, the dice of the Ephod, the official Oracle. There are also diviners who base their work on the study of clouds (Meonim), serpents (Menachesch) or birds. Others use shells, marked lots, knuckle bones, and the divining rod.

While the sacred texts condemn the practice of malevolent magic, the magic of love, and necromancy, they recommend the study of them; for their efficacy was not doubted (for example, Sabbath, 67, cited a case of magic healing). The amulet (*kemea*) was tolerated. Although it had neither the power of the rod of Moses nor that of the magical tetragrammaton, nor, above all, that of the sacred name of God (in 12, 42, or 72 syllables), it served all medical and protective uses against Ein Horra or the evil eye. Water, fire and brass bells also had indisputable protective virtues.

The Golem

Man has always had the ambition to create life. According to the tradition passed down to our day by the common Prague Jew, a new Epimetheus, Rabbi Judah Loew Ben Bezalel, brought about the animation of a red clay statuette in a ghetto of Prague in the 16th century. He thus created the homunculus which occupied the minds of many during the Middle Ages. He was able to animate it, as the Creator, because he knew the secret name of God, which he wrote on the forehead of the statuette.

In the writings of Eleazar of Worms, in the 11th century, were the oldest formulas for creating the Golem, which at first was only animated during the phases of ecstasy of the most saintly rabbi.

Rabbi Loew himself is said to have performed the miracle which rendered him equal to God. Animated, the Golem grew bigger, a kind of Frankenstein's monster. Mongoloid, he was a yellow color, with slanting eyes, and beardless. He was probably used to massacre the assailants of the Jewish community. Whether the Rabbi had forgotten to withdraw the name or whether he had been merely an apprentice sorcerer left behind by the turn of events, he saw the Golem escape and terrorize the town, killing all those he met. Loew had to resign himself to destroying him. The legend has him reappearing every thirty-three years.

The Golem was to be revived in the imagination of the 20th century. Paul Wegener made two films on him, in 1914 and 1930. In 1918 Chaym Bloch produced an apocrypha on the subject, following the curious novel of Gustave Meyrinck, *The Golem*, published in 1916 and again in 1962.

THE REIGN OF THE DEVIL

The Sabbat

The place is sinister. Marshes, stagnant swamps and pestilence surround it. No beast ever appears there; for the ceremony about to take place leaves behind burnt earth where grass will no longer grow! An enormous shadow appears in the sky. The Great

Black Three-horned Goat advances and the ground creaks under his feet. His appearance is diabolical, since he is the devil himself, in the role of Leonard, great patron of sorcerers and witches. He has renounced for this evening (always a Saturday) his metamorphoses of an ox, black bird, red man, tree without feet and evil face. Today, he is the terrifying goat with three horns. He will soon light up the gathering with his middle horn illuminated. A black crown dominates his bristled hair; his face is haggard; his eyes are inflamed and vicious; a monotonous and dreadful voice shakes his beard with each word; his human hands have all fingers equal and curved, like the talons of a bird of prey; his feet are spread out like those of a goose; his tail, as long as that of a donkey, covers the buttocks which are in the form of a face which all the zealots will kiss.

This is the sabbat, not the little sabbat, to which the devil, 'Leonard', would not deign to appear, but the Great Sabbat, at which he presides, assisted by his lieutenant, Master Jean Mullin, and where the sorcerers of the entire world are reunited. Some ride a goat which flies through space, others ride magic brooms which take to the air. Those who have neither goat nor broom are transported by the subaltern devils changed into donkeys or aerial horses. For the voyage must be taken by air. It is equally important that the participants, after having slept, go out through the chimney shrieking several times 'Emen-Hetan' before mounting the goat (ritual in Italy), or the broomstick 'smeared with the fat of a child' (used in France).

Normally, the sorcerer must steal a child and carry it to the sabbat because the devil needs disciples of the very young. On his arrival the child receives from Leonard and Jean Mullin a godfather and godmother, who rename him, causing him to deny God, the Virgin and the saints. Leonard then marks him in the left eye with one of his horns. The child will wear this mark for the whole period of tests, during which he will take care of the magic toads every day of the sabbat. If he manages to pass the tests, he receives another sign in the form of a black cat, hare or toad foot. He can then participate in the dances himself and at the feast of the sabbat and pronounce the consecrated phrase: 'I have drunk from the tambourine, I have eaten from the cauldron, and I have become professed in sorcery'. If he fails, on the other hand, the sorcerers will cut him up and make a horrible stew for the sabbat.

Now to return to the ceremony itself.

The sorcerers embrace the hindquarters of Leonard to signify their allegiances, for which they receive in exchange a little silver. The devil then rises and the master of ceremonies distributes the places for the feast, each according to his importance, but always taking care to alternate the devilkins and sorcerers.

Here opinions differ. Some assert that the cloth is golden and the dishes succulent, others that those attending eat only the bread of the devil, made of black millet, and an assortment of horrible dishes composed of hanged people and young children.

They sing obscene songs all the time. When the meal is over, the sorcerers proceed to a kind of 'auto-criticism', controlled and aggravated by the toads who serve as domestics. The guilty are punished by the armless demons, who roast them over a slow fire or force them to dance with a ferocious cat hanging behind them. The rewards, on the other hand, come in the form of toads. These are adorned sumptuously in red, green or black velvet, and wear a bell on their necks and their right feet. They dance before becoming the servants of the rewarded sorcerers.

Next comes the bacchanalia, frenzied with the worst kinds of debauchery. Before dawn, Leonard does his excrements in a hole and the sorcerers smear themselvs. As soon as the cock-crow resounds, the devil gives leave, and all vanish in haste, dreading the light of day.

Yet another 'night of Walpurgis' has ended.

At least, this is what legend would have us believe. If the cult of the devil was effectively practised in strange ceremonies during the Middle Ages, popular imagination has enriched the tradition with fabulous embellishments, the traces of which will continue to appear in art and literature for centuries to come.

Devil Pacts

The dream of Doctor Faust! Who has not at least once in his life experienced the temptation of the damned: to have eternal youth, beauty, success, even at the price of a contract with the Devil?

. THEY COME RIDING
GOATS . . .

. . . THEY TRAMPLE THE CROSS
UNDERFOOT . . .

. . . THEY ARE REBAPTIZED IN
THE NAME OF THE DEVIL . . .

. . . THEY GIVE THEIR
CLOTHES TO THE DEVIL . . .

. . . THEN THEY KISS THE
DEVIL'S HINDQUARTERS . . .

. . . AND THEY DANCE IN
CIRCLES BACK TO BACK . . .

*Sorcerers at the sabbat—17th century engravings depicting the six main
stages of the sabbat, and a gathering of witches and sorcerers.*

The pact with the devil was much in vogue in the Middle Ages and the Faust of Goethe furnishes a classic example.

Pact was used in a formal sense (direct understanding with the devil) or in a broader sense of an understanding with the sorcerers who follow him in the practice of black magic which could lead to abuse.

It is described in diverse ways, but it always consists of: (1) a preparation (diet of forbidden dishes, nocturnal life, etc.); (2) an invocation (ritual accompanying the sacrifice of a black fowl and a fire, the latter indispensable); (3) a complex assembly of formulas and blasphemy; (4) apparition of the devil (which one prayed would not be too terrifying!); and (5) the signing of the pact with blood from the left arm.

The assembly is so complicated that it is often reduced to tacit pacts or 'equivalents'.

Tradition required that the signatory should 'lose his double', that is to say, in the sun he no longer threw a shadow and a mirror no longer reflected his image. In exchange, he would acquire wealth, irresistible seductive appeal, youth, invisibility, and omnipotence. Generally, his reward does not last throughout his life but for about twenty years, a term which the devil tries to shorten.

The most famous pacts are those of Faust and that of the prior of Loudun, Urbain Grandier, the text of which is kept in the National Library of Paris. At the Arsenal Library in Paris is also a great collection of 'diabolical' pentacles and seals.

The Goety

Goety, or devil magic, pacts with Satan, and little or grand sabbats were common in the Middle Ages and even up to the 17th century. It was, as has been written, the 'reign of the devil' or rather of devils. The book *De Praestigiis* of Jean Wier, published in 1568 at Basle, assures us that there are 7,405,926 devils, divided into 1,111 legions and obedient to 72 infernal princes!

These monsters are everywhere, repugnant, formless. Imagination gets carried away and perceives them even where they could not be. The Germanic forests, the Vendean woodlands,

Contract drawn up in 1631 between the devil and Urbain Grandier.

the Scottish highlands or British moors are full of hideous demons.

The Church launched its outcry: a bull of Gregory IX founding the Inquisition in August, 1233; and a bull of Alexander IV enumerating the main counts of indictment for black magic in 1260. The secular arm burned thirty thousand sorcerers and witches between 1400 and 1504, and not until 1731 was the death penalty for sorcery abrogated in France!

Black Masses

A tribute rendered to Satan, especially in the Middle Ages, the black mass is a parody of the mass.

The altar is surmounted by an obscene Christ or an infernal goat; the candles are of black wax; the bowls contain congealed blood or human fat. Sometimes a naked woman serves as an altar and the celebration is carried out on her buttocks or her stomach. The officiating priest, by preference one who has been defrocked, and the servants are naked under an ornate cassock of Satanic symbols. The offering is black. At the offertory, the ceremony takes place in an atmosphere heavily charged with perfume and incense, and degenerates into convulsive bacchanalia.

The threat of Satan was perceived everywhere in the Middle Ages and many hoped to be freed of their fears by paying homage to him. Obsessed by the sins of the flesh, some believed they saw a return of Dionysus-Bacchus and Aphrodite-Venus in the practice of the sabbat.

As a consequence, black masses continue to exist, but their justification for existence has long since disappeared. On December 9, 1963, a newspaper article described an instance of sorcery in Sussex, England:

Sorcery is again in the news in England. The police of Sussex are busy hunting four individuals caught in the act of conducting a black mass in the old church in the village of Westham, which dates back to the 12th century.

The bell-ringer, Mr. Burstead, was on his way to the church yesterday evening where he had to meet some neighborhood colleagues. He noticed that there was a light in the belfry and, on approaching it, saw four individuals chanting their pagan

Fetish of Mayombe (Lower Congo). The cavity in the centre, enclosed by a mirror, contains some magic charges.

Amulet of New Guinea.

Tibetan Lama, called 'black hat,' master of the unknown, skilled in magic.

Next pages:
Allegory showing different alchemical emblems: the flying eagle, symbol of mercury, the hollow tree and different astrological symbols. (Illustration from manuscript of the 18th century, 'The Five Books of Nicolas Valois'.)

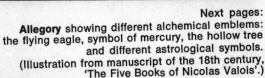

NOS ARABES FIAMM
COLLICVLOS CELS

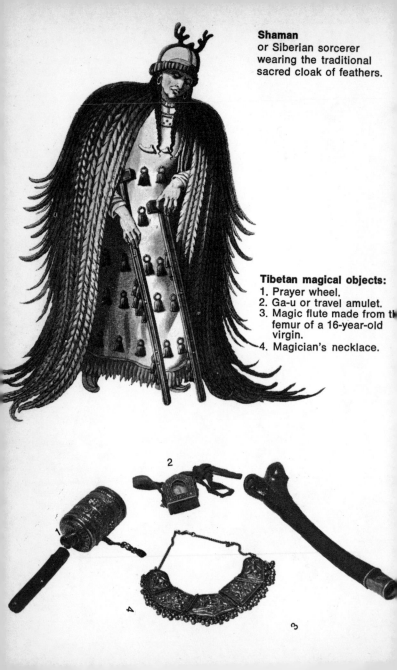

Shaman
or Siberian sorcerer wearing the traditional sacred cloak of feathers.

Tibetan magical objects:
1. Prayer wheel.
2. Ga-u or travel amulet.
3. Magic flute made from the femur of a 16-year-old virgin.
4. Magician's necklace.

Traditional signs of the Zodiac.
Above: Map of the sky
under the sign
of Leo (23 July-22 August).

Virgo (23 August-22 September)

Anatomical Man (following pages):
The signs of the Zodiac
and their affinities
with the human body.
(Pol de Limbourg:
'Tres Riches Heures du duc de Berry'.)

The astrologer attempting to unite the sky and the earth
by a complex system of affinities and symbols.
(Fresco from the Château de Villeneuve, at Lembrun, Puy-de-Dome.)

litanies and invoking the devil in the light of candles of the altar arranged in the form of a cross in the middle of the sanctuary floor.

He immediately alerted the vicar, who was attending a Christmas charity bazaar at the village school. The Rev. Colhurst, aged 79 years, accompanied by Captain Hayden and Mr Pourpre, his churchwardens, and several parishioners, went to the spot. As he was to tell later, the first thing he saw as he went in was one of the profaners spitting on the cross of the altar while the others were continuing to chant in incomprehensible gibberish.

The vicar was knocked down as he tried to end the masquerade and a regular battle began between the faithful and the 'men of the devil', who succeeded in escaping.

The vicar, who, apart from Captain Hayden, was most under attack, later said:

'I am sure that they belong to the same band as those who profaned the churches and cemeteries of Somerset, where some had lit a fire in the churches and others had gone as far as opening a grave.'

The incidents in Somerset were later raised in the House of Commons when the local member asked that sorcery be made illegal. However, the Minister refused to introduce laws which had been renounced during the last century, arguing that it would be taking a step backwards and that the laws in force were sufficient for the maintenance of order.

Sorcery continues to be practised on a large scale in the British Isles.

YOGA, 'SCIENCE OF INTEGRAL MAN'

In 1959, announcements were published that the United States Secret Service was considering contacting some Tibetan yogi specialists in telepathy in order to scientifically study the phenomenon of eventual thought transmission, an exciting domain where scientific experimentation is only just beginning.

In 1960 Russian newspapers reported that a delegation of

Soviet experts had gone to India to meet the most renowned yogis with the aim of studying certain phenomena of reduced metabolism. Indeed, yoga permits its disciples to control, and therefore to accelerate or slow down at will, the normal breathing rhythm and circulation. The latest surgical methods of operation at low temperatures were probably inspired by the techniques of yoga.

Thus, the latest scientific progress matches the experiences of one of the oldest sciences of the world, which had been forgotten, badly interpreted or misunderstood by the West.

It took Freud to discover that the Indian, through yoga, has known of introspection and psychoanalysis for more than two thousand years. But what exactly is yoga?

It is necessary to stress that we in the West cultivate a certain number of readymade and incredibly false ideas about the Orient and the way of life there. Yoga has suffered from these prejudices.

For the man in the street, yoga (which he confuses with yogi or yogin) was, until recently, a strange practice impelling certain Indians or Tibetans to stay motionless and almost naked for long hours on the snowy summits of the Himalayas. Since then, much has been written in the magazines about yoga; and some think of it as a kind of non-tiring gymnastics, mainly for women.

On the other hand, an Oriental expert would define yoga as the technique of ecstasy of the soul.

It is important to understand that yoga is, truly speaking, neither a philosophy nor a simple physical technique, but is an assembly of methods the object of which is to reach very different goals. The simplest of these goals is a good psycho-physical balance. This is generally the result obtained by yoga as at present vulgarized in the West. The most elevated goal, according to Hindu tradition, is absolute deliverance from the cycle of birth and death.

'Specific dimension of the soul' or 'science of integral man', as eminent Oriental men have proclaimed it, yoga has had contacts with shamanism and other native sorcery before being codified by Patanjali and invading all the religions of India.

It contains eight steps or *angas*, which are divided into three plans in the following way:

| Moral plan (two *angas*): | (1) Five abstinences or *yama*. |
| | (2) Five disciplines or *niyama*. |

Psycho-physical plan (three *angas*):	(1) Postures or *asana*.
	(2) Control of respiration or *pranayama*.
	(3) Abstraction of the senses or *pratyahara*.

Mental plan (three *angas*) (*Samyama* in three stages):	(1) Concentration of thought in one single spot or *dharana*.
	(2) Active contemplation on the essence of the object. or *dhyana*.
	(3) Active ecstasy or *samadhi*.

According to the result envisaged the following main yogas can be distinguished:

Hatha-yoga, or physical.

Karma, of action.

Bhakti, of devotion, divine love.

Jnana, of intellectual knowledge.

Laya, cosmic or of fusion with the Universe.

Raja, or royal, the crowning of all.

There is an extract from the *Seven Books of the Wisdom of the Great Path,* 'The twelve indispensable things for becoming a yogi':

1. *An intelligence gifted with the power of comprehension and application of the doctrine to its real needs.*

2. *From the beginning (of a religious life), the deepest aversion for the endless series of deaths and rebirths.*

3. *A guru able to guide you on the path of deliverance.*

4. *Diligence combined with steadfastness and invulnerability to temptation.*

5. *A perseverance to neutralize the results of evil deeds by the accomplishment of good deeds, and the observance of the triple vow of maintaining chastity of the body, purity of the mind and control of the word.*

6. *A sufficiently comprehensive philosophy to embrace knowledge as a whole.*

7. *A method of meditation giving the power to concentrate totally.*

8. *An art of living which allows the use of each activity (of body, mind and word) as an aid on the path.*

9. *A method of practising the chosen instructions to make them more than simple words.*

10. *Particular instructions (by a wise guru) which will permit the avoidance of errors, temptations, traps and dangers.*

11. *An indomitable faith combined with a supreme serenity of mind at the time of death.*

12. *As a result of having practically applied the chosen instructions, the attainment of spiritual powers capable of transmuting the body, the word and the mind in their divine essence.*

Yoga in Hindu Wisdom

The sage of India seeks his deliverance above all things. To reach it he must 'break through his human condition'. Unfortunately, important obstacles stand before him.

Firstly, the law of Karma or of the responsibility for acts, which states that the sins committed in our former lives are atoned for by a series of transmigrations or *avatars,* which can be unlimited.

This cycle of rebirths, the *samsara,* which engenders and maintains the universe is, in fact, an illusion caused by ignorance.

One cannot reach truth without first overcoming this ignorance; in other words, one can only obtain salvation or *nirvana* by eliminating this ignorance, by 'leaving this life' in order to merit deliverance.

Yoga constitutes one of many Indian systems of deliverance. It had two characteristics: training of the initiate, and a practical objective, deliverance.

Suffering on this earth is inevitable, but we can free ourselves from it by Knowledge. Certain techniques allow us to isolate that part of divine spirit which is in us, that which will free us from pain by eliminating our egocentrism.

By disassociating the spirit from our psycho-mental impressions we will be released from the present mind-body association and we will be freed from evil and suffering.

This dissociation is commented on by the Hindu philosopher Vivekananda:

Real man is contained behind the mind; the mind is the instrument in his hands: it is his intelligence which filters through the mind. It is only when you take your place behind the mind that the latter becomes intelligence. When man abandons the mind, the latter falls to pieces and is no longer. You understand thus what one hears by chitta. *It is the mental content, and the* vrittis *are the waves and ripples which are raised on it when external causes come to excite it. These* vrittis *are our universe.*

We cannot see the bottom of a lake when the surface is covered with ripples. We can only have a glimpse of the bottom when the ripples are subdued and the surface is calm. If the water is muddy, or if it is constantly stirring, the bottom will not be visible. If the water is limpid and if it does not have our real self, the lake is the chitta, *the waves are the* vrittis . . .

Thus, leaving a series of 'negations' or 'denials' for the price of a methodical and intensive training, of which *hatha* yoga or physical yoga only constitutes the early stages, the sage must arrive at a deliverance which is not negative, since 'freed of his living' there is nothing more to fear. Actions, in effect, can no longer harm him.

If he voluntarily shuts out humanity, it is to acquire absolute freedom in the Good; if he rejects an illusory world, it is to reinstate all aspects in the Self, in the One.

So explains the *yuj* origin of yoga: 'to put under the yoke', is to impose on oneself an extraordinary discipline in order to 'bind together', to unify one's spirit, so as to fuse it with the universe, with God or Brahma.

Yoga is difficult to export, and we must be suspicious of the many charlatans who, without knowing a great deal, exploit it for commercial ends. The recourse to a spiritual master—the Indians call him a *guru* — will fully avoid all errors and dangers. This cannot be stressed too much. Practised well, yoga unquestionably brings beneficial results: a better psycho-physical balance, a greater certainty of oneself, an intensified resistance to fatigue and a more rapid recovery after exertion, an improvement of circulation and respiration, an art of 'relaxation' or integral rest, and a concentration more effective for intellectual work.

DERIVED FORMS OF OCCULTISM

FROM THE HEALING DREAMS OF ANTIQUITY TO THE MODERN 'KEY OF DREAMS'

Oneiromancy

During the Trojan War pestilence ravaged the Greek camp, and before making a move the Greek leaders tried to find out why the God Apollo was angry with them. The intrepid Achilles recommended the consultation of a diviner of birds or (and one feels his preference was with this divination) of a specialist in oneiromancy, 'for even the dream comes from Zeus' (*Iliad,* I, 63).

However, the king of gods was not the only one to send dreams. To refer to Homer again, but this time in the *Odyssey* XIX, 560:

Through two separate gates our insubstantial dreams
Come to us. One is made of horn, the other ivory.
Those that pass through the gate of sawn ivory are deceptive dreams,
And the words they bring are false.
But those that come through the gate of polished horn tell truly to the mortals that see them of things that really happen.

To criticize, to interpret these dreams and to determine to whom they are addressed, one consults the *oneirocritic* who exercises *oneiroscopy.* Homer finishes by making of the dream an independent person delegated by Apollo, especially by Zeus, and at times by Cronos (the Time), who while restrained on an island was in touch with the thoughts of his son Zeus. Aristotle also believed in the significance of dreams.

Quick to deride the augurs, Cicero (*De Divinatione*) does not, however, mock oneiromancy which was allowed by Artemidorus of Ephesus (his work was the basis for our key of modern dreams), Demetrius of Phalereus, the critic Aristarchus, and Strabo. Synesius, a Christian (360-430), specifies in his *Treatise of Dreams* that 'the state of the soul in eternity would conform to the dreams it experiences. . . . That each registers in his memory all that he has experienced while sleeping' and he had the wisdom to commend avoiding 'the general methods'. A long time previously, the *Book of Dreams* of the new Egyptian Empire said practically the same thing, adding many details that are in our key of dreams.

About 450 the Roman poet Macrobius distinguished five kinds of dreams: (1) any whatever; (2) nightmare; (3) vision; (4) oracle; and (5) divinatory. The most scientific interpretation, in some ways a pre-Freudian psychoanalysis, was given by the Greek doctor Herophilus (360-283 B.C.), who distinguished the dreams sent by the gods and those of obsessions, usually erotic.

Prophetic and Healing Dreams

There have been famous dreams, such as that of Zoroaster, who received from each of the archangels, notably the Spirit of Wisdom, Vohu Mano, revelations which gave him control over the elements. There are also the prophetic dreams of the unfortunate Cassandra, Trojan Princess, which were never taken seriously.

There were also the dreams of Pharaoh, who asked Joseph to interpret them, and Nebuchadnezzar's dream of a fallen tree, which caused him to ask Daniel for its meaning (Daniel's reply made him look foolish!).

The Bible is also rich in dreams: Jacob and his ladder, the fat and lean cows, Balthazar, Booz . . .

Cicero in his *De Re Publica* relates 'the dream of Scipio the African', as Aeschylus, in *The Persians* (v. 181-200), had related that of Atossa, widow of Darius.

Brutus, on the eve of the battle of Philippi, saw a ghost telling him he would be beaten by Antony and Octavius.

Calpurnia, wife of Julius Caesar, predicted his assassination and begged him not to go to the Senate on the Ides of March, 44 B.C.

Some other examples, from Cyrus the Ancient to Hannibal and to Dionysius of Syracuse, are given by Valerius Maximus in his *Memorable Actions and Words* (1, 7).

Healing dreams were practised in ancient Egypt, especially in the temples of Imhotep and Serapis, as was the evocation of the dead to intervene in dreams; in the chambers of dreams of the ziggurats or Chaldean pyramids; under the portico of Asclepius, healer of Epidaurus; in the Greek grottos of Latmos; at the sanctuary of Amphiaraus at Oropos and at Thebes, at that of Dionysius at Amphiclea in Phocis, etc. The act which provoked the appearance of an angel in a dream to obtain either the revelation of the future or, in most cases, a cure, was called incubation.

In antiquity, six circumstances for interpreting dreams were taken into consideration: nature, law, custom, profession, name and time. (The specialists brought them to 250!)

And what of the pills capable of procuring a pleasant sleep, full of delightful dreams? Let us borrow a recipe from the *Formula of Eminent Magic* of Piobb, obviously without guaranteeing anything:

Peel of the root of cynoglossum	15.0
Juice of herbane	15.0
Extract of opium	15.0
Myrrh	23.0
Oliban	20.0
Saffron	6.0
Castoreum	6.0

Syrup of opium proportionally and divide into pills of 0.1; take one or two before going to bed.

Key of Dreams and Psychology

A deep study of dreams is not our purpose. It will be sufficient to note that modern psychology since Freud and Jung has upset previously accepted concepts. We know now, for example, that the dream does not depend on sex, age, or state of health; that there is no sleep without dreams, but most of them are forgotten; that dreams, whatever their length, have an influence on our thinking, and are sometimes an indication of our unconscious; that they often distort reality following complex laws that only the specialized psychologist can interpret according to a series of symbols variable with each case.

Although fanciful and varied, the study of dreams has nevertheless resulted in an attempted elaboration of a traditional symbolism. As an example, the following are some interpretations of dreams borrowed from the *Dictionnaire Infernal* of Collin de Plancy (6th edit., 1862).

DREAM	MEANING
Ass	Resting = wickedness; braying = fatigue; running = misery.
Bath	Clear water = health; troubled water = death of parents or friends.
Bean	Quarrels, lawsuit.
Black pudding	Eaten = unexpected visit.
Black swans	Marriage turmoil.
Bone	Troubles.
Brigand	Loss of parents or friends.
Crow	Flying = danger of death.
Crown	Honor.
Eagle	Good omen; if it lands on you, sign of death.
Eggs	White = good luck; broken = bad luck.
Funeral	Going there = marriage; to see oneself buried = long misery.
Gallows	Success.
Game	Gain.
Geese	Honor.
Hair	Torn out = loss of friends.
Man	In white = good luck; in black = bad luck.
Milk	Friendship.
Mirror	Treachery.
Money	Found = loss; lost = good business.
Moon	Delay in business; dim = torments.
Moving house	Marriage or inheritance.
Murder	Security.
Mushrooms	Long life.
Parrots	Indiscretions.
Peacock	Beautiful children.
Phantom	White = joy, honor; black = grief.
Pork	Eating = victory.
Rabbits	White = success; black = bad luck; eating = health.
Rats	Hidden enemies.
Roses	Pleasures.
Scorpion	Treachery.
Singing	Man = hope; woman = tears.
Specter	Surprise.

DREAM	MEANING
Storm	Discord.
Teeth	Falling out = death.
Tempest	Great peril.
Weasel	Wicked woman.
Woman	Infirmity, except if white.
Wood	Long life.
Violets	Success.
Violin	Peace.

THE POWERS OF THE HAND: CHIROMANCY, RADIESTHESIA AND FLUIDS

In his *Pantagruel,* III, 25, Rabelais attributes to Her Tripa some methods of divination which he makes use of to illuminate Panurge. But Rabelais was scarcely generous. Scores of divinatory procedures or mancies have existed since antiquity, at least seventy of which are known to us today.

Not being able to analyze all (they are described briefly in the dictionary), we will limit ourselves to some powers of the hand.

The hand which writes, which draws, which sculpts, which plays music, was regarded as prophetic. A science of signs (*chirology*) and of divination (*chiromancy*) have come from the study of the hand. (The science which concerns writing is a domain reserved for *graphology*).

Chirology

This is sometimes confused with *chirognomony*, the art of knowing the character of someone by the study of his hand. To be scientific, the chirologist never gives a fixed value to given signs, but always aims at examining them in characteristic groups.

To realize these complexes, he proceeds with different examinations:

(1) Relation between the hand and the wrist.
(2) Position and relative length of the fingers, especially in relation to the thumb.

(3) Characteristic quality of the hand to touch (firmness, suppleness, clamminess, warmth, etc.).

(4) Joints.

(5) Structure of the palm and the back of the hand.

(6) Dorsal and palmar side of the fingers.

(7) Nails (there is a divination concerning them, *onychomancy*).

(8) Relation between the two hands.

The general indications are:

(1) *Wrist:* indicates vital power.

(2) *Fingers:* thumb = adaptation, sexuality; index = form of intelligence; middle = personality in days gone by; annular = enthusiasm; auricular = affectivity, intuition.

(3) *Characteristic quality of the hand:* a complex interpretation, which goes back to Hippocratic medicine.

(4) *Stiffness* = primitiveness, schizoid character; *suppleness* = adaptive character.

(5) *Palm:* relation of the individual with himself (eminence = potential character; wrinkles = realized characteristics and their effects). *Back:* adolescence, relations with the outside world.

(6) *Fronts of fingers and spaces between fingers:* according to each case: activities, timidity, sensuality.

(7) *Nails:* adaptation to the outside world.

(8) *Left hand:* past, especially before maturity. *Right hand:* past since maturity and present activities.

Lastly, *chiropathology* studies the particular pathological signs to each sub-domain: tissues, structure, wrinkles, nails, fingers. These must also be integrated in the whole.

All the signs are thought to furnish indications of the general order capable of illuminating the personality and even the future of the subject studied. It is necessary to admit that too much imagination is often employed in this field.

Chiromancy

This is a divination based on the interpretation of signs revealed in the hand, which nobody can normally change and which the Gipsies studied long before the morphologists. Occultists have practised chiromancy since antiquity, since the hand is above all else the tool of intelligence. The Gipsies took up these techniques, and from the 17th century a general diagram of the hand was established, relating the lines and their astrological affinities (see illustration). It is useless to try to sum up this profusion of what are often absurdities, but we will seek to extract from them an intelligible explanation.

The whole of the hand has wrinkles or lines (ambition, luck, heart, head, life), a central plane (of Mars), and mounts (Jupiter, Saturn, Sun, Mercury, Venus and Moon). These elements can be interpreted separately or in combinations. Others take account of figures in squares, in stars (four intersecting lines), in a cross, and in grills.

Convinced that the planetary influences must also be written in the hand, some astrologers have not only drawn the relief of the hand, but have introduced to it the Zodiac and its houses. Thus, one obtains roughly the following equivalences for this *astrological chiromancy*:

House I—Aries—thumb = ambition, daring.
House II—Taurus—mount of Venus = love, friendship.
House III—Gemini—mount of Venus = love, friendship.
House IV—Cancer—mount of Moon—luck, dreaming, travel, secrets.
Houses V and VI—Leo—mount of Mars = children, contests, intelligence.
House VI—Virgo—mount of Mercury = illness, hesitation.
Houses VII and VIII—Scorpio—auricular = skill, cunning, receptivity, fertility.
Houses VIII and IX—Capricorn—Sagittarius—annular = mysticism, arts, fame, fortune.
House X—Capricorn—middle finger = position, destiny.
House XI—Aquarius—index = commandment.
House XII—Pisces = analysis, judgment.

Furthermore, it is said that the index is the 'divine finger' or Jupiterian, the middle Saturnia, the annular Solar, and the auricular Mercurian.

Chiromancers who take themselves seriously assert that a hand must reveal characteristics of the individual, specifying: (a) his condition, according to his quality of strength and his orientation-structure; (b) the mechanism which motivates him; and (c) the circumstances which have developed these. The hand must also reveal events. Some stipulate that the right hand expresses reality, the left, theory.

Strictly speaking, if one allows the first point, the second is

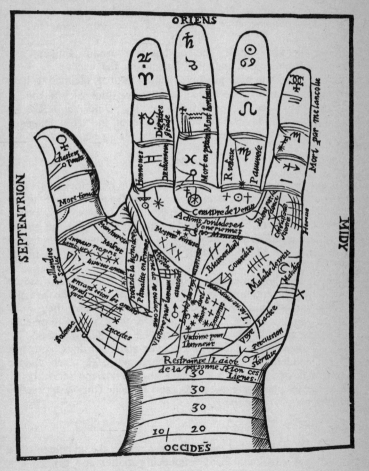

The lines of the hand and their astrological affinities.

confirmed. In practice this is questionable, especially as the interpretations of the specialists are frequently very different.

Rhabdomancy

The use of arrows (*belomancy*), and sticks or rods (properly called *rhabdomancy*) as a means of divination goes back to antiquity.

Since the 15th century the rod has been used in England and Germany to discover metallic deposits in the earth.

In 1692, a Dauphine peasant, Jacques Aymar, claimed to have recognized a murderer thanks to the qualities of his rod; it is true that, since the publication of *The Universal Baton* by Le Royer in 1674, the multiple virtues of the truly 'magical' rod were no longer doubted.

Radiesthesia

Many occultists recognize that the term radiesthesia is badly chosen because it implies *a priori* the existence of waves, radiations, and fluids, of which we shall see that there is no proof.

If one admits that an 'esthesia' or special sensibility can attract a wave, it is difficult to explain how different pendulums, some of metal, some of wood, some of other materials, react in the same way.

The fact is the practitioner 'chooses' for his pendulum those powers which suit him best. The claims of those who are not sincere radiesthesists have become exorbitant, and they work with or without proof, as, for example, with a packet or tube containing material or an object similar to what one seeks.

The radiesthesist claims to discover water, springs, ore, lost objects, hidden treasure and missing persons. He even claims, and this is dangerous, to diagnose and advise the seriously ill. He turns to photographs, cards, and objects (this last practice touches on *psychometry*).

Fluids

A 'fluid' is regarded as a subtle stream, the privilege of a chosen few, and capable of influencing matter and beings. For example, one cannot conceive a fakir without fluid, if not 'solar'

A sorcerer of the 17th century.

at any rate 'personal'. But do these 'fluids' exist? It has often been confused with 'vital breath'—from the 'influx of life' with the Egyptians, the 'prana' of the Hindus, and the 'aura' of the Romans, to the mysterious 'gift of the Kings' which heals scrofula. It is found under the name of *Telesma* in the Emerald Table of the alchemists. Paracelsus called it *spiritus vitae* or *archaeus;* for the Rosicrucians, it was 'the vital universal principle'; for Mesmer and the defenders of animal magnetism, 'the vital fluid or healer'.

It has also had scientific names: *V.* or *vital rays* of Commandant Darget (1847-1923), *N. ray* of Rene Blondlot (announced in 1903), and *mito-genetic rays* of A. and L. Gurwitsch (1927), approved by Andre Meyer in 1934.

To the credulous, this fluid panacea has astonishing powers, but the fakíric fluid, the magnetic fluid and the experiences of hypnosis associated with it on stage, and spectral fluid or 'effluvograms' collected by transcendent photography—claimed as photographs of the apparitions of phantoms or the *ectoplasm* of mediums—have not withstood scientific investigation. Equipment for measuring these fluids has proved unreliable, and the 'fluids' themselves have not lived up to the claims made for them.

CARTOMANCY AND THE BOHEMIAN TAROT

Origin and significance of cards

Cartomancy, or art of divining by the use of playing-cards is a minor popular divination. It is only a poor sister of the Tarot, and its devotees are insignificant.

It is doubtless easy to establish analogies between the two (diamonds ═ wands, clubs ═ coins, spades ═ swords, hearts ═ cups), but it leads nowhere, for the meanings attributed to playing-cards and to those of the Tarot are different.

It is generally believed that cards were invented to amuse King Charles VI (1366-1422) called 'Well-loved' and then 'the Simple', but in reality Alphonse XI had already forbidden them in 1332 in the statutes of the Order of the Band.

The art of divination with cards had a tremendous following in Europe, especially in France at the court of Louis XVI and under the Empire. Sometimes the symbols of the four elements (diamonds = salamanders, clubs = water-sprites, spades = gnomes, hearts = sylphs), were discerned in it, and sometimes a summary of integral alchemy.

Cartomancy used a pack of fifty-two cards, but more frequently a piquet pack of thirty-two cards, in which the figures have only a head.

Following is a list of the main values of the cards, but it is important to remember that a card does not have isolated significance, and that its interpretation depends on the card or cards which precede it.

Diamonds: Generally unlucky; blond or auburn-haired people.

King:	Rather important man who is thinking of harming you; *reversed* (when the head is *inverted*): will harm you.
Queen:	Slanderous or thoughtless woman; *reversed*: will harm you.
Jack:	Soldier, postman (unpleasant news); *reversed*: no letters or disastrous news.
Ace:	A letter.
Ten:	Indispensable and unforeseen voyage.
Nine:	Money delay.
Eight:	Surprising steps, propositions.
Seven:	Surprise; gain if it comes with the ace.

Clubs: Generally lucky; brown or dark-auburn hair.

King:	Just and helpful man; *reversed*: his help will be delayed.
Queen:	Brown-haired woman, important, will help you; *reversed*: jealousy or delay.
Jack:	Young brown-haired man, serious, prospects of marriage; *reversed*: impediment, repulsion.
Ace:	Gain, money, success: *reversed*: theft.
Ten:	Fortune, inheritance; followed by the nine of diamonds or spades: delay, loss.
Nine:	Success.
Eight:	Hopes established, situation.
Seven:	Weakness; followed by a nine: inheritance.

Spades: Generally unlucky; brown-haired or dark auburn people.

King:	Man of law, doctor with whom one would become

	bored; *reversed:* loss of a lawsuit, serious illness.
Queen:	Widow or divorcee who seeks to deceive you; *reversed:* will deceive you.
Jack:	Treachery; *reversed*: some say treachery, others the opposite.
Ace:	Sadness; *reversed*: grief.
Ten:	Imprisonment, obscurity.
Nine:	Delay in business, death.
Eight:	Bad news, sorrow; followed by seven of diamonds: discord.
Seven:	Boredom, quarrels, loss (except if followed by hearts).

Hearts: Generally lucky; blond or auburn-haired people.

King:	Honorable benevolent man; *reversed*: obstacles to his benevolence.
Queen:	Generous woman; *reversed*: nuisance in her intervention.
Jack:	Young man seeking to help you, amorous; *reversed*: lack of freedom, ill child.
Ace:	Pleasant news; surrounded by figures: meal with friends; *reversed*: hostile family.
Ten:	Great unforeseen happiness.
Nine:	Reconciliation, declaration of love.
Eight:	Satisfaction through children, joy in the country.
Seven:	Love, good marriage.

It is also necessary to take into account the most important sequences or series:

Kings:	Four: honors; three: protection, success in commerce; two: good advice, competition of men.
Queens:	Four: scandal, anger; three: jealousy, trickery; two: friendship.
Jacks:	Four: success; three: laziness, complications; two: dispute or approaching marriage.
Aces:	Four: success or a death; three: success, flirtations; two: hesitation, enmity.
Tens:	Four: some say boredom, others success; three: change of situation; two: loss, deception.
Nines:	Four: good deeds, realization; three: boredom, indiscretions; two: hesitation, money.

Eights: Four: checks; three: some say abandon, others marriages; two: disagreements.

Sevens: Four: intrigue, slander; three: pleasure; two: news or pregnancy.

With the exception of spades, a series, particularly of figures, is an excellent omen.

How to Draw the Cards

There are several ways to draw the cards.

The usual method consists of shuffling the cards, having the person for whom it is being done cut them with the left hand, and draw from the pack each seventh card (7th, 14th, 21st, etc.). Each time the six intermediary cards must be put back at the bottom of the pack. When twelve cards have thus been drawn, they are spread out on the table in a semi-circle, from left to right, in the order they were drawn.

One then presumes the king of hearts for a consultant who is blonde and married, the king of clubs for a brown-haired married person, the queen of hearts for a blonde woman or young girl, and the queen of clubs for a brown-haired woman or girl. If one of these cards is not among the twelve drawn, it is sought from the pack and added as a thirteenth. If it is already there, a thirteenth card is drawn from the pack and placed down. One interprets by starting from the card corresponding to the consultant and stopping at each seventh (some say fifth) card.

As additional information, for each important card, a new card can be drawn from the pack.

To finish the reading the thirteen main cards may be picked up, shuffled and cut with the left hand.

Six cards are spread out, the next five placed one on each of the first five cards, so that the sixth remains a single card, and then the last two cards placed on the first two stacks, so that each then contains three cards. The cards are then interpreted on the basis that the first stack concerns the person himself, the second his house, the third what he expects, the fourth what he does not expect, the fifth surprises, and the sixth his thoughts.

Another method consists of drawing four sets each of three

cards and placing them so they form a square, to be interpreted from right to left, setting out from the highest card, which is known as the card of destiny. This method is completed by four cards of 'detail', drawn after shuffling and cutting again.

The Consecration of the Tarot

Probably of Bohemian origin, the Tarot is a special pack of seventy-eight cards (which will be described later). The main figures are called the *major arcana*. They are consulted for a knowledge of the future.

A Tarot must be consecrated. The dedication takes place in a dwelling in complete solitude, with doors and windows closed, at the hour of Jupiter and the crescent moon, seated facing east, on a table covered with white linen.

The one officiating must have purified his hands previously and be clothed in linen and proper garments. Women can only perform the dedication seven hours after the last menstruation and complete and general purification.

It is necessary to strew on the table or burn a little incense of the zodiacal sign which occupies the sun at the date of birth of the person officiating, and taking the complete series of arcana, to pass them progressively, one by one, in numerical order, with the cards facing up to form a complete pack. The fingers of each hand are joined, with the tips of the thumbs and index fingers touching and are placed palm down at a short distance from the pack. They are kept thus for three minutes while maintaining complete mental passivity; eyes and mouth are closed, the body naturally straight, with elbows tucked in and the arms not touching the table. After this period, the arcana are shuffled for another three minutes, put face down in the same way, and the hands are placed as before. After three minutes the same operation is repeated with the cards facing up. Three minutes later the pack must be enveloped in a square of violet silk and left untouched in a sheltered place for seven days, after which the book of Thot is dedicated and can enter into service.

To conserve the impression of the emanation of the hands and to harmonize the officiating one with his instrument, the arcana must not be touched by any other person and must stay in the same silk.

Symbolism of the Tarot

It is impossible to supply, even in abbreviated form, a symbolic study of the Tarot. Its most exalted followers say that the 'Bible of the Bohemians' contains all occultism and is the projection of the collective unconscious; in other words, it is the illustration of symbols accumulated through the ages and even unconsciously by different peoples. Here are some elements of this symbolism.

The attitude of the person represented is either dynamic (standing) or static (seated); each part of the represented body has a particular significance and colors play an important role. Blue, red, yellow, flesh, white, black and green are the seven colors of the major arcana and violet of the minor arcana. Their symbolism is practically the same as it was in the Middle Ages. The twenty-two major arcana express the history of the evolution of the world, of human progress, and the mystical alphabet, while with the exception of the Fool, they all have a number which allows a combination following the techniques of secret numerology. The minor arcana have the following significance:

Sword = air = action.
Cup = water = sensibility, fertility.
Coin = earth = possession.
Wand = fire = life.

The Game of the 78 Cards

Tarot is, for some, a card game and divination; for others, a complex system of logic for improving the mind.

The seventy-eight cards are decorated according to different traditions developed after the Bohemians brought them from Egypt at the end of the Middle Ages. There is a German Tarot, one of Paris, one of Etteilla (Alliette); but the Tarot of Marseilles, issued by Nicolet Conver in the 18th century, seems to be closest to the original.

There are twenty-two main figures or major arcana, all having a number except the Fool.

Their detailed explanation is in the dictionary under the following words: Lovers; Juggler; Chariot; Devil; Emperor; Hermit; Star; Strength; Empress; Justice; Judgment; Moon;

House of God; Fool; World; Death; Pope; Pope, Female; Hanged Man; Wheel of Fortune; Sun; Temperance.

There are four more series or suits of the minor arcana. Each set (cards of Cup, Sword, Rod or Scepter, coin or cycle) comprises fourteen cards subdivided into four figures (King, Queen, Knight, Knave) and ten cards (from ace to ten). From

The Juggler,
first card of the Tarot

these fifty-six cards (knights excepted, leaving fifty-two cards) comes the usual structure of the Tarot. As stated before, rods = diamonds, coins = clubs, swords = spades, cups = hearts.

The following meanings are usually given to the suits: *Red or Scepter* (diamonds): expression of being, creation, procreation, commandment.

Cup (hearts): receptivity and conservation of being, love on all planes, intuition, mysticism.

Sword (spades): combativeness and suffering of being, violence, hate, struggle.

Coin or cycle or disc (clubs): expansiveness of being, munificence.

As for the cards, there is a special significance for each card, which varies according to the systems and the suits.

Divining Technique

There are numerous ways of drawing the Tarot.

The main ones are (the consultant always cuts with the left hand): (1) The technique of the fifteen: the pack is shuffled and fifteen cards are chosen and interpreted from right to left.

The rest are shuffled and another fifteen are taken and interpreted in the same way, being placed under the previous ones.

Lastly, a third interpretation of pairs is made from top to bottom.

(2) The seven stacks: the consultant shuffles the pack and cuts six times to obtain seven bundles, from which each first card is turned for interpretation. Then from each stack the cards are interpreted in order.

(3) The cross: fifteen cards are drawn and set out, three at the top, three in the center, three at the bottom, three to the left and three to the right in the form of a cross. They are interpreted, taking into account that high = question put, center = present life, bottom = consequences, right = social life, left = sentiments.

(4) The method of the major arcana: one uses only these twenty-two cards. They are placed in five lots of two or three cards each, noting that high = situation, center = whole, bottom = possibilities, right = relation with others, left = personal destiny.

MAGNETISM AND HYPNOTISM

It is necessary to distinguish between *magnetism* and *hypnosis*. According to Littre 'magnetism is a series of practices by which one produces on the human body unusual phenomena like those which characterize a magnet'.

Several occultists today prefer to say of magnetism: 'It is the personal action, physical or physiological, of man upon man'. Magnetism can calm and provoke sleep. That is what it has in common with hypnotism, but if the magnetized subject continues to reason the hypnotized neither thinks nor acts independently.

Hypnosis, a term created (from the Greek hypnos: sleep) by the surgeon Braid, of Manchester, in 1845, is a state similar to sleep, characterized by an exaggerated suggestibility and produced artificially with or without glance fixation and passes.

Hypnotism is the scientific study and practice of hypnosis and of methods which relate to it.

The Tub of Mesmer

Mesmer was famous for his tub of magnetism. In the middle of a room would stand the tub—an immense bath on legs four inches above the floor and with a foot of water in it. The bath would be full of bottles containing 'magnetized' water and they lay on a bed of crushed glass and iron filings. From each bottle projected an iron rod, which the patient gripped and applied to the area to be healed.

Chants, accompanied by a harpsichord, gave the ceremony a sonorous background favorable to magnetism. Clothed in a sumptuous robe of lilac silk, Mesmer would stride forward majestically. Standing in the center of the ring of patients he would look at them slowly, imperiously, flourishing an iron wand. Most of the patients would go into trances and Mesmer would then withdraw.

This, then, was how the Austrian, Friedrich Anton Mesmer, born in Germany in 1733 and branded a fool by the Academy of Berlin, performed cures for the court of Louis XVI in his magnificent apartment in the Place Vendome.

The Faculty of Medicine was aroused. It sent a commission of enquiry to investigate. The Commission members included

Dr Benjamin Franklin, then Ambassador for the United States, and Dr Guillotin, inventor of the guillotine. In vain Mesmer protested: 'Magnetism is a universally distributed fluid. It penetrates the substance of the nerves, and affects them immediately. The action and the virtue of animal magnetism can be communicated from one body to another, animate or inanimate'. Fool or precursor, Mesmer was hunted from Paris.

Magnetism

Hypnosis has been known since ancient times. It was probably practised in Egyptian temples four thousand years ago to help heal the sick. Mesmer made it famous by bringing back a theory of Paracelsus.

Paracelsus (1493-1541) spoke of 'animal magnetism', a kind of mysterious attraction which 'explained' a lot about human behavior. Mesmer and his techniques with the healing tub (1778) drew inspiration from this. In 1784 the Marquis Armand de Puysegur studied what he called a privileged state: 'magnetic somnambulism with supernormal perception'. A little later Dr Petetin de Lyon studied 'animal electricity' with 'cataleptic state' and 'senses at the tips of the fingers'. Fluid, magnetism, and animal and human hypnosis were all mixed, and in the 19th century, the magnetist Ricard de Montpellier claimed even to be able to 'direct the clouds'.

To clarify the problem it is necessary to successively analyze animal hypnosis, hypnosis of hysterics, the suggestion of normal people, and 'scinec' or 'fakiric' hypnosis.

Animal Hypnosis

Many differing phenomena have been labelled with the term 'animal hypnosis'. In 1646, Kircher recorded among animals a curious reflex immobilization which Czermack likened to hypnosis in 1873. Preyer studied it in 1880 and disclosed three different causes. A state of fear or cataplexy, provoked by a sudden or violent excitation; a kind of partial sleep, as if the mind kept watch in a sleeping or paralyzed body; or a lethargic somnolence, following a weak but prolonged excitation; and a prostration caused by an intense fixation on a white line or a brilliant object.

On the other hand, from 1874 Kahlbaum had called attention to a state of catatonia, a neurosis accompanied by catalepsy, rigidity and confusion. In 1904, Peters produced something like catatonia with the help of certain medicaments. These experiments were studied by Baruk and de Jong.

There is also 'Javanese narcosis', a kind of constriction of the carotid arteries practised on some fowls by the sorcerers of Java and Sumatra and presented by them at demonstrations of hypnosis.

It should be noted that the term animal hypnosis is used excessively to indicate phenomena which bear little relation to proper hypnotism.

The Hypnosis of Hysterics

At the Salpetriere, Professor Charcot, following many studies of hysterical women, believed he could distinguish three stages of hypnotism. His theories were recognized by Bernheim, Grasset, Luys, Professor Ochorowicz (who invented the 'rigid rays' to explain telekinesis), Berillon, Professor Boirac and others. In fact, Charcot was often duped by these women, who soon learned that a good 'demonstration' was worth double rations. Later several of these subjects confessed to shamming.

The Charcot method was brought into disrepute finally by Ernest Dupre (1862-1921) and Joseph Babinsky (1857-1932), who proved that it was not a matter of hypnosis, but of pithiatism or malady of suggestion.

Although questionable, Charcot's methods served as a prelude to the cathartic method or cleansing of the mind of Breuer in 1880, later to the psychoanalysis of Freud (who had attended several experiments at the Salpetriere), then to the 'awakening dream' of R. Desoille, and, lastly, to the exploration of the collective unconscious by Jung. Progressively, the 'cleansing' was extended from hysterics to normal subjects.

It is difficult to pinpoint the phenomenon of suggestion. Where does it begin? Where does it end?

The Coue method, improved by Eymieu, showed what autosuggestion could do. Suggestion by others, immediate or deferred, sometimes achieves much as, for example, with advertising and 'underground psychology', which has been used by dictators skilfully to control the masses.

Between accepted suggestion and hypnosis there is a thin dividing line. Some fiercely deny hypnotic phenomenon, others put it down to complicity.

It seems, however, that hypnosis is possible only with the consent of the subject. Once consent is obtained, most patients are very amenable to suggestion. In Great Britain alone, 8000 surgeons and dentists use hypnosis for painless childbirth or dental extraction, but disastrous consequences can ensue if the hypnotist is incompetent or a swindler.

Professor Bessemans once remarked that hypnosis is set in motion by the subject himself, with the acceptance of the idea that he is reconciled to it.

Hypnosis, Staged or Fakiric

Hypnosis which is practised on stage, with the single object of offering an unsophisticated public an original spectacle, is always suspect. It is often based on illusion. These demonstrations can have as subjects an animal, an individual who is an accomplice or assistant (hetero-hypnosis) or the person himself (auto-hypnosis), with the apparition 'of a cataleptic coma, of cadaveric rigidity and of concomitant states'.

Techniques of Hypnotism

The techniques of hypnotism are varied, and only the main ones are outlined here:

(1) Prepared dreams and at times a forceful manner were used by healers even during celebrations of mysteries in antiquity (the oracle of Trophonius at Lebadea did not hesitate to abuse his clients).

(2) The tub of Mesmer.

(3) The magnetic passes of the hand (with or without 'emission of fluid'), sometimes combined with 'the action of substances at a distance'. This method is of doubtful authenticity.

(4) The order 'sleep!'.

(5) The fixation of visual attention on a brilliant object (spinning mirror, luminous globe, silver spoon).

(6) The shock manner used by Charcot on the hysterics at

the Salpetriere of Paris (1878-1884), such as violent pressure, surprises, dazzling lights, etc.

(7) The methods of Dr Watson using visual fixation.

(8) Telehypnotism or hypnosis at a distance, with immediate or delayed action. Dr Bjorken, Swedish psychiatrist, could re-hypnotize by telephone. In fact, once a subject accepts a post-hypnotic suggestion, he is sensitive to any sign by the hypnotist or the hypnotist's voice.

(9) The classic method is the fixation of the eyes, with or without passes (these passes are operated with or without contact).

The Three Stages

Hypnosis comprises three phases:

(1): Somnolence, improperly called lethargy. The subject gives the impression of needing sleep and imagines he can no longer carry out movements which his hypnotist forbids. (2): The subject assumes the appearance of natural sleep; this is often accompanied by catalepsy (especially studied by Baruk) enabling the subject to keep the position assigned him (this is far from fakiric rigidity). (3): Automation or hypnotic somnabulation: all the sensory reactions and motives of the subject are inhibited, amnesia takes over and post-hypnotic action, the execution of an order after awakening, becomes possible. This should not be confused with ordinary somnabulism.

These three stages can occur successively, although not necessarily in the order specified, or separately. They are reached either by heterohypnosis (intervention of a hypnotist) or by auto-hypnosis.

SPIRITUALISM

In the little Italian city of Camerino 1500 copies of a journal, Aurora, were published regularly in 1954, which were entirely compiled by spirits. At a seance held each Thursday spirits told twelve spiritists what they had to write down.

Collaborators were not lacking. Dante would dictate a poem in ancient triplets like his *Divine Comedy*, d'Annunzio would deliver diatribes surpassed only by Mussolini, better trained to harangue the masses.

Spirit Seance with a Medium

The room is closed, the curtains are drawn. A seance is about to begin.

The 'faithful' are grouped about a small round or revolving table. They form a chain either by holding hands or placing their hands, fingers open, side by side with little fingers touching those of their neighbors'. Soft music is played or a hymn is quietly sung. The seance takes place with or without a medium, a person who is believed to serve as an intermediary (from the Latin medius: middle) between the spirits and the consultants. Very often the medium, who may be hypnotized, stays isolated in a corner of the room or even in the 'spirit cabinet', a curtained-off area. Some mediums even tie themselves to their chairs to show that they are not physically involved in the seance (but some of these ties are child's play to professionals).

It is important that the group meditate and concentrate completely, for 'unity of thought' is necessary for the coming of the spirits. Patience is necessary, too; for a spirit of quality refuses to inconvenience himself at the first invocation. When attending a seance it is necessary to ensure that the medium is an expert, being in affinity with the beyond, as an inexpert medium may summon vulgar and coarse spirits.

It is essential, also, to believe in a seance, otherwise the spirits will be reticent.

After a period of meditation the medium begins to chant. Sometimes the curtained-off area is opened and a vapor called *ectoplasm* can be seen coming out or an *aureola* (aura) crowning the medium. Some mediums can operate a 'doubling' and, on very rare occasions, proceed to what is called a direct exploration, when the 'subtle elements' of the body explore the superior planes forbidden to mortals. Other mediums are possessed: a spirit takes possession of them and goes out, as a complete ectoplasm, from their mouth. Florence Cook in 1873 gave birth in this way to Katie King, who was manifested for three years, while Neapolitan Eusapia Paladino produced a 'third hand'. Other mediums realize telekinesis (movements of objects without contact from a distance), levitation (the human body defies the law of gravity) or *apports* (materialization of an object believed to be created from nothing).

Swedenborg

Emmanuel Swedenborg, who was called by Balzac the 'Buddha of the North', was born in Stockholm in 1688. A doctor of Upsala University, he was dedicated to occultism from 1744, claiming to have had on the night of April 7 a vision which was to reoccur again in London a year later, a Magus clothed in purple revealing all the secrets to him. Thereafter, he was in contact with Virgil and Luther among other distinguished spirits.

From 1757 he was given the gift of clairvoyance and he claimed to have seen the Last Judgment. His book, *Heaven and Hell*, brought out in 1758, made a great impression. It was to be the foundation of modern spiritualism, which he called *pneumatology*.

He was also one of the founders of hypnotism, since he turned to auto-hypnosis to facilitate his visions. Following him, the German professor Adam Weishaupt, founded in 1766 the sect of the Three Perfectibles, which later on became that of The Illuminated.

The American Renaissance

At Hydesville in the State of New York in December, 1847, Margaret and Katie Fox, aged fifteen and twelve respectively, claimed to hear at their farm knocks produced by a spirit (this kind of knocking was later called raps and 'typtology' the discipline studying such supernatural knocks). There was also the displacement of furniture. It was all due to the ghost of Charles Ryan, called by others Charles Haynes, a hawker, father of five, who revealed that he had been murdered by a neighbour some years before. Counting the raps and entering into conversation with the spirit, the Fox family invented the principle of the spirit alphabet.

This created a sensation in America, despite the protests of the Methodist Church, which banned the Fox family. Margaret and Katie, having become successful mediums under the guidance of their sister Leah, made a fortune first in Rochester and then in New York.

The Spirit Vogue

Spirits suddenly multiplied, eager to manifest themselves. The first Spirit Congress was held at Cleveland in 1852 and two years later there were ten thousand mediums to serve three million devotees in the United States. There were soon twenty-two journals and magazines devoted to the subject alone.

In 1852 a congress of mediums went to England and in 1853 they visited Germany and France.

A commission of thirty-three members of the Dialectical Society of London was nominated to 'crush forever these works of imagination'. However, eighteen months later, it concluded by supporting the reality of spiritist phenomena and the great scientist, William Crookes, wrote: 'I do not say that it is possible: I say that it is'.

In Germany, several university professors quickly became supporters. The Academy of Science of Paris, however, headed by Chevreul and Faraday, took a stand against spiritism from 1854, while the salons, on the other hand, became keen supporters. They had a following of such famous personalities as Victor Hugo, the author, who attended many circles during his exile in Jersey; Boucher of Perthes, the father of prehistory; Lieutenant Colonel Rochas; Dr Charles Richet; and the dramatist Sardou, who presided over the spiritist congress of 1900. Other countries followed quickly: Italy (with, among others, the crimonologist Lombroso), Russia (with Aksakof, secret councillor of Czar Alexander II), and Spain.

Codifier: Allan Kardec

The person to give spiritism its greatest impetus was Leon Rivail of Lyons. Under the English pseudonym of Allan Kardec, Rivail unified and codified spiritism. Thus a religion began, as he said himself 'on the existence, the manifestations, and the information of the spirits'.

Spiritism, according to Kardec, is a spiritualist doctrine in the

sense that it believes in the immortality of the soul and in God.
It is thus incompatible with atheism and materialism. Kardec
contends that the spirits manifest themselves to us in order to
inform us. The Church, however, rejects this.

The Spirits and Their Consultation

The spirits are the souls of the dead, and are divided into
three categories: (1) The imperfect, subdivided into the vicious,
inconsiderate, the neuters and rappers (these last are true agitators); (2) The good, subdivided into benevolent, learned, wise
and superior (these include Jesus and Buddha); (3) The pure,
subdivided into angels, archangels and seraphim.

They live together in Eternity, being grouped by affinity. They
have instantaneity of thought (but it is difficult to accept the
intellectual poverty of most of their revelations) and a certain
ubiquity (they can manifest themselves in several places at a
time 'by a kind of radiation').

During life, the soul is enveloped in a 'perispirit', residing in
the body which it sometimes leaves momentarily, particularly
in a dream.

After death it can be called back and consulted.

This is not new. *Nekyomancy*, later called necromancy or
divination by consultation of the dead, existed in antiquity. Saul
invoked the spirit of Samuel through the mouth of the magician
of Endor (Samuel 1, 28); Ulysses consulted the diviner Tiresias
(10th canto of Homer's *Odyssey*); Atossa evoked King Darius
(*The Persians* of Aeschylus); Gilgamesh, the Assyrian hero,
called back his friend Enkidu; the Egyptians asked the dead for
premonitory dreams (papyrus of the Louvre 3229 and gnostic
papyrus of Leyde); and Tertullian spoke from the turning table
at the Roman senate of the second century.

Today, the raps have been replaced by the *planchette*, or
ouija board, where a pointer indicates the letters of an alphabet.

Since Kardec . . .

To the outsider, two schools more or less make use of the
name of spiritism while practising a wide religious syncretism:
Madame Blavatsky, after acting poorly as a medium, founded

in New York in 1875 the Theosophical Society, of which the initial center was established at Mount Adyar, near Madras. Annie Besant succeeded her until 1933.

In Cochin-china, the Cao-Dai was launched by an official, Ngo-Van-Chieu, and directed by Le-Van-Trung, who died in 1934. The movement today has some 250,000 members. As for spiritists, there are about three or four million in the world today.

Metapsychics

The scientifically-minded have been unable to accept the intellectual weakness of the relevations from beyond, or the manifestations of the dead by the raps or the table turning Scepticism seized some spiritists and they turned away from spirits to study, from 1865, the 'medium faculties' or the special powers of the mediums.

Metaphysics was established in science and the great mediums were to be called to task. (They will be dealt with in the next chapter.)

We cannot finish with spiritism, however, without pointing out the enormous trickery due to prestidigitation (spirit cupboard of the Davenport Brothers in 1860; faked slates of Slade, the medium, at the beginning of this century, etc.), without criticizing the value of spirit photos (Buguet 'photographer of spirits' was denounced by Flammarion) and without insisting on the danger which these practices offer weak minds.

THE GREAT MEDIUMS AND METAPSYCHICS

According to the best specialist in spiritism, its codifier Allan Kardec, the mediums were 'the people accessible to the influence of the spirits and more or less gifted in the faculty of receiving and transmitting their communications'. But, besides spiritists wholly believing in survival and the manifestations of the spirits of the dead (like Lodge and Bozzasnio), many specialists reject ghosts and their survival, but admit that unknown forces are used by mediums.

Many men of science were interested in the phenomenon. A list of great mediums and a report on the controversies they stirred up have been set down by Robert Amadou in his work *The Great Mediums*. Here are the main parts:

Angelique Cottin, 14 years old, of Bouvigny (Orne), in 1846 produced several examples of telekinesis—the movement of objects at a distance and without contact.
However, the report of the commission of the Academy of Sciences, directed by Arago, concluded on February 16, 1846, the non-existence of telekinesis by the young girl. It concluded also that there was some cheating and 'brisk and violent movements of chairs on which she was sitting'.

Margaret and Katie Fox, who were dealt with earlier in this book, must be regarded with caution. In 1888, Margaret, then Mrs Kane, declared in effect before the Musical Academy of New York that all her accounts were false. Her sister, then Mrs. Sparr, confirmed this in November of the same year. However, they retracted these statements in 1892.

Daniel Dunglas Home (1833-1886) produced throughout his life and in some ten countries the most curious phenomena of telekinesis, of levitation (the body defying gravity), of raps (paranormal knocks), of materialization and even of ghosts. The most amazing thing is that he worked in light, surrounded by spectators. He became a favorite at the court of the Czar at St Petersburg and at that of Napoleon III at the Tuileries.

If allowance is made for legend and if the objective inquiry made by Louis Figuier in 1860 is studied from the journals of the time, we must view his performances with an open mind. Almost all accounts came from people little experienced in occultism and prestidigitation (Home refused to work before the French conjurer Robert Houdin). But to be fair the assertions of 'Dr Phillip Davis' (his real name is not known) in his book, *The End of the Spirit World*, are too anti-spiritist to offer the guarantees desired for accuracy.

The real problem lies in the experiences of Home, controlled by William Crookes, from 1869 to 1873. The examination of these experiences does not lead to a conclusion as to their veracity. Faraday said there was no value in the experiences and even today, Dr D. J. West, director of Research of the Society for Psychical Research, underlines the lack of control by Crookes.

Florence Cook: Crookes was unbelievably naive about this woman, and her claims, too, must be treated with the greatest caution. From January to May, 1874, this medium made a fool of Crookes by making a spirit appear which she had signalled from 1871 and materialized from April 22, 1872, under the name of Katie King, whose name in the other world was Annie Morgan, and who died during the reign of Charles II. The controls for the experiments were non-existent, but Crookes persisted in the belief that he could hear their hearts beat and that it was actually possible to photograph them.

Stainton Moses, who adopted the pseudonym of M.A. Oxon, was an honest man, but the phenomena which he produced from 1872 with the Speers or Frederick Myers are challenged by Charles Richet and by a president of the Society for Psychical Research, W. H. Salter.

Eusapia Palladino (1854-1918), daughter of Abruzzi peasants. She had a painful childhood, which explains her nervous disorders. Her case was studied by different experts (notably Cesar Lombroso) from February, 1891. Some spoke of telekinesis, of phosphorescent apparitions, of materialization of hands, of teleplasty or imprints at a distance on a block of mastic, etc. Some of her experiences took place in Naples (Professor Wagner, 1893), in Warsaw (Professor Ochorowicz, forty seances in 1893), and in France (Professor Richet, 1894, and Count Rochas). Metapsychic critics from Cambridge University under Hodgson, however, concluded that her experiences were a systematic fraud. This did not deter Maxwell in 1895, or the Italians and the French in 1896, from reaffirming the authenticity of the phenomena. After numerous experiences in different parts of Europe, a scientific report was prepared in January, 1908, by a number of learned scientists, among them Pierre and Marie Curie, Henry Bergson, A. d'Arsonval and Branly. Despite what numerous occultists have affirmed, it is essential to point out with Amadou that neither Branly nor the Curies asserted that they were scientifically convinced of the authenticity of the phenomena. If, *a priori*, some of these phenomena of Eusapia seemed curious, her work was often tinged with gross examples of trickery, which were denounced and explained.

Kathleen Goligher, of Belfast, particularly interested Professor

W. J. Crawford who, between 1914 and 1920, wrote many words on mediums' experiences. In 1922 Charles Richet underlined the 'decisive value' of the works. Since then, the naivety of Professor Crawford, who committed suicide on July 30, 1920, has been proved and nobody believes the 'teleplastic phenomena of Belfast' nor the psychic influence of Miss Goligher, capable of lifting tables.

Martha Beraud offers history the most comical and unlikely of mediumnistic experiences. Some of her experiences were at General Noel's villa at Algiers, where to the general and his wife appeared not only an army of occultists but the ghost of the Hindu Grand Priest Bien-Boa and his sister Bergolia; Areski, the coachman; an actor-comedian of Kursaal; and a chambermaid. All were incarnated by Martha Beraud. Her experiences must have been convincing, for the great scientist Charles Richet was duped by them and some occultists still cite these apparitions as evidence.

Professor Schrenck-Notzing and Dr Geley, between 1916 and 1918, believed in the phenomena. However, Robert Tocquet proved the photographs taken were suspect and indicated that the electroplasm was faked.

Ladislas Lasslo in 1923 produced paranormal phenomena which were convincing to all who witnessed it at Budapest. The controls were strict, but before he left for a world journey he disclosed that it had been imposture.

Pasquale Erto, Neapolitan medium, controlled by Dr Sanguinetti and Dr Mackenzie in 1922, offered some good examples of 'rays' and 'luminous phenomena'. At Paris in 1923 Dr Geley gave assurances that all precautions had been taken to prevent trickery, and people believed in the phenomena until five seances from April 16 to May 2, 1924, at the Sorbonne, exposed him. It was proved that he concealed steel and cerium for writing, particularly in his fingernails.

Mrs le Roi Goddard Candon, called Margery, produced, from 1923 to 1929, according to Dr Prince, president of the Society for Psychical Research of Boston, 'the most ingenious and fantastic fraudulent effect in the history of metaphysics'. An inquiry at Harvard in 1925 also discredited her.

Stanislawa P., was patronized by the ever-credulous Schrenck-Notzing. Ochorowicz marvelled at her 'rigid rays'. Dr Osty exposed her at Paris in 1930.

Franck Kluski (1874-1944) began by producing ghosts, then, at forty-six, became a successful medium in Warsaw. Experiences in Paris, led by Dr Geley and Professor Richet, very often in total darkness, lacked control; darkness was maintained under the pretext that otherwise it 'was not suitable for Franck'. Amadou proved that the results of the experiences were not indisputable; however Kluski refused to submit to an examination by Paul Heuze and his collaborators.

Jean Guzik (1876-1928), Polish medium, after questionable demonstrations in Poland and Russia, he went to Paris and, under the direction of Dr Geley, gave thirty seances in 1922 and fifty in 1923. Some thirty-four reports mentioned two main categories of paranormal phenomena: telekinesis and contacts. G. Mendel underlined the imperfections of the control, and the challenge of the conjuror Dicksonn to the medium was not accepted.

Moreover, the phenomena ceased when experiences were requested at the Sorbonne by Paul Heuze. Was this because the control in this case was relentless? Although his trickery was exposed at Cracow in March, 1925, Guzik was, nevertheless, recalled to Paris by Dr Osty, but, after forty-one seances, Dr Osty confessed that even if the phenomena appeared valid to him 'it is certainly not a certainty'.

The brothers *Willy and Rudy Schneider,* in Braunau on the Inn, near the Austrian-German border, created the appearance in 1918 of Olga, ghost of Lola Montez, favorite of Louis II of Bavaria. Following experiments with Schrenck-Notzing at the University of Munich (the deficiency of controls by Schrenck-Notzing is well known) Willy gave a number of seances in London in 1924 and these luminous phenomena appeared convincing to Dr Dingwall. However, Willy always refused to allow himself to be photographed in action.

His younger brother, Rudy, worked in Vienna and was exposed in 1924 first by Professor Przibram, and then by Dr Leukei. However, eighty-eight seances were conducted in Munich,

Vienna and Prague in 1926, and from these favorable reports were obtained, although they were not very detailed. On August 26 that year Vinton concluded that the experiences were a fraud. The Paris seances, controlled by Dr Osty, after the 'production of an invisible absorbent substance', produced nothing more in the last seventeen experiences. There were fifty-five more experiences from October, 1933, to March, 1934, in London which also yielded little. His gift as a medium disappeared in 1934 and did not return. He died in 1957.

FAKIRISM

The Indian Rope Trick

The Indian rope trick has acquired more fame than any other. Earliest references to it go back thousands of years in Hindu, Buddhist and Mohammedan writings.

However, the most striking description of it comes from the Moroccan explorer and geographer, Ibn Batuta (1304-1378), who saw it at Hang-Tcheou in the gardens of the Great Khan. This is his description:

'When the feast was over, one of the entertainers took a ball of wood which had several holes and through which passed a rope. He threw it in the air and it went up to a point where we could no longer see it, finally to be held there without visible support. When there was only a little end of the rope in his hand, the entertainer told one of his assistants to hang on to the rope and climb into the air, which he did, until we could no longer see him. The entertainer called him three times without response then he took his knife in his hand, as if he were angry, grabbed the cord and disappeared also. Next he threw on the ground the hand of the child who had climbed the rope, then a foot, after that the other hand, then the other foot, the body and the head. He came down out of breath, his clothes tinged with blood. . . . After the Emir whispered to him something, the entertainer took the limbs of the young boy and put them down on the ground in their original position. Then he gave the mutilated body a slight kick and there was the child, who got up and stood quite straight, completely whole.'

The 19th century attempted to explain the phenomena ration-
ally and turned to scientific explanations, thereby stirring up
some lively controversy.

Firstly, the theory of collective hallucination was advanced;
that is, because of certain fortuitous or provoked circumstances,
a group of observers believe they see or hear something which
does not exist.

Hypnosis was remarkably successful around 1885, making
possible collective suggestion, which can best be defined as the
success in creating in the minds of spectators, with or without
staging and by the power of speech and gestures, a representation
which does not correspond with reality. The Indian fakirs were
the most expert in hypnotic manifestations.

In August, 1890, an article in the Chicago Daily Tribune,
signed S. Ellmore, attracted much attention. In company with
a painter named Lessing, this graduate of Yale University was
sent to India to study the Indian rope trick. They had, they
reported, seen the rope trick. Lessing had even drawn it in six
sketches and Ellmore had photographed it, but nothing appeared
on the film, which was developed normally. They therefore
concluded that the trick was a 'hypnotic influence'. They did
not call it 'collective suggestion' but 'collective hallucination'.

Months later the newspaper confessed that the story was pure
invention, aimed solely to catch the curiosity of readers and,
as a consequence, to boost sales. The newspapers added that the
name of the author of the story should have alerted readers,
as phonetically it meant 'sell more'.

The tests of Charcot at the Salpetriere and the better understanding of hypnosis produced the second stage of explanations
around 1920. The hypothesis of collective hypnosis had been
rejected, as it had been proven that part of any audience was
always resistant to hypnosis and even to suggestion. It was therefore contended that there remained the explanation by collective
illusion, which can be defined as any skilful staging or trickery
which gives to a collection of people a false idea of reality.

On February 5, 1919, Colonel Elliot told the 'Magic Circle',
of London, of which he was president, that the Circle had not
been able to find anyone who could do the Indian rope trick
under scientific control for a prize of 500 guineas. The 'Times

of India' and the English magician Branson had also offered prizes for a demonstration of the rope trick by amateurs, but had not had any takers.

The conclusion that the trick could not really be done was arrived at a little quickly, for Hindu fakirs do not generally read the newspapers and the offer thus probably escaped them.

However, the defenders of the rope trick have never admitted defeat and the hypothesis of collective hallucination has again been advanced. Even today the fascination of the Indian rope trick remains.

Other Miracles

Among the best known of the tricks of the Fakirs are the cord that cannot be cut; the multiplication of pieces of gold; the miraculous growth of a mango seed (the mango trick); animal hypnosis (such as snake charmers); the swallowing with impunity of nails, stones, needles, cactus, scorpions, etc.; spontaneous germination and the accelerated hatching of eggs; trances and levitation; the swallowing of crushed glass; the braving of sharp points, heat, intense cold, electric charges and even firearms, and firewalking. There are also the classic instances of body rigidity and concomitant states, the burial or immersion in water of fakirs with suspension of bodily functions, followed by resurrection.

REPUTED PARANORMAL POWERS
THE PSI FACULTIES

TELEKINESIS AND PARAPHYSICS

Telekinesis is the art of moving objects at a distance without any contact with them.

Between the extremes of those who condemn telekinesis and those who support it, there is a place for moderates. Renowned researchers like Lombroso, Professor Charcot, the physicist William Crookes and even the great Charles Richet were often duped by skilful charlatans. There are widely differing opinions about the authenticity of telekinesis, even among scientists. It is interesting, therefore, to restate the opinions of two authorities who cannot be suspected of being opposed to reputed occult phenomena.

The first, Professor Tocquet, a member of the committee of the Institut Metapsychique International, retains as valid only those telekinetic experiences of Eusapia Palladino at the Institut General Psychologique; of Stella C. with English illusionist Price, and some personal tests with a 'young medium' not named.

The second comes from one of the most renowned representatives of the modern school of Parapsychology, Robert Amadou. 'Nobody', he says, 'can affirm that the paranormal phenomena with physical effects attributed to the mediums does not exist. But if we require that they meet the demands of modern scientific proof, neither can anybody affirm the authenticity of these phenomena. After rejecting obvious trickery, there still remains a probability of fraud or illusion, but no one will ever be certain that certain experiments were worthless.

'The tests conducted with the great mediums have never brought rigorous scientific proof of paranormal material phenomena. Parapsychology is a scientific discipline in the modern sense of the term. It follows the rules of science and adopts its criteria. Whether or not there exist paraphysical phenomena, similar to those which the great mediums had the reputation

of displaying none has ever been observed in conditions capable
of convincing scientists.'

Parapsychology can assert no more. Robert Amadou also said,
'Let us therefore take care that we do not assert that the
reputedly paranormal physical phenomena do not authentically
exist. Let us just say that proof of their existence has never been
given'.

This conclusion of Amadou is the view of modern science.
Is it not also commonsense?

We add our own thoughts: in the immense mass of reports
about telekinesis, in the many experiences that it has claimed
to present to us, we could find nothing giving irrefutable proof
of it.

PSYCHOKINESIS OR P.K.

Psychokinesis is a term invented by Professor J. B. Rhine, of
Duke University in North Carolina. It describes the direct action
of thought on matter without any known material intermediary.
Objectively, it can be defined as a coincidence not explainable
by chance, or a mechanical action, or a rational or sensorial
influence between the desire or thought of an individual and an
objective event. The desire or thought of an individual may
be determined by an aleatory agent, the objective event
being produced independently of the aleatory process which produced the desire or thought of the individual. Parapsychologists
abbreviate it to *P.K.*

More simply, psychokinesis is the possibility of influencing a
physical system by the use of the mind alone.

Rhine studied what he called 'the *psi* functions' comprising
E.S.P. or 'extra-sensory perception', in other words, the possibility of perceiving other than by the senses, at the same time
as P.K. or psychokinesis.

Seeking to classify the reputed classic paranormal phenomena,
Professor Rhine decided to examine the manifestations of
telekinesis.

In an article in the *Journal of Parapsychology,* of Durham,
U.S.A. (March 1946), which summarizes his work, he states:
'The belief in P.K. or the direct action of thought on matter is

common in primitive societies. . . . In a new branch of medicine, the psychosomatic, are reports of healing which seemed impossible yesterday and are still inexplicable today. The observations and experiences collected by the societies of psychical research have added their contribution to the background of P.K. Certainly it would be difficult for those who know this subject well to reject the arguments in favor of P.K. as totally inadequate and valueless. On the other hand, it would be impossible to establish a convincing case from the arguments even if they were considered in their entirety. Their experimental control was insufficient and the repetitions and observations were too few to lead to definite conclusions that the P.K. effect could work on those around and on society. It would need new experiments with better controls.'

The encouraging experiments of Professor Rhine on E.S.P. led him to believe that this unusual form of sensation implied a psychophysical relation of which P.K. could represent another aspect. It was a matter of verifying this hypothesis: would not the supposed action of an object on the mind bring a symmetrical action of the mind on the object?

To clarify the question Rhine worked out a number of tests. A subject tried, by thought alone, to act on a tossed dice, to make it fall on a previously chosen number, or a fixed total. The results obtained were interpreted according to the rules of probability.

The first of these results was clearly positive, but Kaufmann and Sheffeld criticized the conditions under which the experiments were conducted. Rhine strengthened his controls. The dice were mixed in a container, moved around a central axis by an electric motor and the number not chosen by the subject but by different procedures governed uniquely by chance. This time the results did not differ enough to be able to discount chance.

F. Nicol and W. Carrington hardly did better in 1947, with 115,200 tosses of the same dice by eight subjects each not knowing the goal they were to aim for. Dr McConnell, Professor of Biophysics at the University of Pittsburg, using photography, eliminated all influence of the experimenters in controlling the dice at each stop.

These unimpressive results, together with the scepticism and reservations of many scientists, the admission by Rhine himself, and the criticism of the American Scarne, the famous expert in trickery, led to the conclusion that the experiments with the dice do not prove the existence of P.K.

It seems reasonable to accept the conclusion of Amadou: 'Too few experiences have been fulfilled to date to make evident psychokinesis, such as has been described by Rhine and his students. In most of these experiences the experimental conditions are far from satisfying to an impartial critic. In others the level of the results evaluated statistically is too weak to exclude the action of chance. In certain cases the researchers—especially the European researchers—did not obtain the success claimed by Rhine and his students. It is, therefore, not possible to decide if the P.K. effect is an authentic paranormal manifestation or if these apparent manifestations are due solely to chance, to mathematical singularities, to faults in the organization of the tests, to subtle manifestations of E.S.P., or a combination of these three factors'.

EXTRA-SENSORY PERCEPTION AND TELEPATHY

E.S.P., or extra-sensory, or extra-sensorial perception, allows one of several kinds of communication between people, given that they do not use any known means of sensorial contact. At present, this communication is inexplicable to science.

When studying E.S.P. it is wise to dismiss *a priori* the words clairvoyance or other analogous terms which imply the taking of a predetermined stand. The analyses seem to prove that pure clairvoyance does not exist, even in a 'state of trance', but that spontaneous telepathy is an established phenomenon. On stage, the examples of provoked telepathy are always faked. Everyone knows of cases of spontaneous telepathy, but the extent to which vanity, voluntary or involuntary fabrication, or error, has tainted the truth of such accounts must be taken into account.

If spontaneous telepathy is an established phenomenon, but rarer than we think, it is still difficult to control. It is therefore important to study it anew with discretion and with the maximum of scientific accuracy.

The Future of Parapsychology

The reader will perhaps be tempted to accuse the authors of exaggerated circumspection. However, none of the available evidence allows us to draw rash conclusions.

If we are so rigid in our analysis of the reputed paranormal phenomena it is because we want to preserve it from manipulation; for we are convinced that these phenomena are capable of throwing a new and fruitful light on the subject.

In the numerous disciplines of occultism (we prefer this word in preference to the more pretentious term occult science), it seems that in setting out judicious observations those responsible have often drawn excessive conclusions. Of all the disciplines studied, only the following appear to us to stand up to a critical examination:—

1. All classic yoga.

2. Some fields of suggestion (we include here medical hypnosis and the 'underground or subliminal psychology' applied notably in advertising.

3. Spontaneous telepathy (a mother who suddenly senses her child is in danger or a friend who senses that his companion is in immediate need of help).

4. Certain experiences that have been practised among the Tibetans (for example, the *Tou-mo* or art of warming oneself naked in the snow, the *Loung-gom* or art of running without fatigue) which deserve a deep study.

It is this small part of the subject which escapes condemnation and on which, in our opinion, rests the future of parapsychology.

This future is exciting, even if it makes a clean sweep of the mysterious, of the 'supernatural'. We must bear in mind the admirable maxim of Plotin, who, teaching the 'liberating experience' leading to wisdom, asserted that it is wise to distinguish the ecstasy to which it leads from the para-phenomena which only produce an illusion of it.

CONCLUSION

Occultism forms an extremely complex domain. Amazing as it seems in our scientific age, it enjoys a good deal of support. In the magazine *Paris-Match* (October, 1961) there was a report stating that there existed in Paris 'six thousand professionals in occult sciences giving, each day, fifty thousand consultations and earning fifteen thousand million francs, and there are also, some two thousand mystical associations'.

An English journal at the end of 1960 declared: 'If one believes the statistics of the London Society for Scientific Research in a study of popular superstition, there exists in England ten thousand turning tables, three hundred and twenty-five ghosts and eight hundred and twenty-five spirits. About thirty thousand English people claim to be in constant contact with their dead parents, eighty thousand participate, at least once a year, in a seance and more than two hundred thousand believe in telepathic power. In the United States there are six million members of the "new church", five hundred astrology shops in New York alone and two thousand astrology columns in newspapers each day. At Benson, Arizona, thirty members of a society have been living underground since the society directed them to do so on July 4, 1961'.

Attraction of the Occult

The attraction of the occult for the human mind remains undeniable. At all stages of a civilization which is constantly evolving, occultism is present for better or for worse. The progress of science has not eliminated it. If the assembly of beliefs and practices known as occultism included only eccentricities it would still be worth the trouble to study it, on the one hand, as a history, singularly rich and revealing, of multiple deviations of the human mind, and, on the other, for the extreme ingenuity often marking its trickery.

Mechanism of Credulity

If the effect of the occult on the human mind is unquestionable, how can we explain this attraction? How can we examine the mechanism of this credulity?

It has often been claimed that when a faith wavers or weakens, occultism triumphs. This statement does not explain everything. It would be too simple to plead the equation: occult = recoil or absence of religion.

Credulity, we believe, rests above all on two factors, one *innate,* the other *acquired.* In the first instance it is almost always through a primitive fear response that one turns to the occult. As a way of seeking power over the unknown, it is both simpler than prayer, which postulates both faith and humility, and more radical, since prayer asks, whereas magic, sure of its formulas, imposes. The responses of primitive man, who, fearing the elements, tried to conjure unknown powers, reappears in modern occult practices.

Reinforcing this primitive impulse are the circumstances in which modern man finds himself living: haunted by the insecurities of his urban culture, trapped in a civilization which he himself has fabricated, terrified of the implacable mechanization which he has let loose, he searches frantically for an escape from the machine age.

A New Dimension in Living

Occult investigations have often led to some unforeseen results of progress, as Egyptian, Hindu and Tibetan art, poetry, several scientific inventions and important discoveries in medicine indicate.

Perhaps there does not exist a paranormal phenomenon in the strictest sense of the term. Perhaps what appears to be so today will one day, when our knowledge is greater, enter into the pattern of a hyper-psychology.

It seems, although nothing is yet formerly and scientifically proven, that in some privileged areas rigorous inquiries enable the discovery of 'something' notably in hypnosis, telepathy and yoga. This totally new 'thing' (*psi* faculty if you like), could, if one were to reach, discover, surround and perhaps cultivate it, renew the possibilities of our minds and give to man an unknown ability. As the American psychologist William James said: 'We are only half awake'.

THE GREAT FIGURES OF OCCULTISM

Through history there has been an enormous number of people with a deep interest in the occult doctrines. Their importance can be considered as decisive or debatable, according to one's point of view. We limit ourselves in this list to twenty-six names which appear to us important.

Chronologically: The list will not include people (mythical or real) of antiquity (e.g., Pythagoras, Hermes Trismegistus, etc.) or, for obvious reasons, contemporary people. Our list ends roughly at the beginning of this century.

Geographically: We mention only people of Western civilization, leaving aside the Hindus, Chinese, Arabs and others.

Doctrinally: We avoid citing people whose doctrine or occult activity was largely inspired by existing theories and whose originality, for this reason, is questionable. We leave out most of the personalities of the eighteenth and nineteenth centuries who were not devoted occultists.

For the same reason, there is no mention of men whose occult doctrine is often only a minor component of a literary, philosophical, religious or metaphysical theory (Rene-Guenon, Rudolph Steiner or others).

AGRIPPA de NETTESHEIM, Cornelius (1486-1535). Born in Cologne, he instructed in theology at Dole, was a professor at Pavia after graduating as doctor of laws and medicine, and took part in the Council at Pisa. After taking part in wars in Italy, he was an advocate at Metz, then a family doctor in Savoy, and lastly an historian of Charles V. Leo X named him a 'very cherished son', although the Dominicans clashed fiercely with him, and he was also regarded as a charlatan.

He was passionately interested in the cabala and in magic which, he said, 'allows communication with the forces of a superior plane, and allows one to rise above those of an inferior plane'. He divided the macrocosm into three worlds, each ruled by magic: physical, astral and religious. To reach these it is necessary 'to die unto the world'.

Nostradamus,
astrologer and doctor,
author of the celebrated prophetic work
'The Centuries' (1555).

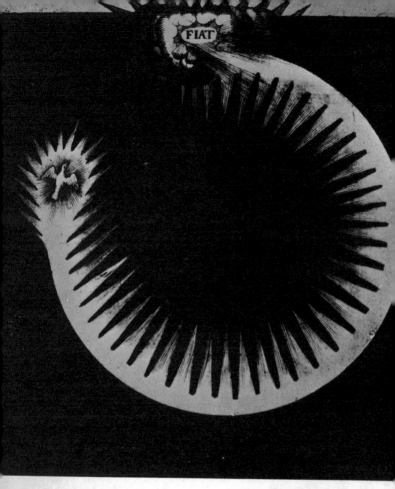

**The circle, symbol of the universe
and magical figure.**
Above: The Creation, as seen
by the occultist Robert Fludd.
Right: Aztec image
of the cosmic circle.

Above: Symbol of evolution
and the cyclic return of the great ages,
the circle is here formed by two dragons
eating one another's tails.
It encircles a magic hexagram
with astrological symbols and has the power
to dispel the 'evil eye'.

Left: The talisman of Agrippa:
In the center, the sacred word 'Ararita'.

A symbol of the sacred book of the Cabalists, the Zohar. Here it distinguishes two levels in man: the pure soul or 'neshama', turned towards the heavens, and the animating and vital function or 'nephesh', turned towards the earth.

Paracelsus, alchemist and father of hermetic medicine (born in Switzerland in 1493).

The Count of Saint-Germain was an ambassador for Louis XV and practised occultism in the courts of Europe.

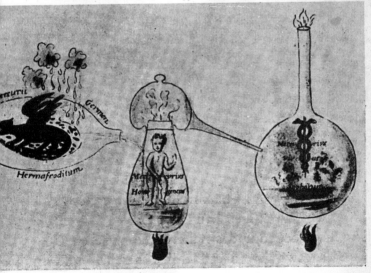

The Homunculus:
pursuing their theories of transmutation and their ambitious dreams, the alchemists attempted to create in the laboratory a 'little man'. On the right mercury; on the left an hermaphrodite bird.

The alchemist and his workshop
(below, engraving of Teniers).

The Resurrection theme, illustrated with alchemical symbolism (painting on silk from the 18th century).

The Street of the Alchemist in Prague. During the Middl￼ Ages the alchemists pursu￼ their experiments under the protection of the emperor.

Chief work: *The Occult Philosophy*.
He died in Grenoble.

ALBERT THE GREAT (1193-1280). Born on the banks of the Danube, from the illustrious line of Bolestadt, he became a Dominican and champion of Aristotelian philosophy. He wrote twenty-one volumes after attending different universities at Pavia, Padua, Bologne and Cologne. An exemplary monk, he was drawn to occultism through astrology and alchemy. Legend added to his stature, and he was represented as one who evoked the dead (before Frederick II) and as author of two rather mediocre treatises: *Les Secrets Du Grand Albert* and *Les Secrets Du Petit Albert*, apocrypha of the 18th century which, plagiarized in the 19th century, became veritable manuals of sorcery. The creation of an astral automaton which responded by words and signs was also attributed to him.

He was the teacher of the great Thomas Aquinas (1225-1274), to whom some have attributed occult activities.

BACON, Roger (1214-1294). Born at Ilchester in the county of Somerset, England, he became a mathematician in Paris, then a Franciscan at Oxford. A general scientist, he was the first European to verify the basis of chemistry in his *Mirror of Alchemy*. He put his trust only in experience. An English legend also attributes to him the creation of a mysterious android. In his *Treatise of the Secret Works of Nature and of Art* he predicted inventions which were later realized (flying, suspension bridges, horseless vehicles, etc.), but this work brought imprisonment for sorcery.

BLAVATSKY, Madame H. P. (1831-1891). In November, 1875, with Colonel Olcott, she founded the Theosophical Society in America, the headquarters of which were established in Bombay in 1878 and, later, Mount Adyar, near Madras. Aim: religious syncretism and development of the latent potential of man. Their review, *The Red Lotus,* published the writings of Papus (see this name), and of Colonel Olcott. In 1909 Annie Besant succeeded Madame Blavatsky, whose writing on the Indians testified to much naivety in her interpretation of 'fakiric phenomena'. Around 1930 the Theosophical Society claimed about fifty national divisions. Their headquarters are in Adyar.

CAGLIOSTRO (1743-1795). Born on June 2, 1743, in Palermo. He was called Joseph Balsamo-Bacconieri but took the name of his godmother, Vicenzia Cagliostro. He began as an assistant apothecary at the Convent of the Brothers of Charity, whence he fled to lead a life of debauchery under assumed names (Tischio, Belmonte, Pellegrini, etc.). He later appeared in England, where he was arrested for forecasting the winning numbers of the Royal lottery and for theft. He then travelled in Europe, and in Warsaw presented himself as the Grand Kopht of the Egyptian Rite, being received into the Masonic lodges. In 1781 he was professor of occultism at Strasbourg and his cures became famous. His recipe for 'physical regeneration' made him a friend of the naive Cardinal de Rohan and introduced him to Paris and the court, where he succeeded Mesmer. He called himself Count and his wife Lorenza the Second. He gave lessons in Magic at 100 louis a person.

Although innocent in the affair of the Queen's necklace, the couple had to leave Paris following the disgrace of the cardinal. They resumed their success in Rome, until suddenly Lorenza denounced, at the Holy Office, the falsehood of her husband, who was condemned to death, but instead imprisoned for life in the Fortress of St Leo in 1791. After predicting the revolution, he died miserably in prison on August 26, 1795.

CROWLEY, Aleister (born 1875). He was initiated in 1898 in the society of the 'Hermetic Order of the Golden Dawn' directed by S. L. Mathers, who had translated into English *The Clavicles of Solomon* and who practised an Egyptian ritual based on *The Book of the Dead,* perhaps following an idea of Cagliostro. In 1905 Crowley created the *A.A.,* or *Astrum Argentinum,* a new magical order reserved for prophets. During a trip to Cairo in 1904, where his wife had a vision of the god Horus, he wrote *The Book of the Law* extolling a new religion which his disciple Smith propagated in California.

Crowley revived some Graeco-Egyptian Hermetic invocations which he mixed in 1905 with conceptions of yoga, collected on a voyage through Asia. For him 'each man and woman is a star' and their supreme goal must be to 'traverse the abyss'.

He was against collective meetings, and recommended auto-initiation, received from 'unknown superiors' and which resulted in the 'destruction of the self'. He also taught that 'existence is pure joy' and, having founded in Sicily about 1920 the 'abbey of Theleme' he appeared under numerous eccentric disguises, dressed as an Asiatic, smoking tobacco soaked in rum and indulging in drugs at the 'sacred orgy'. He sometimes signed himself 'the beast', claiming to be the devil.

His dubious activities (many of his concubines had to be hospitalized) led to the closing of the abbey, where American Kenneth Anger had been able to photograph some paintings realized by the master in a 'second state'.

FAUST. Perhaps real, probably legendary, Faust has been made the prototype of the man who has sold his soul to the devil in return for youth and honor. George Sabellicus Faustus, Junior, the future Dr Johann Faust, would have known Paracelsus and Agrippa.

He practised magic at Prague, invoked spirits at Wittemberg, claimed to have made a journey to Hell with Beelzebub for a mount, and then claimed to be able to make himself invisible. He related to his friend Dr Jonas of Leipzig tales of his excursion in the cosmos in eight days, practised alchemy at the Manual Bronn Abbey (where he had a magic dog!) and caused several people to appear in Innsbruck for Charles V.

In 1525, he brought out a large cask by magic from the vault of Auerbach at Leipzig, made Helen of Sparta appear to some students, and claimed later to have had a child by her called Justus Faustus. He was hunted from Inglostadt for magic in 1528, and returned to Prague and Erfurt where he invoked the Trojan heroes. In Venice he is said to have performed levitation. He made some miraculous cures in the Netherlands, was imprisoned, cursed by Luther and proclaimed 'arch magician'.

At the end of the pact he experienced a horrible death at the hands of the devil. This did not prevent his appearance several times to his faithful servant, Christopher Wagner (or Waiger). His story appeared in the *Livre Populaire* in 1587. In 1590 the English dramatist Marlowe made a hero of him, but he was popularized by the drama of Goethe and the operas of Berlioz and Gounod.

FLAMEL, Nicolas (1330-1418). Born in Pontoise, France,

and lived in Paris. A conjuring book drew this simple man to occultism in 1357.

After studying at Bologne with 'Master Canches', he succeeded in transforming a half pound of mercury into silver on January 17, 1382. On April 25 of the same year the same quantity of mercury was transformed into gold! It is said that he negotiated with Charles VI to supply gold to the State. In any case, he disposed of considerable sums for such a simple commercial dealer. If indeed he had not found the philosopher's stone, only his relationship with the Jewish usurers could explain his wealth. He died in 1418.

GUAITA, Stanislas de (1861-1897). He was a Marquis, descended from a great Lombardy family, a poet friend of Maurice Barras, and a cultivated mystic. He was attacked by J. K. Huysmans, who accused him of casting spells. He was considered a specialist of the Tarot and of the cabala.

In 1888 he re-established in Paris the 'Supreme Council of the Cabalistic Order of the Rose-Cross', with Sar Peladan as his assistant. He was a member of Papus' group and was said to be a direct successor of Eliphas Levi and an admirer of Paracelsus (*See* these names).

He claimed that one could communicate with the dead only by a 'spiritual communion' reached in an ecstasy invoked by music. According to him, the workings of evil were explained by the law of opposites. In his *Serpent De La Genese*, he justifies magic by the influences of the mind and of magic fluid. He died in 1897.

GURDJIEFF, G. I. The amazing Gurdjieff is one of the most mysterious characters of the early part of this century. The details of his life are little-known, but Louis Pauwels dedicated an important biography to him.

He was probably born in Asia Minor of nomadic parents. He was a spy for several great powers, profiting by numerous Asiatic travels. He created, in a castle at Fontainbleau, a kind of philosophical community where the guests sometimes had to do odd tasks. The novelist Katherine Mansfield, a consumptive, came there to be nursed and was given little better accommodation than a stable. Besides his farfetched philosophies, Gurdjieff also expressed some original theories.

His disciple, Ouspensky, who died in London in 1947, summarized the main points of his philosophies in *Fragments of the Unknown Teacher*. Gurdjieff, while selling carpets, first organized secret groups for research at Moscow in 1914 (theme: 'man is a machine'), then in 1915 at St Petersburg (theme: 'man can be freed by four methods: those of the fakir, of the monk, of the yogi, and of the artful man, which has yet to be found'). In the revolution of October, 1917, he left for the Caucasus and set up institutions at Rostov, Tiflis and Constantinople.

He spent 1920 in Germany, 1921 at Fontainbleau and 1924 in America. He died in Paris in 1949. On his death bed he said to his disciples: 'I leave you in a fine mess'.

KARDEC, Allan (1804-1869). Born in 1804 in Lyon, his real name was Leon Denizard Hippolyte Rivail. He was educated privately in Switzerland. He opened a teaching institute in Paris, and, at the age of twenty-eight, married an instructress. Ruined, he became an accountant and wrote teaching manuals for a livelihood.

Rivail was also convinced by spiritualism and, claiming to be the reincarnation of Allan Kardec, he published *The Book of Spirits,* with the 'collaboration' of Socrates, Swedenborg and Napoleon. Soon the *Revue Spirite* also included contributions by St Augustine, St Louis, Luther and Pascal! His numerous other works, *The Bible Spirit, The Book of Mediums, What is Spiritism?*, had a great international success, despite an auto-da-fe in 1861 by the Bishop of Barcelona. Their theory of the 'fluid' launched the mediums.

He died when his *Revue* had made more than a million converts in Europe. The menhir of the Celtic Druids marks his grave at Pere-Lachaise.

LEVI, Eliphas (1810-1875). Alphonse Louis Constant, son of a cobbler, was presumptuous and self taught, a poor songwriter, a nondescript painter, a mediocre poet, a deacon unfrocked before ordination, and imprisoned several times for anarchy.

In July, 1854, he evoked the spirit of Apollonius Thyaneus, a Pythagorean philosopher in London, devoted himself to the cabala, and became associated with the English Rose-Cross. He met the Polish Wronski, inventor of the prognometer or predicting machine.

Back in Paris he called himself 'master' under the name of Eliphas Levi Zamed. He edited *la Revue Philosophique et Religieuse,* on which Michelet and Littre collaborated and which was banned in 1858.

He next published *Le Dogme et le Ritual de la Haute Magie* and initiated disciples by correspondence. His 'key of the great mysteries' was considered extravagant and dangerous by officials in Paris.

LULLY, Raymond (1235-1316). A Catalonian born in Palma and a protege of James II, he attended the universities of Montpellier, Rome, Paris, Palermo and Naples. Seneschal of this king, he was also a great swashbuckler and *trouvere,* or medieval poet of Northern France. Converted, he was initiated into the Cabala. He studied Arabic and was perhaps in contact with the Mohammedan sect, The Brothers of Purity. Most of his alchemical writings have been questioned.

At 70 he was a member of the household of England's King Edward II. He published widely on the topic of science. He believed his work on the Cabala was capable of converting the unfaithful. He founded numerous chairs of Oriental languages. At 80 he went on a personal crusade, and was made a prisoner at Bougie in 1315; was stoned by a mob and died on a Genoese boat which had rescued him. His contemporaries called him Dr Illuminatus. His tomb is in the chapel of the St Francis' Church in Palma.

MESMER, Frederick Antoine (1733-1815). Born at Iznang, near Constance. His thesis, *de l'influence des astres sur le corps humain,* published in 1766, was considered the basis of judicious astrology. His theory on the healing power of magnets ('magnetic cures') was founded on animal magnetism, but in Vienna an Englishman named Hall accused him of having stolen his procedure. He dedicated his system to three academies, but those of Paris and London did not acknowledge it and the Academy of Berlin declared him a fool. However, the success of his cures was such that rich patrons set him up sumptuously in the Hotel

Bullon, Place Vendome, Paris, in the spring of 1788, where his famous tub drew huge crowds. Although supposedly limited to 20 people, each seance was actually attended by about 50, bringing him much extra money.

He took Dr Deslon on as an assistant and he soon became his rival, accusing him of swindling.

Mesmer then founded the 'Society of Harmony' near his hotel, where he instructed future magnetizers, among them the Marquis de Puysegur. He established branches at Lyons, Strasboug and Bordeaux. He also became a member of The Illuminated and some called him 'The Superior Unknown of the Supreme Order'.

Marie Antoinette was going to protect him and asked Mesmer to form a 'magnetic clinic', but the Academy, as well as the Press, incited by the doctors, succeeded in quashing the plan. The 'animists' had triumphed over the 'fluidists'. Mesmer went into seclusion and died in 1815.

NOSTRADAMUS (1503-1566). His real name was Michel de Notre-Dame. Grandson of the doctor of King Rene d'Anjou, son of a notary, he was a Jew from Provence, France, converted to Catholicism. A doctor, he was said to have repelled the plague in the South of France. He was a great traveller, and he passed for a spy of France, of Lorraine and of Savoy.

Summoned by Catherine de Medici to the court following the publication of his prophetic book, *The Centuries*, he recited to her the famous quatrain on Henry II:

'*The young lion shall overcome the old,*
On the field of war, in single combat.
He will pierce his eyes in a cage of gold.
This is the first of two loppings, then he dies a cruel death.'

Four years later, Henry II, at the time of chivalric duels celebrating the marriage of his daughter, Elizabeth, had his eye pierced with a blow from a lance. He had been wearing his gilt casque, and it was during a second reprisal against the Earl of Montgomery. He died as a result.

Menaced by the religious wars of the following year, 1560, Catherine summoned Nostradamus back to her mansion at Soissons, where she practised occultism. He went in the spring, and after forty-five sittings had the Angel appear to predict for the queen the future of her three sons.

He then published *Prognostications* or almanacs. His 'prophesies' or *Centuries* have run into innumerable editions, the first being dated 1555. These three hundred and fifty-three quatrains, grown to 4,780 verses, are deliberately obscure. This made it possible for the exegists to read whatever they wished into them. With each war they come up again, for they predict the future to 3797 A.D.

PAPUS (1865-1916). Born at Corogne, in Spain, of a French father and gipsy mother, who claimed to be descended from Cagliostro.

His true name was Gerard Encausse. He spent his youth at Montmartre, Paris, leading a happy life with the song-writers. In 1882 he commenced medicine and was initiated into Martinism. From 1887, he became a member of the Hermes Theosophical Society of Paris, and founded his own review, *Le Voile d'Isis,* in 1889. He became a doctor of medicine in 1894. He became a spiritualist, created numerous occult societies (of which 'the independent group of esoteric studies' was directed against the theosophists), and practised a 'secret medicine', exported from India.

He was proclaimed a disciple of Saint-Yves d'Alveydre (born 1842), who extolled synarchy or ideal scientific government, and of Nizier Philippe, of Lyons (born 1849), a theurgist who was said to be the 'intermediary unconscious' between God and humanity.

He became a successful inventor with the help of Lepine and published many works.

He was said to be clairvoyant and from 1900 enjoyed the protection of the Tsar Nicolas II, residing in St Petersburg, where his cures were successful, until his death in 1916 from tuberculosis contacted in the army. His name of Papus is the name of a medical demon.

PARACELSUS, Theophrast Bombast von Hohenheim (1493-1541). Born in Switzerland, at Einsielden. He studied medicine at Ferrara, and soon provoked doctors and learned men. He travelled widely, and became a lecturer at the University of Basle. He offended all with his nonconformity and was much criticized. He was a great magician, and practised alchemy with Abbe Jean de Tritheim. Using the loadstone, he was the fore-runner of magnetism and Mesmer. Praising the total power of faith, he inveigled against Luther. Renewing medicine, he extolled the comprehension of nature, the study of remedies (theory of the 'signatures' based on homeopathy, explained subsequently by Hahnemann), clinical observation, and general pathology (in his *Paraminum*). He died in 1541.

PELADAN, Josephino (1850-1915). Born in the South of France, he became the disciple of his elder brother, Dr Adrien Peladan, who left him a vast hermetic library.

He helped Stanislas de Guaita to found the cabalistic Order of the Rose-Cross in Paris in 1888. Breaking with Guaita in May, 1890, he was named Supreme Hierarch of the Third Order of the Catholic Rosicrucians and took the title of Sar Peladan.

After attracting crowds of Parisians to his concerts and artistic expositions at the 'salons of the Rose-Cross', he died in 1915 and was soon forgotten.

PIC DE LA MIRANDOLE (1463-1494). After studying at the Sorbonne, he became a friend of Laurent the Magnificent and led the life of the great men of the Renaissance. He claimed to be 'wise in all things understandable and some others'.

He invited all the scientists of the world to the court of Rome for a discussion on his nine hundred theses. Having written damaging comments on his judges, he had to flee Italy and was incarcerated in the Tower of Vincennes.

On his study of the practice of magic he declared: 'Magic is the most notable part of the natural sciences'. He did not believe in the philosopher's stone, but some detecting equipment for auriferous bearings has been attributed to him.

He was a member of the Academy of Florence, but the friendship of Savonarola failed to convert him to a Dominican. He died in 1494, having greatly influenced Thomas More and Jean Reuchlin as well as the Christian cabala.

RAIS, Gilles de Laval de (1404-1440). Gilles de Rais, baron of Machecoul, was the grand nephew of the Lord High Constable of Guesclin. He fought on the side of Joan of Arc and was named Marshal of France at Rheims when twenty-three years old.

After the capture of Joan of Arc, he fought on and then suddenly devoted himself to a life of great luxury, living in magnificent surroundings at Tiffanges and Machecoul. He rapidly ran into debt and, to procure gold, became involved in alchemy. Soon, he called Francois Prelati from Florence, an expert in the forbidden art of geomancy, with whom he evoked 'evil spirits' and signed a pact with the demon Baron. Following his lack of success, he commenced to sacrifice children to win over Lucifer. More horrible murders followed until the Inquisition stopped him in 1440, and he was hanged, then burned, on October 26, 1440, at Nantes.

SAINT-GERMAIN, Count (?-1784). Nothing is known of his origins. He arrived in France from Germany in 1743 with the ambassador of Louis XV, Marshal of Belle-Isle, for whom he established a 'magic laboratory' in outlying Saint-Antoine. He was said by some to be a Jew from Portugal, by others the son of a doctor of Strasbourg, and by yet others to be from Savoy. It was even said that he was a defrocked Jesuit, or the eldest son of King Frederick II Rackoczi. He fostered the doubts as to his origin and told nobody his age.

His knowledge was extraordinary and he practised all the arts. He would have astonished Rameau at the harpsichord, and was familiar with all the countries and most of the languages of the period.

A guest of the nobility, he would arrive sumptuously dressed, but would never receive them at home. He contented himself with giving balms and especially health elixirs to women (he did not claim to rejuvenate but to 'conserve'!). The king showed him particular favor and had two laboratories built for him at Versailles and the Trianon, where they often secluded themselves. He was imprisoned in London for spying in 1745, but was back in Paris ten years later, protected by Pompadour. He was officially disclaimed in 1760 during his stay at the Hague where doubtless he served as a spy.

He next travelled to Germany and Russia where, as a member of the Rose-Cross, he helped the king of Prussia.

According to Mme d'Adhemar (in *Souvenirs*, perhaps apocryphal) he warned Marie-Antoinette of the Revolution.

He was seen in Paris, in Vienna, Constantinople and in Russia in 1762 as a revolutionary. Not knowing where he had vanished to, he was even·identified as 'Major Fraser', who, in the last years of Louis-Philippe, claimed to have known Nero and Dante!

Saint-Germain himself claimed to have once lived in the time of Henry IV. He announced to Casanova that he would invent the steam boat in Holland in the following century. The two theosophists, Mme Blavatsky and Mrs Besant, claimed to have met him at the end of the 19th century.

He died in 1784 at the home of Charles de Hesse-Cassel, devoted to occultism.

SAINT-MARTIN, Louis Claude de (1743-1803). Born at Amboise, writer and philosopher, convinced by the illuminism of Jacob Boehme, about whom he published *The Triple Life*. He became acquainted with Swedenborg. His treatise *Tableau naturel des rapports qui existent entre Dieu, l'homme et l'univers (Natural Table of Relations which exist between God, Man and the Universe)* is famous and extols absolute spiritualism.

He modified certain rites of Freemasonry and created his own school, Martinism, which had a marked success among the nobility. As he had been the secretary and assistant of the Martins of Pasqually, their respective adepts were often confused under the name of Martinists.

In 1755 he published *Des erreurs et de la Verite (Of Errors and of the Truth)* under the pen-name of the 'Unknown Philosopher', a name which has stuck to him.

A Rosicrucian and Freemason, he established himself at Lyons and his fame became widespread. His disciple, Joseph de Maistre, praised him widely, as also did Sainte-Beuve and Prince Galitzine, who propagated his theories in Russia. He became attracted to Christianity, which he called 'transcendant', and attacked Catholicism. He died at Aunay, near Paris.

SCOT, Michael (1170-1232). Born in Scotland around 1170. Nothing is known of his youth. Tutor of the future Frederick II, 'the baptized Sultan', he dedicated two of his works to him. At Toledo he translated some Arab works and tried his hand at necromancy before returning to the court of the Emperor as adviser and astrologer. Some 'miracles' in Florence have been ascribed to him, but it is not known if these were the result of illusions or hypnotism. He purified 'the medicine of the physicians'.

After becoming suspect, he was offered the distant See of the Archbishop of Cashel in Ireland. He turned it down and went to Bologne, Paris and Oxford to prepare a translation of the Arab Avicenna. When he was praying in the church of his native village a falling stone ended his life in 1232.

His many activities were forgotten (notably his treatise on alchemy) and he was remembered only as a divining magician. Dante (*Inferno*, XX, 115) even ranges him with the sorcerers in the eighth circle of Hell. Sir Walter Scott evoked him in *The Lay of the Last Minstrel*, in which the knight Deloraine opens his tomb to obtain his *Book of Power*.

SWEDENBORG, Emmanuel (1688-1772). Son of a Lutheran bishop, he was born in Stockholm in 1688, and became a doctor in theology from the University of Upsala at 21 years of age. He worked in England with Newton, then in Norway, and devoted himself to occultism from April 7, 1744, following a nocturnal vision of a Magus who dictated a mission to him, and he was said to be in contact with the spirits of Virgil and Luther. In 1757 he declared that he had seen the Last Judgment, and from 1759 aspired to clairvoyance under auto-hypnosis.

He wrote seventeen treatises. His *Heaven and Hell*, published in London in 1758, is the ancestor of spiritism, which he called 'pneumatology'. His theories were very successful in Scandinavia. He was also one of the forerunners of hypnotism, since he turned to auto-hypnosis to facilitate his clairvoyance. He died on March 29, 1772, in London, the day he had forecast. Balzac named him 'Buddha of the North'.

TRITHEIM, Abbe de (1462-1516). Johannes Heidenberg was born near Treves, at Tritheim, from which he took his name. He became a Benedictine at 22, then *abbe* of the convent of Sponheim in 1483. A book lover, he devoted himself to the unknown sciences, especially astrology and magic. He was said to be a disciple of Albert the Great.

In his *Chronique du cloitre (Chronicle of the Convent)* he told the most extraordinary stories, notably that of the 'golden nose of Charlemagne'. In 1505, during an illness at Heidelberg, the monks burned his books on magic. He refused to return to Sponheim, and went direct to the Abbey of Wurtzburg, where he resumed his secret teaching and extolled the cabala. His *Stenography* disclosed how to win over Orifiel and the spirits. He devoted himself to alchemy with some other prelates, strongly influencing Paracelsus and Agrippa.

In 1500 he divided magic into three branches: natural, cabalistic, and satanic, and the history of the world into seven stages presided over by the seven angels of the apocalypse of St. John.

He narrowly escaped the stake.

VILLENEUVE, Arnaud de (1235-1312). Born of an obscure family of Catalonia, he studied medicine and natural science.

He accomplished the first regular attempts at distillation. He had a great reputation for healing, making his remedies with the use of alchemy, establishing the astral theme for his patients, and, through his knowledge of the cabala, giving them preservative amulets. His works on hygiene displayed a wide knowledge of the human body.

The Dominicans proclaimed him a heretic and he escaped the stake only because he was counsellor of two kings (Frederick II of Sicily and James of Aragon), and private doctor of three popes (Boniface VIII, Benedict XI, Clement V). He resigned himself with difficulty to being only a doctor to the popes. He was several times proclaimed a visionary. This allowed him to influence Frederick II of Sicily in his democratic reforms. After a journey to Avignon in 1309, which put him on bad terms with James II, he died in 1312 during a crossing of the Mediterranean.

THE DICTIONARY

ABIGOR: A superior demon, a fine cavalier bearing a standard or a scepter, mounted on a winged monster. Commands sixty infernal legions. Knows the future, the secrets of war, and the art of making himself liked by his soldiers.

ABIOSE: In occultism, a state of apparent death.

ABLUTION: In a great number of religious and magic ceremonies water* has a purifying value (lustral water). Before these ceremonies, the believer purifies himself by washing part or all of his body. This is not only (in some cases not at all) a requirement of hygiene. The most important religious bath takes place every 12 days in India at Allahabad (last in 1954) and is called 'Kumbh Mela'. It involves about six million believers who come to bathe, and to offer a lock of hair to the confluence of the three sacred rivers. The Buddhist monks of Thailand wash their idols completely, except for the head.

ABRACADABRA: *See* Abracax. It is presented like this:

    ABRACADABRA
    ABRACADABR
    ABRACADAB
    ABRACADA
    ABRACAD
    ABRACA
    ABRAC
    ABRA
    ABR
    AB
    A

Pentacle*, to which certain sects, especially Persian and Syrian has given a numerical meaning (total $=$ 365) or a medical significance (cure for intestinal maladies and, especially, for fevers). Was worn around the neck, written on parchment or on a thin piece of metal. The alchemists used it to make a triangular symbol of the cosmic All.

ABRACAX or ABRAXAS:

(1) The most ancient of the gods, according to certain Syrians and Persians. The Basilidians, heretics of the second century, made him the chief of the 365 genies ruling the days of the year. He would have sent Christ to earth as a 'benevolent spirit'. His name has given us Abracadabra*, a magic formula used as a charm. (2) In a broad sense, the engraved stone worn as an amulet in the Orient since the second century. *See* Loadstone. (3) In demonology became a demon with the head of a cock, a large belly, feet like

Gnostic cameo.

serpents, and a knotted tail. He was pictured carrying a whip.

ABSINTHE: A strong anise-flavored alcoholic drink. It was formerly believed that if the palms of a child under 12 years of age were rubbed with the juice of absinthe, he would never become too cold or hot.

ABSTINENCE: Antique magic claimed that the great magicians could abstain from eating and drinking. *See* Fasting.

ACQUISITIO: A figure of geomancy* symbolizing growth, material or moral success. Corresponds to air-Jupiter. It is also called Gain and, in popular language, Fortune. To the Arabs: clenched fist.

ACTION AT A DISTANCE: *See* Ectoplasm, Fluid, Telekinesis.

ACUPUNCTURE: Chinese medical practice of treating illnesses by piercing the skin with fine needles.

ADAM KADMON: *See* Polypsychism.

ADEPT: (1) *See* Alchemy. (2) Partisan of a doctrine, of a sect. An initiate to the secrets of a philosophy or a science.

ADJURATION: Formula of exorcism.

ADRAMELECH: President of the High Council of Devils, supervisor of the stool of

Satan. He is represented in the form of a mule, with a human torso and a peacock's tail. At Sepharviam in Assyria children were burned on his altars (the same is said of Sardon: the cry of the children was the sardonic laugh. Another tradition has it that such laughter was caused by the ingestion of a noxious weed from Sardinia).

AEGAGROPILE: *See* Bezoar.

AEROMANCY: The art of predicting the future by the observation of aerial phenomena (air, winds, clouds); in the case of the Greeks by the play of the wind on a liquid in a basin placed in an elevated position; for the ancient Persians, by the air or effervescent liquids. For many, a comet is the sign of death of an important person. *See* Chaomancy.

AEROSOME: See Body (a).

AETITE: Also called the stone of the eagle, because it was believed that eagles sought it as far as India to put in their nests to facilitate the hatching of their young. That is why it was used to hasten childbirth (attached above the knee of the mother) or to delay it (on the chest). Dioscoride also says that, reduced to powder and put in a special bread, it gave away thieves, because they could not swallow it.

AFFINITIES (Fr.: *Correspondences*): Natural symbolism allowing analogies* according to the tables of affinities (names of divinities, animals, plants, minerals, etc.). *See* Space. Those interested in these details consulted especially the tables reproduced by Marianne Verneuil in Practical Dictionary of Occult Sciences. The author has borrowed from it the table of geomantic affinities. *See* First Part, Numerology. *See also* Homosophy, Space, Zodiac.

AFFLICTED: In astrology*, said of a planet which is in poor aspect.

AGATE: The Ancients believed that it warded off the plague and snake and scorpion bites; that it strengthened the heart.

AGENT: Person who, in spontaneous telepathy*, saw the conscious or unconscious experience felt by another person, the perceiver*. In experimental telepathy, a person from whom the experience is reputed to act on the perceiver.

AGLA: Magic word, shortened cabalistically from *Aieth Kadol Leolam Adonai* which means: 'The Lord will be great in Eternity'.

AGUARES: Grand duke of the Eastern part of hell. Sparrow hawk on his wrist, dressed in a tunic, he rides a crocodile. He commands thirty-one infernal legions, teaches languages, makes the spirits of the earth dance, and overthrows enemies.

AIGUILLETTE: Knotting of the aiguillette or knotted aiguillette: a practice of sorcery to render an enemy powerless. The rabbis attribute this invention to Cham. Greeks and Romans knew of it, but it was especially common in the Middle Ages and in the 16th Century. The occultists recommend rather carrying the teeth of a dead person or eating a roasted woodpecker, or having a ring in which is set the eye of a weasel, or yet, to write *Avigazirtor* on some fresh parchment for nine days, before sunrise. *See* Pegging, Entanglement, Ligature.

AIR: *See* Aeromancy, Chaomancy.

AITHESIS: Name sometimes given to clairvoyance* or seventh sense.

ALASTOR: (1) Malevolent genie of the Ancients. (2) A severe demon, incarnating Nemesis (divine vengeance of the Greeks) and good fortune. It has been confused by some with Azazel, by others with the exterminating angel, and by others with Raum.

ALBERT (Great or Small): Alchemist monk of the 13th century, master of Thomas Aquinas. To him are attributed, probably incorrectly: (1) *The admittable secrets of Albert le Grand or Grand Albert,* a mixture of cosmogony, medicine, physiognomy and various practical recipes with which to predict sex. (2) *The solid treasures of Petit Albert* or *Petit Albert,* a mixture of sorcery and the key to dreams.

ALBUS: In geomancy, figure expressing purification, purity, serenity. Corresponds to Venus.

ALCHEMIST: Practitioner of alchemy*; the alchemists called themselves philosophers, trustees of the foremost science, which had been revealed to man by Hermes, 'philosophus per igneum', philosophy by the fire. They are sometimes divided into simple empiricists or 'chemists', and adepts or true alchemists, the Great Initiates. The Rose-Cross mystic is always called Adept, with a capital.

ALCHEMY: (1) Practical alchemy, the application of theory, the search for the 'philosopher's stone'*. The two essential powers of this stone were the transmutation of metals into gold, which constituted the great work in the restricted sense of the term, and universal medicine (thanks to the panacea), secret doctrine or 'black art', which claimed to realize the union or 'marriage of opposites': water-fire, gold-silver, sulfur-mercury,

Alchemists at work.

steady-volatile, sun-moon, king-queen, male-female, red rose-white rose, red man-white woman. The androgynous being or hermaphrodite often symbolizes it. It watches over initiations, and triumphs over the dragon, toad or initial matter. It is also represented by a blooming rose. The phoenix is the manifestation of this rebirth. Issue symbolized also by the Town and the Child. (2) Mystic alchemy aims to know the quintessence of things, to get rid of base metals (passions, sins), to discover the spiritual gold, to find again the lost paradise after rebirth. In short, to become a superman, which sometimes involves seven grades of perfection, by *The Great Voyage*. The Great Art (*Ars Magna* or Royal Art), especially from the 15th to 17th centuries, consisted for alchemists in bringing about the 'mystic work', the work of the Phoenix*, rebirth by choosing the 'path of the absolute', by reinstating man in his primordial

Medallion commemorating a transmutation at Prague in 1658.

dignity through giving him perfect knowledge (*See* Gnosis), regenerating the world. It is 'the art of man', said Paracelsus in the 16th Century. (3) Common alchemy simply sought transmutation. The Greeks called the doubling of the weight of a precious metal by making an alloy with a base metal 'diplosis'. The result of the transmutation of an alloy of gold and silver was called asem or electron. The alchemists were its practitioners. Teniers scoffs at them in his engraving *The Pleasure of Madmen,* as also did Brueghel the Elder. In his *Basilica Philosophia,* Mylius shows an assortment of their apparatus. It is too simplified to say that alchemy is the primitive or erring form of chemistry.

ALECTORIUS: Stone taken from a four-year-old capon. It renders one invincible.

ALECTRYOMANCY: Divination with the aid of a cock placed in the center of a circle or square divided into 24, each with a letter of the alphabet and a grain of wheat. Interpretation follows the order of pecking up the grains.

ALEUROMANCY: Divination by flour spread on the ground, following the patterns thus formed, or by the dough of cakes destined for sacrifice. The latter was called Crithomancy.

ALEXIPHARMAC: The name formerly given to remedies able to counteract the effects of poisons.

ALKAHEST: Universal solvent of alchemists. Obtained by means of the philosopher's stone and capable of dissolving all bodies and, in some cases, of giving them a liquid state.

ALOCER: Grand Duke of Hell, represented as a horseman with the head of a lion; commands thirty six legions. This horse, with the legs of a dragon, is enormous. He teaches the secrets of the sky and of the liberal arts.

ALOMANCY or HALOMANCY: Divination by salt, dissolved in a liquid or thrown into a fire.

ALOUETTE: Female symbol of joy, health. According to Vincent de Beauvais (13th century), Leonardo da Vinci relates that she refused to look at someone who was going to die, but that she cured a sick person when she chose to look at him.

ALPHABET: (1) See Arithomancy, Dactylomancy, Gyromancy. (2) There has been much speculation on letter-number affinities*. The cabalists* have established relations for the twenty-two letters of the Hebrew alphabet.

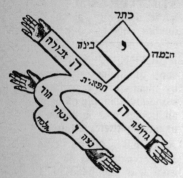

Cabalistic ideogram of the Hebrew letter 'Aleph'.

ALPHITOMANCY: Divination according to the way in which a suspected person ate a cake made from flour of wheat or barley. From this comes the popular saying: 'May this piece of bread choke me if I am deceiving you.' *See* Alveromancy.

ALRUNE: Succubus*. Magic puppet, doll*. Made of hard roots, covered in runic characters.

ALUDEL: For alchemists*, the name of the 'philosopher's vase', where the great work of creating the philosopher's stone was accomplished.

ALVEROMANCY: Divination analogous to alphitomancy*.

A M B E R : The electro-magnetic properties of this hard fossilized resin (called in Greek 'electron' and dedicated to Apollo, the sun) have been known since Antiquity. As loadstone attracts iron, amber rubbed with a piece of cloth attracts neutral bodies. Its 'clear' qualities (warming, fertilizing, bactericidal) have given it a great reputation as a cure. The Bretons believe that an amber necklace warms children and protects them against throat infections. The Chinese sculpted it into animal forms to promote fertility. The Middle Ages used it for love potions. The Magic Pharmacopoeia used it, burnt, to help difficult confinements and, in powdered form, against boils, goitre, and nose bleeding. *See* Loadstone.

AMBIVALENCE: Magic theory requiring that each of our tendencies be balanced by its opposite.

AMBROSIA: Divine food 'nine times sweeter than honey' which gave immortality and youth. It was usually made as a solid substance with a nectar potion; sometimes a liquor with a honey base. The divinities used it to render incorruptible the bodies of heroes.

AMDUSCIAS: Grand Duke of Hell. Commands twenty nine legions. Has the head of a unicorn, but a human body. Gives invisible concerts: 'the trees bend towards his voice.'

AMEN: Hebrew magic word, of which the cabalistic value is ninety nine. Became the 'so be it' of Christians. Its origins lie in the Hindu *Aum* or *Om*.

AMETHYST: Violet variety of quartz, stone of knowledge and of light, reputed to prevent drunkenness, to give prophetic dreams, and to ward off impure thoughts. Symbol of wisdom, of lucidity.

AMISSIO: Figure of geomancy*, expressing diminution, failure, loss. In popular language: shameless. For the Arabs: an open fist.

AMITY: In astrology* two planets are said to be in *amity* when their influences are not in opposition. In enmity they are in opposition.

AMNIOMANCY: Divination by the examination of the membrane or caul which sometimes envelops the head of a newborn child.

AMON or AAMON: Marquis of Hell. Commands forty legions. Head of a wolf spewing flames, tail of a serpent. Appears sometimes with the head of an owl and a human body. Knows the past and the future.

AMULET: From the Latin *amuletum*. Object which one carries on one's person and to which superstition attributes magic properties. Pliny the Elder, XXVIII, 25-29, wrote that some carried a living fly in linen as protection against eye diseases. Passive protector against 'influences'. Uses a natural object (powder, grass) and allows its particular properties to act. *See* Pentacle, Talisman (active), Charm, Gris-gris, Fetish.

ANAGRAMMATISM: Divination finding destiny in the letters of a name from which comes an anagram. Very fashionable in the 15th and 16th centuries. *See* Onomancy.

ANALOGY: Analogies express the permanence of a relationship between two similar concepts. In magic they signify correspondence.* It is through them that most numerological speculations attempt to attain reality.

ANANCOLOGY: Science of destiny. Term proposed by Arsene Lenormand to designate morphological study of individual destiny advocated by the Hungarian L. Szondi, called 'the psychologist of the anti-chance', disciple of Freud.

ANANISAPTA: Initials of a formula against contagious illnesses. The written word must be carried on one's person.

ANARETE: Certain authors give this name to the worst

planet of an astrological*
theme, especially to that which
has a poor relationship with
the House of the Dead.
Erroneous appellation, since
any planet can have this role.
It is the aspect which decides.

ANDRAS: Marquis of Hell.
Commands thirty legions. Head
of a screech-owl, bare body of
a winged angel, mounted on a
black wolf and brandishing a
sword.

ANDROGYNE: *See* Alchemy
(1).

ANDROID: In magic, designates all artificial human beings. *See* Golem, Homunculus.

ANGA: Members or divisions
of Yoga*.

ANIMALS: *See* Zoomorphism.

ANTHROPOMANCY: Divin-
ation by the examination of
the entrails of sacrificed men,
women or children. Menelas
Heliogabalus and Julian the
Apostate were accused of having practised it. *See* Aruspex.

ANTHROPOSOPHY: Move-
ment founded at the beginning
of the 20th century by the
ex-theosophist Rudolph Steiner
and admitting reincarnation.

ANTITHEAS: At the height
of Greek antiquity, evil genies*
who deceived men by illusions.

ANTONINISM: Very vague
spiritualistic* doctrine. Launched in 1888 at Jemeppe, on the
Meuse, by a Belgian metallur-
gist, Louis Antoine, who called
himself a medium and healer.
Since 1910 there have been
some 150,000 adherents.

AOB or AOD: *See* Azoth.

APANTOMANCY: Divin-
ation by interpretation from
animals or objects presenting
themselves unexpectedly.

APOLLO: For the Greeks,
and then the Romans, the
great God of divination*. His
most famous oracles were at
Delphi (the Pythia)*, Colo-
thon, Xanthos, Branchides, the
Didymeion temple of Miletus,
Delos, and Claros in Asia
Minor, where the temple in
excellent condition has recently
been discovered.

APONE: Italian fountain near
Padua, supposed to confer
divinatory gifts.

APPARENT MOVEMENT:
In astrology*, apparent movement of planets by rapport
with the earth (geocentric system), subdivided into direct
(or D) and retrograde (R =
bad omen). The sun and the
moon are never in retrograde.

APPARITION: Hallucinatory
image of a living person. (*See*
Doubling) or more often of a
dead person. (*See* Phantom,
Poltergeist, Specter) this generally on a Friday or Saturday
night. The oldest recorded case
seems to be that of the appari-

tion of Basilide to Vespasian, related by Tacitus (History, IV, 81). The most famous among the dead (some are deceptions) are Katie King (with the medium Florence Cook, at the house of William Crookes) and Bien-Boa (produced at the Villa Carmen, the house of the Noels in Algiers, by the medium Marthe Beraud, who became Eva C). By extension, visions in general, not to be confused with unions* arising from a complex mental-preparation: expectant attention and auto-suggestion* (for example, the Tibetan technique of migs-pa).

APPLICATION: In astrology*, indicates that two planets are approaching their conjunction. According to the case, it is qualified as simple (two anterograde planets), double (an anterograde and a retrograde), complete, incomplete (or unachieved, bad omen). See Separation.

AQUAMARINE: Stone favorable to Gemini and to Pisces, symbolizes innocence, youth.

AQUARIUS: One of the twelve signs of the Zodiac*. See Astrology, Part One.

ARC OF CLAIRVOYANCE: Line on the hand ending in the form of an arc at the base of the little finger. On the left hand only it indicates potential clairvoyance; on both hands, efficacy.

ARCHEE: Spirit of the universe.

ARCHETYPES: According to Jung, 'the precise factors of organization of the unconscious psychic processes'.

ARITHMOMANCY: Divination* by numbers, practised in multiple ways. The Chinese Ha-Do used mancy* in giving to numbers symbolic values derived from Pa-koi. The Chaldeans divided their alphabet into three decades and changed the name of the consultants into numeral letters. Pythagoras explained everything by the harmony of numbers. The Greeks compared the value of letters, as did many ancient Oriental people, their numbers being letters. The Cabala* and the Tarot* have given an arithmomancy consisting in an analysis of the qualitative characteristics of the numbers. Arab geomancy* has developed a numeral symbolism. Some occultists assert that materially One is incomplete, malevolent, but that Two reassures by its symmetry. On the other hand, metaphysically, One is benevolent (monotheism, unity, ace); Two is incomplete, diabolical (the goat as opposed to the unicorn); Three is stable, balanced (trinity, tripod).

ARITHMOSOPHY: In number systems, philosophy of the numbers or key to wisdom through numbers. The two biggest schools are the ancient Pythagoreans and the modern Cabala. Too many gratuitous speculations have tainted it. The practitioner is called an arithmosophist.

Parts of the human body arranged in relation to their secret number.

ARMOMANCY: Divination from the shoulders of sacrificed cattle.

ARROWS: *See* Belomancy.

ARS MAGNA or ROYAL ART: *See* Alchemy, Great Art.

ART OF THE SPIRITS: Swedenborg's method of invoking spirits.

ARTHAME: Magic cutting instrument.

ARUSPEX or HARUSPEX: Soothsayers who practised in Rome, following the Etruscans, utilised a form of divination by the examination of the entrails of animals, especially those with horns, and later by the study of lightning. They studied (a) the behavior of the animals before the sacrifice; (b) its agony; (c) its entrails, especially heart and liver (of which the disappearance is a bad sign), lungs, spleen, kidneys, and stomach; (d) the flame which burns them (which should be light-colored, silent, pyramidal) and (e) the water, incense, wine, and flour used at the sacrifice. Their pronouncements often had a bearing on opinion as to the destiny of Rome, contrasting with the augurs*. They were officially consulted when the auspices* were insufficient. They accompanied the armies during campaigns. To avoid charlatans, they were grouped in a sort of free academy of about sixty members.

ARZEL: Horse with a white mark on its right foreleg. Reputed to be bad luck in battle.

ASANA: One of the eighty four basic poses of yoga.

ASCENDANT: *See* Horoscope.

ASEM: *See* Alchemy (3).

ASMODEUS: Sometimes identified as Samael, the serpent which seduced Eve. Prince of Hell with three heads: those of a bull, of a crowned man breathing fire, of a ram; feet of a goose, tail of a serpent. Mounted on a dragon; commands seventy two legions. Superintendent of gaming houses, he sows error and dissipation. Conquered by Solomon, who made him help to build the temple.

Asmodeus.

ASPECT: (1) In geomancy* one examines the resultant aspects of the relative position of the two houses of the theme: (a) The aspect of company or contiguity (houses II and III, for example); (b) The aspect of opposition: difference of six houses (II and VIII,

for example); (c) the trigonal aspect or threefold regard: difference of three houses; (d) the quadrant aspect: difference of four houses; (e) the sextile aspect ties by an intermediary two separate houses. *See* Astrology, First Part.

(2) In astrology* it is said that the planets have (or are in) a particular aspect, according to the arc which separates them on the Zodiac*. Two planets of the same angle are said to be in conjunction; at opposite angles (separated by an arc of 180 degrees) they are said to be in opposition. When their declination north or south is the same, two stars are said to be in parallel aspect.

ASS: The Persians sacrificed it to the God of War, the Greeks to Priapus. For the Egyptians it symbolized the god of the evil, Typhon, to whom were offered presents bearing his image. The Romans considered a meeting with it as unlucky. It symbolizes stubbornness, courage, procreative power, stupidity. Apollo gave King Midas ass's ears and a number of demons have them. Often the ass is involved in operative magic.

ASSUMPTION OF THE OAK: Magic in country areas has it that a sick person can be cured of a suppurating wound if one of the dressings is hidden, with the appropriate rite, in a hole hollowed in an oak tree and sealed up. It is dangerous to cut down the tree. *See* Vergraben der Krankheit.

ASTAROTH or ASTAROT: Grand Duke of the West of Hell. Represented as a wreathed angel, naked, puny, holding a viper in his left hand and mounted on a dragon; infernal treasurer. Sees the past, the present and the future; detects secret desires, and accords protection to the great.

ASTRAGALOMANCY: Divination by bones marked with letters practised in Greece and Rome. It was later played with dice. Its practice has continued. On throwing 1 = A; 2 = E; 3 = I, Y; 4 = O; 5 = V; 6 = B, P, V; 7 = C, K, Q; 8 = D, T; 9 = F, S, X, Z; 10 = G, J; 11 = L, M, N; 12 = R. The combination of letters obtained gives the answer.

ASTRAL: (1) *See* Body. (2) Astral is used to describe the visible plane and the plane of invisible forces which circulate between the stars.

ASTRAL JOURNEY: *See* Doubling.

ASTRAL or CELESTIAL VISIONS: Apart from the armies claimed to have been seen in the sky, there have also been reports of a fleet (in 1140), a comet (falsely) in 1480, three suns (1492) and rain*.

ASTROITE: According to the oracles of Zoroaster, a stone having the power of subduing the terrestrial demon, invoking genies and in obtaining a desired result.

ASTROLATER: Star worshipper. This adoration is called *astrolatry*.

ASTROLOGER: Practitioner of astrology* called sometimes 'spiritual pilgrim'. Since the 17th century, thanks to the 'Rodolphine Tables', has no longer to observe the sky.

ASTROLOGICAL HOUSE: Division adopted in astrology* according to the twelve signs of the Zodiac*. Each has an analogical relationship with an aspect of the life and destiny of the consultant. Tradition gives the twelve houses numerous and sometimes divergent values. Roughly, here are the most current:
(1) Life of the body, enterprise. (2) Gains. (3) Relatives, not ascendants, mail. (4) Patrimony, heredity. (5) Children, pleasures, games, clothes. (6) Illness, servants. (7) Marriage, contracts, war. (8) Death, wills. (9) Religion, philosophy, occultism. (10) Honors. (11)

Astrologers at work.

Friends, plans. (12) Hidden enemies, various miseries, griefs.

A rearrangement has been proposed of Angular houses (1,4,7,10), succeeding (2,5,8,11) and falling 3,6,9,12. It is better to relate them to the signs of the zodiac*.

ASTROLOGICAL THEME: Theme disclosing the future; it is established at birth, as a consequence of the position of the stars. *See* Part One, Astrology.

ASTROLOGY: Art of predicting events by the stars. It is necessary to distinguish: (a) Symbolic or onomantic astrology, which prolongs, in a fashion, mythological symbolism and even natural symbolism. It does not aim at application to human life. (b) Traditional or analogical or Babylonian astrology, the heritage of ancient techniques and some attributed to Cham, Noah's son. (c) Scientific astrology, which claims to adapt the early methods to be useful in modern life.

From the point of view of the areas of application, astrology is divided into (a) genethliac or individual or judicial astrology, which makes a judgment on people, is the most widespread, and studies individual destiny; (b) sociological or worldwide astrology, which analyzes the relationships between stars and societies (works of Armand Barbault and the tables of Pierre Maheu); (c) meteorological astrology (works of Dr. Maag); (d) medical astrology, following the school of Salerne in the Middle Ages and (e) vegetal astrology, which believes in the influences of the stars on vegetation.

For the symbols; *See* Zodiac. cf. also Decan, Degrees.

ASTRUM ARGENTINUM: Secret society founded by the Englishman Alister Crowley (born 1875), who preached auto-initiation and destruction of self, necessary 'to cross the abyss'. Abuses (injuries, sexuality) in his 'Abbey of Theleme', founded in Sicily in 1920, discredited him.

ATMOSPHERE, HUMAN: *See* Aura, Fluid.

AUGMENTATION or DIMINUTION OF WEIGHT: Claim by certain mediums and fakirs. The latter have exploited the trick on stage, dubbing it 'unliftable man'. (Done in Paris by Johnny Coulon).

AUGUR: Roman theologian (not priest) in charge of conserving the traditional rules relating to the observation and interpretation of natural signs constituting the auspices (phenomena of the sky, the flight of birds, hens). Their emblem is the 'lituus', a spiral baton. The college of the augur (soothsayers) comprised three to nine members. It made judgments on tangible events. (*See* Aruspex).

Cicero said that two augurs could not look at each other without laughing (De Divinatione 11,24). The augurs' books finish on twelve points (to correspond to the Zodiac). By extension: Presage. *See* Auspices.

AULI: Statuette or image made and consulted by the Opanotates, priests of Madagascar.

AURA: *See* Fluid.

Colored emanation (blue for the evolved things, reddish for the primary things), rays of light or 'human atmosphere'; visible manifestation of the vital fluid or of the astral* body that certain clairvoyants perceive around the body (or just around the head) of each person. This vital energy permits the action of the mediums in material effects. Its existence was discredited by the experieces of Hoffman (1919).

AUSPICES: For the Romans the generic term designating the public signs sent by Jupiter to make his will known. More or less synonymous with pres-age; natural signs from which one foretells the future. *See* Augur.

AUTOMATIC: Writing, drawing, language, painting, etc. Done by a medium in a state of unconsciousness or of lessened consciousness, without the exercise of his will. It is sometimes the expression of clairvoyance or telepathy*. *See* Automatic writing, Trance.

AUTOMATIC WRITING: Device employed by medium* (in a trance*) to allow the spirits of the dead to express themselves. Boirac (1893) incorporated it with *spiritism* in *cryptopsyche*. Andre Breton and the surrealists have practised it.

AUTOMATISM: (1) *See* Somnambulism. (2) In psychology, a complex act accomplished unconsciously. Can be of an abnormal origin. (3) In parapsychology, sensorial automatism designates a certain automatic functioning of the senses, of a hallucinatory nature, which may or may not reveal the activities of p.s.i. functions.

AUTOMATON: *See* Android.

AUTOSCOPY or ENDO-SCOPY: The faculty of seeing what is happening in one's own body. In someone else's body: hetero-endoscopy. Most often hallucinatory, it may nevertheless reveal the truth. Yoga has developed an auto-scopy that is not imaginative, but based on internal knowledge.

AUTOSUGGESTION: Hypnotizing oneself to influence one's actions.

AVATAR: From the Sanskrit *'avatara'*, descent. In the Hindu religion, an incarnation of a god. By extension, reincarnation of a dead person. *Karma* (expiation of past faults) rules it. *See* Metempsychosis, Palingenesis.

AVIGAZIRTOR: *See* Aiguillette.

AXINOMANCY: Divination by an axe balanced on a round post. One turns around saying the names of suspected people. The axe falls when the name of the guilty person is said.

AYM: *See* Haborym.

AYPERSON: Infernal prince, commands thirty six legions. Represented as a vulture. Discloses the future.

AZAZEL: Chief of the fallen angels (Book of Henoch).

AZOTH: (1) To show that the philosopher's stone* was the principle and the end of all bodies, it is symbolized by 'Azoth', initial 'a' and final letters of the Latin, Greek and Hebrew alphabets. Represents the predominance of Mercury.

(2) The 'Traite de l'Azoth', by the monk Basile Valentin, or the documents preferred by alchemists*. (3) For the theosophists* it is *the Light*, a unique substance which has engendered everything. It is manifested by the 'Physical Quaternary': heat, light, electricity, magnetism. It is animated by a perpetual double current: of projection (positive, AOB), of absorption (negative, AOD).

BACCHARIS: Herb, commonly called 'Notre-Dame glove', which is used against enchantments*.

BACIDE: Bakis was the name of an ancient Boeotian diviner. By extension, a diviner inspired by the nymphs. In the feminine, it is Sibyl or Pythia.

BACILLOGIRE: Bearer of rod capable of finding treasures in subterranean waters.

BACKWARD ATTRACTION: This alleged manifestation of fluid or hypnosis is explained by the experience of Dr. Moutin: one places two hands without pressure on the shoulders of a person standing up straight. When the hands are taken away slowly, the person follows their movement. Its practice, with at least one principal, on a line of eight to 10 people, is called a magnetic chain.

BAEL: First king of Hell, reigns in the Eastern part. Commands sixty six legions. He has three heads: cat, crowned man, toad. His sturdy body has the legs of a spider. Renders invisible and cunning.

BALAN: King of Hell. Sometimes with three heads: bull, man with eyes of fire, ram. Most often naked and horned, a sparrowhawk on his wrist, and mounted on a bear.

BALL: Of glass or crystal. Polished and perfect, used in clairvoyance: by auto-hypnosis, by the images that one sees in it, or by the play of a flame from a candle placed behind it.

BANSHEE: Fairies of Ireland and the north of Scotland. In the form of old women, they announced the death of an important person. There are also some who carry to heaven the souls of new-born children.

BAP or BAPHOMET: Idol venerated by the Templars*. Of unknown origin, the Baphomet had a white beard and two rubies for eyes. His cult was secret and immoral.
See Black Mass, Teraph.

BARKERS: Women or men struck by a delirium during which they bark like dogs. Especially in use in Brittany, France.

BARROW OF DEATH: In low Brittany mainly, it is heard when someone is about to die. It is sometimes seen, driven by skeletons and covered in a white sheet.

BAT: In magic, signifies twilight, androgynism*, mystery. Participates at the Sabbat*.

BATON OF COMMAND-MENT: Since prehistoric times, decorated batons used by sorcerers and from which, perhaps, the magic wand is derived.

BATON, UNIVERSAL: *See* Rhabdomancy.

BEANS: Antiquity reserved them for funeral offerings and believed that black beans contained certain souls of the dead.

BEARDED: *See* Laetitia.

BED OF NAILS: The classic bed of the fakirs*, made of nails (close together and often blunted), on which they sit or stretch out.

BEDOUH: *See* Ring (of Solomon).

BEE: Symbolizes activity, purity, vigilance, refinement. Certain Greek priestesses of the mother of the gods were called 'The Bees'. Greco-Latin mythology involves it in legends concerning the birth of Zeus-Jupiter in the cave of Dictre, in Crete. Childeric and Napoleon took it for an emblem. Certain popular Breton beliefs in France have it that when the master of an apiary dies it is necessary to veil each hive with black crepe and to say softly. 'The master is dead'. Without this precaution, the bees will die or go away. In the case of a marriage or a feast, the apiary must be adorned with a piece of red cloth. Honey is, in many circumstances, a sacred basic element, like butter, water, milk. It is used in the making of hydromel and perhaps of ambrosia* and nectar*.

BEELZEBUB: Prince of the demons; the first after Satan. The Lord of the flies, from which he could deliver men and whose appearance he sometimes took. Colossal, puffy-faced, crowned with a band of fire, horned black and menacing, hairy with bat's wings, duck's feet and the tail of a lion. The Syrian tradition made him the king of the demons.

BEHEMOTH: (1) Colossal, marvellous ox which the Jews said was kept back at the meal of the Messiah. (2) The Middle Ages made of it a demon in the form of an obese elephant.

Behemoth.

BELIAL or BELIAR: The most vicious of the demons, very charming. Appears on a chariot of fire. The Apocalypse calls Belial 'the beast'.

BELOMANCY: Divination by arrows, especially among the Chaldeans and Arabs.

BELPHEGOR or BAAL-

PHEGOR: Adored by the Moabites on Mount Phegor. Sometimes a young woman, more often a hideous, horned demon, seated nude. Distributed riches and ingenious inventions. Some rabbis state that homage was rendered to him on the commode.

Belphegor.

BERITH: Demon who, according to certain alchemists, was capable of changing all metals into gold.

BERYLISTIC: Divination interpreting the images formed in special mirrors (Berylli).

BETYLE or BAETILES: Little round stones, probably aerolites, venerated in the Orient, in Greece and in Rome. They are considered as a god's dwelling, often the divinity itself (black stone of

Cybele). Cybele swathed one of them to make her husband, Cronus-Saturn, devour it in place of her son, Zeus-Jupiter. Synonym: *Abadir*. *See* Omphalos.

BEVERAGE OF HATE or MISETRA: For poisoning, comprised the plant promethea and the gall of four animals.

BEZOAR: (From the Persian 'Badzahar'), or aegagropile. Stony concretions forming in stomachs (antelope, wild goat, llama, vicuna), and used as a talisman against plague and diverse dangers. It was made in the West in the Middle Ages. *See* Aetite.

BHAKTI: Mystic devotion. A form of Yoga* based on divine love.

BIBLE: Certain occultists see in it three magic keys: the five books of Moses, the prophecies of Ezekiel, and the Apocalypse of St. John, named sometimes the Christian Cabala.

BIBLIOMANCY: The person suspected of sorcery was placed on one tray of a pair of scales, the Bible on the other. He was burned for sorcery if the scale leaned on his side.

BIDENTAL: Monument consecrated after the flash of lightning by the sacrifice of young sheep, called Bidens.

BILOCATION: *See* Doubling.

BIOMETER: *See* Magneto-meter.

BIOSCOPE: *See* Magneto-meter.

BIRD: (1) *See* Ornithomancy. Euripides calls birds 'messengers of the gods'. (2) Thunder Bird: *See* Manitou, Wakan Tanka.

BIRTH: *See* Amniomancy.

BLACK: (1) Very often, in magic*, a malevolent aspect, or of consecration of the demon (black magic). (2) In symbolism, it has the sense of sable in heraldry and in astrology*, Saturn. (3) For some occultists, it expresses subterranean fertility, the hidden riches. (4) Antiquity kept black animals for sacrifices to infernal divinities (they did not hesitate to tint them if they were not dark enough). *See* White.

BLACK ART: *See* Alchemy (1).

BLACK HEN: (1) *See* Pact Diabolical. (2) It is said that for a black hen sacrificed to him at midnight, towards the east, at an isolated crossroads, with the 'Great Call', a cypress brush in hand, the devil would sometimes give a hen (black) with golden eggs. The Jewish banker, Samuel Bernard, who died in 1739, was accused of possessing one. (3) Magic book, sometimes added to the *Red Dragon* (edition of 1521).

See Clavicle.

BLACK MASS: Parody of the Mass in honor of the devil* (Beelzebub). Celebrated on the back then on the stomach of a naked woman as an altar, using black ornaments. Babies were sometimes sacrificed. An analogous mass, 'the service of vain observance', has been attributed to the Templars*.

BLUE: (1) Symbolizes royalty (royal tattooing = 'royal blue'), nobility (blue blood), water (Pisces, the fish in astrology*), the night in its decline. Color of Zeus-Jupiter in astrology* and in heraldry (azure). (2) Evokes the feminine element (royal; blue of the Chinese Yin-Yang).

BO'AZ: One of the two columns of the Temple of Solomon, in magic. It is feminine, passive, black or white. It corresponds to the moon. White = wisdom, victory. Black = royalty. *See* Yakin.

BODY: Occultists distinguish in the physical body: (a) The 'fluid body' or 'etheric body' (however, intersideral ether does not exist). Immaterial but coincidental in normal life with the material body, sometimes visible, this body can leave the being momentarily, or can be materialized voluntarily. Bosc called it *aerosome*.

(b) The 'causal body', immaterial, connects our eventual diverse existences. (c) The 'glorious body', radiating mystic ecstasy. In legends this body defies natural laws: goes through walls, for example. (d) Certain metapsychists and the spiritists* also distinguish the 'astral body' or 'perispirit'. Nature for them being triple (matter, spirit and perispirit) participates at one time in the body which allows bilocation (*See* Doubling). Many authors re-arranged these divisions. Most of the moderns adhere to the division into three of St. de Guaita (physical body, mediator, astral body, soul).

BODY RIGIDITY: *See* Catalepsy.

BON or PON-PO: Sect of Tibetan magicians prior to the arrival of Buddhism, propagated in the seventh century A.D.

BONES: *See* Astragalomancy.

BOOK TESTS: Mrs. Osborne Leonard claimed that one of her second personalities was capable of revealing the contents of a page of a book she had never seen (and that, to avoid a current of telepathy*, the experimenter did not know it either). Her experiences were directed by C. Drayton Thomas from 1917 to 1922, but seem to have lacked scientific discipline.

BORTISM: A kind of spiritualism* developed in the 19th century by Pastor Bort of Geneva. This cult is celebrated on a fixed day with the help of three mediums, three 'influences' who, placed around a revolving table, communicate to the faithful 'mysterious, divine revelations'.

BOTANOMANCY: Divination by writing one's name and questions on leaves of a tamarind, a fig tree, or verbena, that are exposed to the wind. Only the remaining leaves are judged to have a favorable response.

BOUNTY: See Fortuna Major.

BOY: See Puer.

BRAID, James: Manchester doctor who invented the term *hypnosis** and studied the mechanical processes leading to this state.

BREAK: Superstitions: white glass = happiness; mirror = seven years' bad luck. The wishbone of the chicken is broken to decide which wish will come true.

BRIEFS or BREVETS: Magic formulæ carried by sick men or animals. Also called letters or characters.

BRIZOMANCY: See Oneiromancy.

BRONZE: Alloy of copper, silver and tin, it is considered a purifier. Several religions use it, to the exclusion of all other metals, to make bells. A magic legend claims that the hinges of the gates of hell are of bronze. It symbolizes intrepidity or purification. The Jewish tabernacle includes the sea of bronze, a pool of lustral water.

BROOM: See Sorcerer.

BROTH OF THE SABBAT: On the day of the Sabbat*, the witches* boiled up dead children, flesh of hanged people, frogs, black millet and magic powders. They drank the broth, saying 'I have drunk from the cauldron and I am practised in witchcraft'. This allegedly allowed them to fly, to cast spells and to predict the future.

BUER: Secondary demon, commanding fifty legions. Head of a lion, five goats' legs, advances by rolling on himself. Expert in medicine.

BURIAL OF THE LIVING: See Lethargy (2); Resurrection, Fakiric; Suspension of vital functions.

CABALA or CABAL: Secret science reserved for the sages of Israel. Mysterious interpretation of the Bible by the initiates* (opposed to the Talmud: ritual of the external practice of religion). There have been numerous speculative texts. Among recent ones, the 'Zohar' or 'Book or Splendor' is a good example. In the 15th century Isaac Lorin of Jerusalem created a magic ritual, the beginning of the modern Cabala, which was divided into three main sections.

Symbol of the Christian cabala showing the union of Judaism, Christianity and Islam (1516).

CABALISTIC: Having a connection to the Cabala*. By extension, mysterious, magical: Cabalistic formulae.

CACTONITE: Stone analogous to cornelian, favoring divination and victory.

CADENT: *See* Signs.

CADUCEUS: Rod of gold given by Apollo to Hermes-Mercury in exchange for the lyre with seven strings. Regarding the magic character of the Egyptian Hermes-Thoth, a magic wand was made with them symbolizing, by its two interlaced serpents, reconciliation. The alchemists* saw in this the reconciliation of mercury and gold.

CALCEDONY or CHALCE-DONY: Natural translucent silica, bluish or yellowish, many varieties; possesses magic qualities in the Orient and in the Mediterranean.

CALCHAS: Son of Thestor, one of the most famous of Greek soothsayers. Received from Apollo the ability to see into the past, present · and future. Accompanied the Greeks in the Trojan war. His oracles led to the sacrifice of Iphigenia (so that the Greeks would have a favorable crossing), and the seclusion of Achilles. He knew his fate: to die when he met a soothsayer more skilled than he. This was Mopsos.

CAMAIEU: Stone bearing natural signs to which a magic value was given.

CANCER: One of the twelve signs of the Zodiac*. *See* Astrology, First Part.

CANDELMAS: Superstition: at this time, to obtain money one turns around a piece of crepe while holding a piece of gold in the right hand.

CANDLE: *See* Ball, Gastromancy.

CANTILEVER: *See* Fluid.

CAO-DAISM: Oriental form of spiritualism*. Founded in 1926 this syncretic doctrine developed especially in Vietnam. It has over a million followers. Besides Cao-Dai, the personal supreme God, it venerates Buddha, Confucius, some Chinese heroes and . . . Victor Hugo! The cult consists of ritual invocations; then two mediums, symbolizing the principal Chinese male and female (Yin-Yang), give revelations from above.

CAPNOMANCY: Divination by the interpretation of smoke, either from sacrifices or by throwing jasmine seeds on a fire.

CAPRICORN: One of the twelve signs of the Zodiac*. It symbolizes the peak, solitude, rigor, permanence, mature plans. Corresponds to: dry, cold, earth, mountain, night, violence, sterility, system.

CAPUT DRACONIS: Figure of the geomancy* symbolizing peace, fruitfullness, the products of natural forces.

CARCER: Figure of geomancy*, expressing all that restrains, imprisons, isolates. Corresponds to: earth, Saturn. In English and French: a prison; in Arabian: tripping (or dirty trick).

CARD: *See* Tarot*.

CARD TRICKS: Part of prestidigitation* using normal or trick cards (marked ones, for example).

CARMINA: *See* Dardanian.

CARTOMANCY: Popular divination by cards, using a pack of 32 or 52, usually practised by a woman. It had great vogue under Louis XVI. The ways of drawing the cards are numerous, the interpretations many. Normally a card only has significance in relation to what has preceded it. The succession of figures is beneficial except with spades. It is said that the card game was invented by Jacquemin Gringoneur as a distraction for the madness of Charles VI, but the Spaniards knew of it earlier, since Alphonse XI forbade it in 1332. For the differences with the Tarot*. *See* First Part.

CASSANDRA: Trojan princess, daughter of Priam and Hecuba, last sovereigns of Troy. She repulsed the advances of Apollo, who had given her the gift of clairvoyance. He therefore condemned her to being disregarded when she correctly predicted the future. Notably, she predicted the famous wooden horse in which the Greeks hid to capture Troy. She also predicted her own death with that of Agamemnon on the return to Mycenaea. *See* Sibyl.

CASSIEL: Chief of the spirits invoked in *The Book of Spirits*.

CASTELMEZZANO: Small mountain area held to be the capital of magic in Southern Italy.

CASTER OF SPELLS: Sorcerer who casts malevolent magic on men and animals. Calls himself healer. One combats him by 'making horns at him' and, in Italy, by protecting oneself with a piece of coral.

CASTING SPELL: To bring bad luck by magical means.

CASTOREUM: 'Resin of castor' used in magic.

CAT: (1) Because of its 'magnetism'* and its behavior and appearance it plays a great role in magic. It is benevolent as a protector against rodents which symbolize destruction. It is malevolent, especially the black cat, as an accomplice of the devil*. *See* Sorcerer. (2) Superstition: in some countries, if it crosses the path = bad luck. However, in other countries meeting or seeing a black cat means good fortune. (3) In oniromancy* it personifies the hidden, disloyal adversary, and anguish.

CATALEPSY: (1) In fakirism*, rigidity because of the 'second state'; also called 'cadaveric rigidity'. (2) In reality, catalepsy is a state (hypnotic or associated with mental or nervous unbalance) where the subject keeps his limbs in the position in which they have been placed. *See* Hypnosis, Hypotaxia.

CATAPLEGY: State of fear which prevents the limbs being moved, a kind of paralysis. *See* Reflex Immobilization.

CATATONIA: (1) Neurosis close to hysteria, described by Kahlbaum in 1874. The catalepsy* is accompanied by a consistent stiffness and an active resistance to movement, by violent excitement and organic disorders, with serious mental troubles. (Studied by Baruk).

(2) Experimental or animal catatonia: provoked by a medicament. Pointed out by Peters in 1904, and rediscovered by Froelich and Mayer in 1920. Studied especially by Jung and Baruk.

CATHARSIS: Among the Ancient Greeks a magical rite of 'purgation' to deliver from a former fault either an individual (Orestes in the *Eumenides* of Aeschylus) or a number of people or community (Thebes in Sophocles' *Oedipus-Rex*).

CATOPTROMANCY: Divination by mirrors or a shiny surface (in the 'Archanians' of Aristophanes it is a shield coated with oil). At first by simple observation, then by magic invocations. *See* Crystallomancy.

CAUDA DRACONIS: Figure of geomancy* symbolizing instinctive, pernicious and destructive forces, discord, betrayal, etc. Affinities: Earth, Saturn, Mars. In French: Dragon Tail; in Arabian: the threshold.

CAUSAL: *See* Body.

CAUSINOMANCY: *See* Fire Divination.

CAYM: Demon, Great President of Hell. Appears as an elegant man, with the head and wings of a blackbird.

CEPHALOMANCY: Divination by practising different magical rites over the cooked head of a donkey (in Germany), or over the head of a goat (in Lombardy).

CERAUNOSCOPY: Divination according to the observation of lightning; known in Greece. Introduced into Rome by the Etruscans.

CEROMANCY: See Ciromancy.

CHAIN, ANALOGICAL: *See* Symbol.

CHAIN, MAGNETIC: *See* Backward Attraction.

CHAIN, SPIRITUAL: In the practice of spiritualism*, a chain is formed by the hands of the participants being placed flat on the small round table around which they sit. *See* Spiritualism, First Part.

CHAKRA: Mysterious centers situated in the backbone between the base of the backbone and the top of the head. There are seven principal ones for the Hindus, four for the Buddhists.

CHAMBRE ARDENTE: Name given in France to the courts which judged cases of sorcery.

CHAOMANCY: According to the alchemists*, divination based on aerial visions. *See* Aeromancy.

CHARACTER: One's character, in astrology, is deduced from the dominating factors and the Aspects* at the moment of birth. *See* Typology.

CHARIOT: Seventh major Arcana of the Tarot*; an enthroned person, with a crown and scepter, on a chariot pulled by two horses, one red, the other blue. Represents destiny*, unification by movement. Affinity: Mercury.

CHARM: From the Latin *carmen*, inspired singing. Magic enchantment. Name generic of magic spells of witchcraft and phylactery, more especially a process to obtain some magic effect. *See* Dardanian, Gris-Gris, witchcraft, Philter.

CHARMER: Trainer of certain animals, notably snakes.

CHAX: *See* Scox.

CHEESE: *See* Tyromancy.

CHELA: *See* Guru.

CHILDBIRTH: The Greeks claimed that a sorceress could retard a birth by standing in front of the mother's door, legs and fingers crossed.

CHIMNEY SWEEP: Superstition: to encounter brings luck.

CHIROGNOMY: Art of telling character by study of the hands. Analagous to Chiromancy*.

CHIROMANCY or CHIROSCOPHY: Divination from the signs revealed in the hand and the study of the lines. Especially practised by the gipsies. A mass of disparate doctrines, certain of which involve astrology*, claim to explain the past and the future of an individual from his hands. It is necessary to emphasize that hand 'characteristics' have different significance in different people. Chiromancers study the mounts and lines* (of life, intelligence, heart, etc.).

Astrological chiromancy has ceded its place to a physical chiromancy (where the lines have clairvoyant properties). Not to be confused with chirology, which is the art or practice, especially among the deaf and dumb, of communicating thoughts by signs made by the hands and fingers.

CHRESMOLOGER: Collector and peddler of oracles in the Ancient world.

CHRESMOLOGY: See Divination (enthusiasm).

CHRYSOPEA: See Philosopher's Stone (in gold), Great Work.

CHRYSOPRASE: Variety of whitish green agate, which is supposed to have the property of making people joyful and of strengthening sight.

CIROMANCY or CEROMANCY: Divination by melted wax spilt on a damp table or in a vessel filled with water. Same processes for Molybdomancy*, divination by melted lead.

CLAIRAUDIENCE: Aptitude for divination by hearing.

CLAIRVOYANCE: Aptitude for voyance*, especially by sight. Sometimes called *cryptesthesia*, *telesthesia* or double sight, *lucidity*, *metagnomia* (Boirac). Part of E.S.P.*. One speaks of *mind reading*, if it is exercised on subjective events. It also designates the processes and its results.

CLAVICLE: Small key. In a figurative sense is only used in magic for Solomon's clavicle, a collection of sorcery formulæ, called *True Conjuring Book* or *Secret of Secrets*. See Albert (2), Red Dragon, Black Hen.

CLEDOMANCY or CLEDONISM: From the Greek *Kledon;* in Latin, *omen*. Divination according to words heard fortuitously. The Ancient Greeks used it often. The oracle of Hermes Agoraios, the Bearded One, operated in this manner at Pharai in Archaie. The movements of the human body also have a cledonistic value (hence the importance of epilepsy as the 'sacred illness'), as also does sneezing, favorable when heard on the right, unfavorable on the left.

CLEROMANCY: The drawing of lots manifests the will of the gods (used in the seventh song of the Iliad to point out the Greek champion who took up Hector's challenge). Cleromancy is divination by the drawing of lots: the throwing on the ground or on a table of lead strips, stones, peas, black or white beans. According to the objects used, it is divided into pisomancy, psephomancy, etc. Dedicated to Hermes-Mercury, it was practised at Carpanos, Dodona and Delphi. At Skiron, in Attica, the oracle of Athena used dice. In the Roman Empire books were used.

CLIDOMANCY: Divination

by keys*. Often a paper bearing the name of a suspected person was wrapped around a key; the person was guilty if the paper became unwrapped.

CLIMACTERIC YEAR: Probably according to the Pythagoreans it was believed that the body and nature completely renewed themselves every 7 or 9 years. Thus, 49 (7 x 7) and 81 (9 x 9) are very important. Being the multiple of 7 and 9, sixty three year would be the fatal age or climacteric year.

CLOCK: Instrument used by radiesthesists and sorcerers. A detector, the clock is made of a ball, often of metal, suspended by a thread. Its oscillations give indications of concealed mental states or of diseased organs.

CLOVEN FOOT: Like that of the devil*, in the shape of a goat's foot.

CLOVER: Superstition: a four-leaf clover brings good luck.

COCK or ROOSTER: Symbol of vigilance, of glorious activity. Certain popular beliefs consider the blood of a white cock is infallible for giving sight to the blind, but black magic uses the blood of black cocks. *See* Alectryomancy.

CODES: Enable secret communication, which may be by

word, by gestures, or by a combination of both. The most ancient code known is that of Julius Caesar, who displaced the alphabet by beginning it with D, so A became D and Z became C, etc.).

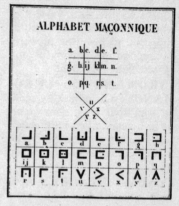

ALPHABET MAÇONNIQUE

COFFEE MARK: Residue of coffee left in the pot. Fresh or old, it must be almost dry to allow the reading of one's fortune. You take a clean, dry, white plate. The mark is warmed while adding a glass of water to dilute it, and stirring with a spoon, is poured progressively on the plate, filling only half of it. It is agitated gently for a minute, then the liquid is drained off. What remains on the plate is interpreted from the different patterns formed. Here are the main outlines: (1) few round forms = grief, many circles = money; (2) squares = trouble, several 'windows' = theft; (3) one triangle = good employment, three = good omen; (4) several ovals = success in business; (5) prominent or multiple straight lines = good old age; (6) a disengaged stripe = travel, more or less long, according to the size of the stripe; more or less difficult, according to whether or not it is accompanied by dots; (7) undulations = reverses; (8) cross in the middle = calm death; three crosses = honor; many crosses = conversion; crown of crosses = death in a year; (9) figure in H = poisoning; (10) four points in a circle = a child; (11) figure of a quadruped = chagrin; of fish = good dinner; snake = betrayal; bird = luck; dog = friendship; horse = help; (12) figure of rose = health; bush = setbacks; four flowers = the best of fortune.

COIF: *See* Amniomancy.

COINCIDENCE: An affinity between two distinct events which permits the establishment of a relationship between them. It is necessary to emphasize that people nearly always accept only those favorable to the thesis they are defending.

COLORS: (1) There are many interpretations of the value of colors. The popular tradition is: red = love, green = hope, blue = wish, etc. Oriented symbolism is the inverse of western symbolism (for example, in Japan, mourning = white, in the west, black). In magic, black is associated with the devil*. (2) Some occultists have established a table of affinities of colors with planets.

COMETS: Although astrologers do not usually allow them any significance, they represent, in popular opinion, a foretelling of calamity.

COMMUNICATOR: Name given to a spirit* incarnated in a medium*. *See* Control.

COMPOST: For the alchemists*, a secret mixture cooked and metamorphosed in the globe of hermetic crystal (Philosopher's Egg) from which comes the Philosopher's Stone*.

CONCOMITANT STATES: *See* Insensibility, invulnerability, Suspension of vital functions.

CONJUNCTIO: (1) Figure of geomancy* expressing coordination, union, concord, association, construction, profitable meetings. Concordances:

Mercury, Earth. In French: the reunion; in Arabian: the meeting. (2) Conjunction of opposites. *See* Alchemy.

CONSTELLATED: Made under a certain constellation.

CONTROL: Term designating the incarnate spirit, the usual guide of a medium* in a trance*. The other spirits* who eventually can be incarnated in him are called communicators. The guide generally presents them. *See* spiritism.

CONVULSIONS: Nervous crisis accompanied by noisy manifestations and tetanization (stiffness). The great cases of convulsionists are: (a) In the 9th century, near a church at Dijon, in front of a pseudorelic refused by Bishop Theobold. (b) At the cemetery at St. Medard, in Paris, in 1732 on the tomb of the deacon of Paris, of which Carre de Mongeron has written in his three illustrated volumes, *The Marvels*.

COPPER: In magic, a benevolent metal. The Spartans believed that it warded off impure spirits and phantoms.

CORAL: Hard calcareous substance found in tropical waters, supposedly has the power of avoiding the evil eye, of safeguarding against lightning, and of stopping bleeding. In Italy it is carried often in a horn as a talisman* or to protect virility.

CORRESPONDENCES: *See* Affinities.

CORRIGANS: *See* Fire Goblins.

CORYBANTS: Mysterious fallen genies* who, according to Plutarch, were condemned to remain in a human body. Often confused with the *dactyls* (mythical characters, frequently identified as the curates of Mount Ida) or *telchines*. (2) Companions of the priests of the goddess Cybele, mother of the gods in Antiquity.

COSCINOMANCY: Divination by the rotation of a sieve suspended by a thread.

COUNTERCHARM: (1) Superstitions: to counter bad luck it is variously thought to be necessary to touch wood, cross the hands, make the sign of the cross, spit on the ground and count up to thirteen, change your path, refuse to cut in cards, throw some salt over one's left shoulder, or tear up some paper. In Italy, make horns with the fingers. (2) Object reputed to have the power of warding off bad luck.

COUNTERSIGN: At the time of spells* the law of countersigns indicated what it was necessary to avoid for three days so as to prevent the effects of the spell.

COURILS: Small, vicious dancing demons of the Finistere. It is necessary to avoid them at night or they force you to dance to the point of exhaustion.

CRANE: Symbol of vigilance, prudence. Favorable omen.

CRIERIANS: Phantoms* of castaways who are heard (bad omen) on the island of Sein, in Brittany.

CRITHOMANCY: See Aleuromancy.

CROSS: (1) In magic, its horizontal bar symbolizes the terrestrial plane or the passive axis; the vertical symbolizes the celestial plane or the active axis. Different magics have used these main crosses. (See diagram

    the *tau* or double gamma, T or Phoenician cross.

    the Egyptian cross of life, ♀ or *Ankh*.

    the cramped cross or *swastika*, warding off the evil 卐 eye in Central Asia and the Orient.

(2) Superstition: Two crossed knives announce sorrow or a quarrel.

CROSSED CORRESPONDENCES: Communications coming from several mediums*, frequently separated by a considerable distance or enormous time lapses. The spiritists* attribute this to the activity of the spirit. Parapsychology sometimes reveals manifestations of telepathy* or clairvoyance*.

CRO(M)MYOMANCY: Divination with the help of an onion. Practised especially on Christmas Eve to learn the health of absent people, or, in Germany, to name one's future spouse.

CROW: In antiquity, sixty four inflexions of different values were distinguished in its cawing, for purposes of divination*. Bird of bad omen. See Putrefactio.

CROWN MAGIC: Crown of wax and wool placed on the head of divinities one wants to placate, or on those beings one wishes to protect.

CRYPTESTHESIA: Designates broadly a faculty which is 'sensitive to hidden things', strictly the art of knowing a hidden fact. Richet includes in this all the phenomena of the 'vibration of the real', or subjective paranormals, known through a 'sixth sense'. See Psychometry.

CRYPTESTHESIA, TELEPATHIC: New version of the energy theory proposed by Raphael Incherumian in Paris. See Intercepters.

CRYTOGRAM: Sign written in secret characters or in cipher.

CRYPTOMNESIA: Designates 'underlying memory', according to Emile Boirac.

CRYPTOPSYCHE: Synonym for clairvoyance, metagnomia.

CRYSTAL: In magic it symbolizes lucid thought (ball* used for voyance*) dignity, victory. It gets rid of nocturnal terrors, cures the kidneys, brings rain. With linen, it signifies natural wisdom (the diamond* signifies spiritual wisdom).

CRYSTALLOMANCY: Divination using fragments of crystal set in a ring or cylinder. *See* Catoptromancy.

CUCKOO: Popular magic holds it to be an omen of silver if it is touched, or gold if its song is heard.

CUMBERLANDISM: Willing-game. Pseudo-telepathy* of the theater exploited by the English magician, Cumberland, and based on the unconscious movements of the wrists of a subject whose thoughts he pretended to read.

CUSPID: *See* Peak or Point.

DACTYLS: *See* Corybants.

DACTYLIOMANCY: Divination with the help of special rings*, often suspended by a thread above a round table on which are written the letters of the alphabet. (Certain of the rings gave the power of invisibility.) *See* Rings (3).

DAGGER: Often used in magic to ward off the evil eye or demons.

DAGYDE: Wax doll or effigy used in magical spells.

DAPHNEPHAGES: Greek soothsayers who would eat the leaves of the laurel trees (the laurel was dedicated to Apollo, foremost oracular god) to obtain a state of intoxication which promoted voyance.

DAPHNOMANCY: Divination according to the way a laurel branch thrown in a fire burns. *See* Pyromancy.

DARDANIAN (Arts): Name given by Jean Spies (1587) to indicate necromancy* (necromantia), magic words (carmina), prophecy and clairvoyance (vaticinia), and charms (incantation).

DEAD ONES: *See* Hand of Glory, Mummification, Necromancy, Phantom.

DEATH: Name of the thirteenth major arcana of the Tarot*. Represented by a formalized skeleton, with a red scythe having a yellow handle, two heads, two hands, two mown feet. Symbolizes change, renewal, risk, death.

DECAN: In astrology* division of each sign of the Zodiac* into three parts. There are, therefore, thirty six decans, each measuring 10 degrees of the arc, governed by a planet, and subdivided in variable terms, from third to eighth. *See* Astrology, First Part.

DEDAL: Name given to automaton — statues, of licentious reputation, made in Crete and Rhodes. They were chained at night. From the name Daedalos, Athenian architect of the Cretan labyrinth destined to shelter the Minotaur.

DEFIXIO: *See* Necromancy*, Spell*.

DEGREES: In astrology*, subdivision in each sign of the Zodiac, in masculine, feminine, honorific, empty, luminous, dark degrees. This classification comes from Robert Fludd.

DEMATERIALIZATION: Total disappearance by the power of the mind. Fakiric* claim.

DEMIURGE: Officiating priest of the divinity.

DEMON(S): *See* Devil.

(1) For the Ancients, entities*, good or bad intermediaries between men and the gods

Portraits of various demons after a 16th century work.

(also called *genies*). Sometimes souls of the dead. Since Plato, or a kind of 'guardian angel' (philosophic aspect). (2) The demon of Socrates (he called it his 'daemon': a kind of interior voice which told him what he must do). (3) According to Michael Psello, there exist six categories of demons: of fire, air (and storms), earth (enticing humans), water (tempests and shipwrecks), subterranean (earthquakes, mine disasters), darkness. From this division some western cabalists* have named four classes: the Salamanders* (fire), Sylphs* (air), Nymphs* (water), and Gnomes* (underground). (4) Contemporary: fallen angel, devil.

DEMONALITRY: Religion which venerates Satan, the demon.

DEMONERY: Intervention of a demon; commerce with demons.

DEMONESS: Feminine of demon, now little used.

DEMONIACS: Those with a relationship with a demon or possessed by a demon.

DEMONISM: Belief in demons.

DEMONOLOGY: Science which studies demons. Also called *demonography*.

DEMONOMANIA: (1) Magic demoniac practices. *See* Goety. (2) Title of work by the lawyer Jean Bodin (1580). (3) Mania, in which one believes oneself to be possessed by a demon (the victim is a *demonomaniac*).

DEMONOPATHY: Physiological or psychic troubles imputed to a belief in the intervention of a demon.

DENDROMANCY: Divination based on plants and trees.

DESTINY: Chain of events, inevitable and unknown; destiny of an individual. For the Ancient Greeks, close to *Nemesis* (jealousy of the gods punishing the *Hybris* or insolence of men). Homer saw in it a pernicious and inevitable force, the *Moira* or *Aisa*. Hesiod made of it the three daughters of *Anagke*, the necessity, or the three *Moirae* or *Parcae**: Clotho, Lachesis, Atropos. Beside this ordered and immutable force existed the *Tyche,* or unforeseen fate, which was personalized and called 'good' to placate it. Among the Romans, Moirae became *Fatum* and Tyche became *Fortuna*.

DETERMINED: *See* Rubeus.

DEVIL, The: Fifteenth major arcana of the Tarot*. The Devil is represented winged, blue, gold-horned, androgynous, unsheathed sword in the

The devil, key personality of the occult world.
An assembly of demons: on the left, Belial, small monster
with donkey's ears, who commands eighty infernal legions.
(German manuscript of the 15th century.)

Following pages: A miniature of 13th century
illustrating the pact of the monk Theophile with the Devil.
(Ingleburg Psalter, Denmark.)

Ego ſū homo ueꝛuſ

MESSES NOIRES

satanistes
et lucifériens

matutano

The cult of the devil
n its most sacrilegious form—the black mass.
Satan, in the guise of a winged goat, presides over the sacrifice.

Sorcerer from Central Africa.
Following pages:
Dance of the witchdoctors, aborigines of Australia.
The Great Goat Leonard, the devil incarnate,
presides over the witches' sabbat (Goya, Prado Museum).

Leaving for the sabbat. According to tradition, the bodies of the women are smeared with the fat of a child (on the left); a witch rides an infernal goat (in the centre), while others straddle their brooms.

Armchair used in China to exorcize the possessed.

left hand, by the larme. He dominates two chained characters. He represents the forces of evil, or rather accepted risk, opposite of wisdom.

Imprint of the devil's hand.

DEVIL(S): *See* Demon(s), Dragon. (1) The spirit of evil, inspires sin and black magic*. Anthropomorphic representation, often frightening: horns, goats' hooves, long, forked tail, eye of fire, goat's beard. (2) There exist many demons. The principal ones are: Abigar, Abracax, Adramelech, Agu-ares, Alastor, Alocer, Amduscias, A(a)mon, Andras, Asmodea, Astaroth, Bael, Balan, Behemoth, Belial or Beliar, Belphegor, Beelzebub, Buer, Caym, Leonard (or the Great Black Goat or the Great Negro) (cf. Sabbat), Leviathan, Mammon, and Moloch (cf. Golden Calf), Stolas, Ukobach, etc. Their great masters are Satan, Lucifer and Mephistopheles. Some writers claim there are 72 infernal princes and 7,405,920 demons (see *Le Cabinet du Roy de France,* 1581). Others name 6 demoniac legions with 66 cohorts of 666 companies of 6,666 demons (666 is the number of the devil).

DEVIL'S REIGN: Denotes the period in the Middle Ages and the Renaissance during which the devil was the object of a powerful cult.

DEVIL'S TRILL: See Trill, Devil's.

DEW: In alchemy*, symbolizes the purity of 'water and its purifying role.

DHARANA: In Yoga*, concentration of thought on a single point. (First stage of Samyama).

DHYANA: Yogic meditation. A type of yoga*, which studies the powers of thought. Used by the Chinese Buddist sect *C'han* and the Japanese *Zen.*

Active concentration on the essence of an object (second stage of Samyama).

DIAMOND: Precious stone to which legend attributes the power of engendering and reproducing itself. Symbolizes uncreated divinity, purity, strength, vigilance, divine wisdom, unity. Magic believes the diamond to be favorable to the right eye, and attributes numerous qualities to it: purifier, anti-spasmodic, calms fever, keeps away terrors and savage beasts, gets rid of ghosts and poisons. According to astrology*, favors Leo (Louis XIV had 9,547 of them) and Taurus especially.

DIAPSYCHE: Name given by Emile Boirac to the faculty of communicating between one psychic person and another. *See* Metagnomy; Telepathy.

DIPLOSIS: *See* Alchemy (3).

DISINCARNATED: Elevated and spiritually removed from one's body (of flesh). *See* Entity, Spiritism.

DIVINATION: The art of foretelling. There are many varieties. (*See* mancies). Plato admits its truth (in his *Phaedo*) in the case of certain chosen people.

Cicero (*De Divinatione*, 1) gives the following table: (1) External, artificial, or inductive divination (by the observation and interpretation of external signs, sent by the gods). (a) according to the intention one distinguishes exceptional wonders, the meaning of whose signs is agreed upon in advance, and fortuitous signs, to be interpreted after the event; (b) according to the natural phenomenon observed one distinguishes ornithomancy (birds), ophiomancy (reptiles), dendromancy (plants and trees), cledomancy (man's instinctive acts), hepatoscopy or art of Aruspex (entrails), pyromancy (fire), hydromancy (water), observation of meteorological phenomena (lightning), astrology (stars), chiromancy (hand), and numeromancy (mathematics). (2) Internal divination, natural or intuitive: the great oracles (direct divine revelation, without external signs), oneiromancy (dreams, simple or with 'incubation'), necromancy (dead), chresmology (sacred delirium called *enthusiasm,* by the great oracles).

DIVINER: One who claims to discover hidden things, or especially to predict the future. The most famous, in Ancient Greece, were Calchas, the blind Tiresias (whom Oedipus and Ulysses consulted, and whose tomb became the seat of a reputed oracle); Mopsus, who, with Amphilochus (son of Amphiriaraus, soothsayer of the Argonauts) founded the oracle of Apollo at Colophon, in Asia Minor. *See* Prophet, Mancies.

DIVINER-BIRDS: Birds which are supposed to have taken a horoscope to Agra (India), Nikko (Japan), and Oaxaca (Mexico).

DIVISION INTO TWO: *See* Doubling.

DJINN: *See* Genie.

DOG: (1) Ally of man, emblem of fidelity, and even deified. The dog is used in black magic rites and regarded as the companion of the devil (yellow dog of Mephistopheles). (2) Often symbolizes the guardian, submissive instinct and equilibrium.

DOLL: *See* Dagyde.

DOMICILE: *See* Exile (astrology*).

DOMIFICATION: Astrological operation to fix the position of the twelve Houses of the sky at the time of birth (natal theme).

DOMINANT: In astrology*, characterizes the principal value of the theme. Some distinguish the elementary, planetary, and zodiacal Dominant. Similar meaning: planetary signature.

DOPPELGANGER: In German legend a double*, es-

pecially one who appears to horsemen in mortal danger.

DOTS, POINTS: Name given to the tracing in geomancy*.

DOUBLE: (1) The Ka of the Ancient Egyptians. *See* Astral Body. (2) *See* Doubling. (3) *See* Doppelganger. (4) *See* Spell (captation of double).

DOUBLE CAPTATION: *See* Spell.

DOUBLE SIGHT: *See* Clairvoyance.

DOUBLING or BILOCATION: Voluntary or not, in a trance, the possibility of being in two different places at once. Investigation of the *fluidic body* which momentarily leaves the material body. *See* Body. Also called 'Astral voyage'. Hornell Hart called it a projection of E.S.P. and Allan Kardec *bicorporeity* or *clairvoyance,* to distinguish it from subject-division and from schizophrenia.

DOWSING ROD: Divining rod.

DRACONITE: According to Pliny the Elder, a fabulous stone found in the head of a dragon (*Legends of Treasures*).

DRAGON: (1) A kind of winged serpent; appears frequently in legend. The devil is sometimes referred to as *The Ancient Dragon.* According to Philostratus, the Arabs ate the heart or liver of a flying dragon

Dragon, guardian of the underworld, from the Kircher demonolog (17th century).

to become diviners or sorcerers. (2) *See* Alchemy. (3) Religion associates it with evil and with the devil, but the gnostics* see in it the symbol of an external beginning, bringing the best *eons,* or emanations of the spirit. The most famous dragons were killed by Cadmos (Boeotia), Hercules, Jason (to gain the Golden Fleece); St George (at Mons), St Michael (at Brussels); and the Tarasque (subdued by St Martha in Provence)

DRAGON, RED: One of the classic books of western magic of the Middle Ages. *See* Albert, Clavicle, Black Hen.

DRAGON TAIL: *See* Cauda Draconis.

DREAMS: *See* Oneiromancy. (1) Assembly of images or ideas, or hallucinatory experiences, more or less consistent and coherent, produced during sleep. Often casting light on the workings of the unconscious*; studied by Jung and Freud. Robert Desoille also analyzed the 'waking dream'. (2) In occultism, a dream implies prediction. Homer especially believed in this form of divination, used in Ancient Greece at Oropos, at the sanctuary of Amphiarus on the skin of a sacrificed ram, or at Epidaurus at the sanctuary of Asklepios, to heal the sick. The symbolism of dreams often has been taken to absurd extremes. The Ancients specified that one could only hope for a prophetic dream after asceticism, aimed at loosening the restrictive influence of the Ego. (3) Many famous dreams have been handed down to us from antiquity: those of Gilgamesh and his friend Enkidu, Zoroaster, Darius, Pharaoh, Jacob (illustrated by Rembrandt), Booz, the mother of Alexander, Buddha, Julius Caesar, etc., and the healing dreams of Epidaurus (by nocturnal 'incubation'*). Artemidorous of Ephesus relied on the 'dream-keys'* in the Roman era, succeeding Aristotle, who had written a small treatise, *On divination by Dreams*. (4) Homer (*Odyssey, XIX, 560*) distinguishes deceitful dreams 'passed through the gate of ivory', from the truthful, 'come through the gate of horn'.

DRUGES: For the Persians, these were female demons, of whom the most vile was Nasu, the 'Black Fly of Cadavers'.

DRUID: Administrative priest of Gaul. The *druidesses* prophesied, notably by examining the entrails and the flow of blood of human victims. They have been gratuitously credited with magic powers. Their religion is *druidism*.

DUKHOBORS: Mystic sect originally from the Caucasus, Russia, which rejects the divinity of Christ. Numbers emigrated to Canada in the early part of the century.

EAGLE: (1) The bird *par excellence*. Dedicated to Zeus-Jupiter, it became the emblem of several empires, the arms of the emperor of the Tarot*. Many primitive tribes, especially American Indians, venerated it as the *thunder-bird*. Its qualities and the symbolism which come from it are evident. (2) Eagle stone: *See* aetite.

EAR: *See* Right, Left.

ECSTASY: Delight of the soul which takes away the realities of the world. *Shamanism* is the technique of ecstasy. The soul directs itself 'away from the self'. *See* Enstasis.

ECTOPLASM or **TELEPLASM:** For some, manifestation of the *psychic fluid* either by molding or by the production of vaporous forms by the medium in a state of trance. Term invented by Richet. *See* Materialization, which is the term usually reserved for the process itself.

ECTOPLASY: A term initiated by Myers in 1904. Synonymous with *materialization* or *telepathy*. Richet called it *ectoplasmy*.

EEL: According to the Grand Albert, the eel, macerated in vinegar mixed with the blood of a vulture and placed under a dunghill, has the ability to resuscitate.

EFFLORESCENCE: *See* Fluid.

EFFLUVIOGRAPHY: Study of the effluvia (*See* Fluid) that certain mediums reputedly release. Sometimes synonymous with scotophotography, formerly reserved for the paranormal photography of spirits.

EGG: Since Roman times, many magicians have claimed that it is necessary to break the shell to destroy spells and to avoid demons lodging in it. *See* Oomancy: Black Hen.

EGREGORE or EGGREGORE: Magic vapor of collectivities (the 'flying saucers' and the 'suns of Fatima' would be some of these). Called sometimes *thought form*. Collective magic being.

EKAGRATA: In Yoga, concentration of the senses on a single point.

ELECTUARY: Remedy. In magic, special potion or ointment. *See* Mithridate.

ELEMENTALS: (1) In magic, semi-intelligent spirits of nature, 'living coagulations of astral light'. (2) From the great psychologist, Jung, they stand for the early stages of evolution, summed up in the individual by the Collective Unconscious.

ELEMENTARY: Entity from beyond. For theosophists*, stellar groups, human remains disintegrating.

ELEMENTS: The ocultists add to the four traditional elements of water, earth, fire and air, a fifth called life, dynamism, time, blood and, for the Chinese, the *center*.

ELEPHANT: Symbolizes temperance, patient power, wisdom, intelligence, longevity. The hair of the elephant, in an ornament or trinket, is supposed to bring good luck.

ELF: In Scandinavian mythology, aerial sprite who symbolizes air, fire, earth, etc. Divided into elves of light (immortal) and elves of darkness. *See* Sylph.

ELIXIR OF LIFE: Name given by alchemists to the *mercurial water* coming from the Philosopher's Stone* by liquefaction or reduction. Also called *fifth elixir,* it rejuvenates old people, resuscitates the dead, prolongs existence without illness (*See* Panacea), but does not give immortality. It is symbolized by the Tarantula*. Cagliostro claimed to have found the elixir: wine of Malmsey with a distillation of sperm of certain animals and the sap of plants.

EMBRYO, METALLIC: *See* Homunculus.

EMERALD: (1) Precious stone from which the famous magic Trismegistus Table* of Hermes, containing the Kybalion*, was made. It was found in a tomb. Since the twelfth century a short translation appeared in the West (*Tabula Smaragdina*), probably translated from Arabian (tenth century), from the original Greek (fourth century) in twelve short verses and about thirteen doubtful ones. Its name of *Telesmer* symbolizes the sun and also love and hope. (2) Some French peasants believe it facilitates childbirth, and protects from dysentery and snakebite. Favors the signs of Cancer and Sagittarius.

EMET: *See* Golem.

EMPEROR: Name given to the fourth major arcana of the Tarot*. Seated, in profile, turned towards the left, on a throne bearing an eagle with outspread wings. Holds a scepter in the right hand. Symbolizes material energy, conservation, static power. His white hair and feet indicate that he is a tool of destiny. *See* Empress.

EMPRESS: Third major arcana of the Tarot*. Enthroned, clothed in blue and red. Symbolizes material energies*, translates the evolutive power of fertilized matter. *See* Emperor.

EMPUSE: Demon of midday, who appears especially in August and breaks the bones of those who refuse to venerate him. In a broad sense, specter, vampire. Probably related to 'Empusa' of Antiquity, a monster with a donkey's foot of brass, which was sent to earth by Hecate and took on hideous forms to terrify men. *See* Hecate.

ENCHANTER: Magician. The prototype is Merlin.

ENCHANTMENT: Magic procedure, advantageous or not, commonly called a spell. Same etymology as incantation.

ENCHANTRESS, GREAT: For the initiates in ancient Egypt, the *Uraeus* or double serpent of the scepter.

ENCHIRIDION: Collection of magic formulae, ascribed to Leo III.

ENDOSCOPY: *See* Auto-scopy.

ENERGUMEN: Formerly, one possessed.

ENGASTRIMANDERS: Diviners of Apollo, who rendered oracles 'by their prophetic bellies' without moving their lips.

ENOPTROMANCY: Divination by a magic mirror which reveals the future, even to those whose eyes are covered or shut.

ENSTASIS: A form of meditation in the recesses of the soul practised by Yogis*. Sometimes called *statis*. *See* Ecstasy.

ENTANGLE, TO: To produce a spell which prevents movement. *See* Aiguillette, Pegging, Ligature.

ENTITY: That which constitutes the essence of a being. In magic: disincarnated human spirits, demons, etc.

ENTRAILS: See Anthropomancy, Aruspex, Ichthyomancy.

ENVOUTEMENT or HEX-ING: Magic practice of love or, more especially, hate, to influence or injure a person. Is carried out on an image of wax or a doll symbolizing the person to be hurt or influenced. For hate, a malevolent attack is made, using nail or hair clippings of the enemy. *See*

Nails. Practised by primitive peoples, and in Europe at least since the thirteenth century. In 1315 Enguerrand de Marigny was hanged for having put a spell on an effigy of Louis X.

EON: For gnostics, the emanation of the eternal intelligence, a force symbolized by the dragon, allowing 'incompatible souls' to improve.

EPARGE: *See* Dagyde.

EPHISIA GRAMMATA: Magic formula of the Ephisians, bringing immediate fulfilment of wishes. Some, on lead, were slipped into wells, tombs, etc. Their oldest known words are, in Greek: *askion, lix, tetrax, damnameneus,* and, in Roman times in North Africa, *aurara, bazagra.*

EPHOD: Jewish oracle. Casket fixed to the shoulders of the magician by thongs. It contained two dice made of emerald: the *ourim* and the *tummim.*

ERGON: *See* Parergon.

ERRORS: Pradines distinguishes the errors of affectivity (auto-suggestion), of the senses (hallucination) and of reason (magic, outward will-power). *See* Fraud.

ESOTERICISM: Secret doctrine, reserved for *initiates.* Opposite of exotericism: The word profane (*pro fano*) indicates those who had to stay 'in front of the temple', not being admitted inside as were the initiates.

E.S.P.: Name given by Rhine to the parapsychological faculties. Extra-sensory perception, also called *Psi-Gamma*. The general or G.E.S.P. comprises, following a convenient but disputed division: clairvoyance* and telepathy.* The Germans say A.S.E. (*Ausserinnliche Erfahrung*); the French speak of 'perception extra-sensorielle'. *See* Psychokinesis or P.K.

ETHERIC: *See* Body.

EURYNOMOS: Superior demon, Prince of Death. A statue in the temple of Delphi represented him sitting on a vulture skin, black with wolf's teeth. He was next imagined covered with sores and partially clad in the skin of a fox.

EVIL: *See* Cauda Draconis.

EVIL EYE: *Mal Ojo* in Spanish, *jettatura* in Italian, *ein horra* in Hebrew. Eye that brings misfortune. The eye has such a magic value that the Rabbi Simeon ben Yochai with a single glance transformed a man into a heap of whitened bones (*Pessikta* 90b); Jochanan did the same to his brother-in-law.

EVOCATION: An operation which makes divinities, the devil, the dead, spirits, appear by charms. (*See* Devil, Medium, Spiritism.) Distinguished from *invocation*, a prayer of attendance.

EXALTED: Said in astrology* when a planet is at a particular point of its course. It is stated as 'exalted in such a degree' or, more simply, 'in such a sign of the Zodiac'.

EXILE: In astrology, a planet which occupies the Zodiac sign totally opposed to that which is its *domicile* is said to be in *exile*.

EXORCISM: Religious ceremony designed to banish demons by prayers. Magical process to liberate a haunted house, to undo a spell, to return something to the devil, etc. *See* Possession.

EXORCIST: Cleric who has received the third minor order. Priest or specialist who exorcises.

EXOTERICISM: *See* Esotericism.

EXPLORATION: *See* Medium.

EXTENIC FORCE: *See* Fluid.

EXTERIORIZATION OF SENSIBILITY: Name given by Colonel Albert de Rochas (1891) to the possibility, for some subjects, of 'projecting their nervous fluid, in certain conditions, out of the body.' This same force could produce *telekinèsis**. Of doubtful validity.

EXTERIOR THRESHOLD: *See* Cauda Draconis.

EXTISPEX: Divination by the examination of the entrails. *See* Aruspex, Hieromancy. Probably arose in Etruria.

EXTRA LUCIDITY: *See* Lucidity.

EXTRA-RETINAL: *See* Paroptic.

EXTRA SENSORY PER-CEPTION: *See* E.S.P.

EYE: Symbolizes intelligence, understanding, knowledge (the *third eye* of the Hindus, Tibetans), conscience (the eye of God in a triangle), but it also represents the anguish of being seen, the fear of chastisement (whence the *pantacles**, representing the 'evil eye*' perceived), guilt, feminity. There is great use of the representation of the eye in magic, which makes it a bringer of good luck: in Persia, the eye of a slaughtered sheep, covered with wax, hung around women's necks; in Egypt, a mystic eye at the wrist; in Italy, 'vetro del occhio', glass in the form of an eye. In France, in the Middle Ages, the right eye of a weasel was carried in the bezel of a ring, against the knotting of the aiguillette*.

FA: Practice of erotic divination in Dahomey.

FAIRY: From the Latin *fatidica*. Some people claim they are the descendants of the druidesses. Legendary beings endowed with remarkable powers, thanks to their *wands*. Omniscient, they appeared in the most varied forms. They obeyed a queen who, to judge them, called them together annually. Immortal, except for one day each year when they must take on an animal form (zoomorphism). The western cabalists have called them *sylphids*. They can be good or bad. A cloud, a griffin or a Spanish cat transports them at the speed of lightning. There are fairy grottos; for example, those of Chablais and Ganges (Languedoc). The fairy Morgan le Fay is celebrated in the annals of chivalry.

FAKE: In prestidigitation, to include trickery apparatus (false finger, false tongue, etc).

FAKIR: (From the Arabian *fakir*, poor). Moslem or Hindu magician reputed to have miraculous powers. Among his many tricks are: the accelerated growth of the mango tree (the mango trick), resting on a bed of nails, immersion or burial, and the celebrated Hindu rope trick. The Paris journalist, Paul Heure, their great adversary, proposed classifying the tricks thus: (1) The fakir acting on himself: catalepsy, immobility, insensibility, invulnerability, suspension of vital functions. (2) The fakir acting on other living things: acceleration of growth of animals or vegetation. (3) The fakir acting on objects: telekinesis, rope trick, dematerialization.

FAKIRIC IMMERSION: *See* Resurrection, Suspension of Vital Functions.

FAKIRISM: Technique and tricks of the fakirs. Can be divided into objective fakirism or physical effects, and subjective fakirism or mental effects.

FALL (or the DROPPING of an object): Superstitions: scissors = announcement of another task: knife, spoon = a visit; comb = disappointment (in England), thought of someone (France); sewing object = pleasure.

FASCINATION: Art of attracting or bewitching a person by a look. As the serpents and the Gorgons 'fascinated' (the three sisters, Medusa, Euryale and Stheno petrified those who looked on them), the Ancients feared the evil eye*. To combat it, the most frequently used amulet had the form of the phallus. ('Fascinum' in Latin.) To spit on the clothes was also advisable.

FASTING: Apart from the fakirs and the cases cited in hagiography, one can mention the marvellous fasts of Marie Pelet de Laval, who lived in le Hainaut, Belgium, for thirty two months (from 6 November, 1754, to 25 June, 1757) without eating or drinking; Anne Harley, of Orival, near Rouen, who, for twenty years, drank only a little milk that she vomited almost immediately; and Mac Swiney, Lord Mayor of Cork, and Michael Murphy, who succumbed in prison: the first in London after seventy four days of fasting and the second at Cork after seventy six. The Italian Angelo Gasti fasted in a Nazi camp for ninety one days.

In fakiric fasts, the principal records (usually badly controlled) are those of Mia-Lu (44 days), Lys Chelys (57 days), the Hungarian Nadia Goya (Genoa, 1951, sixty two days, beating the Triestin, Delfo), Heros (the Geran Willy Schmitz, 1950, 81 days), Burma (Frenchman, Roger Brun, 1951, 94 days), and the Brazilians Silki and Urbano (1955, 100 and 101 days respectively). The Dutchman, Sacco, died in Blackpool in 1929 after 65 days.

FEAR: The Ancient Greeks deified fear under the name 'Phobos'. A cult developed around it, notably in Sparta. In the Dark Ages it became an important demon in magic and sorcery.

FEET: See Podomancy.

FETISH: From the Portuguese *fatiara*, witch. Material object, venerated as an idol by primitive people. By extension, object considered to bring good luck. Different from amulet*, gris-gris*, pantacle*, talisman*.

FETISHISM: Cult of *fetishes*, linking the religious idea with the object which symbolizes it.

FIG (GESTURE OF THE): A gesture designed as a counter-charm, the fist clenched, with the thumb between index and middle fingers.

FIGURINE: See Dagyde, Envoûtement.

FIND: Superstitions: (1) A piece of money (especially pierced) means good luck; (2) a button in the street means success; (3) a four-leaf clover means good luck.

FIRE: See Fire Divination, Ignispicine, Phlogiston, Pyrology, Pyromancy.

(1) *Ignis Fatuus*: emanations of phosphorus of hydrogen gas in marshes or cemeteries, superstitiously believed to be goblins or troubled souls. Some add that they lead travellers astray in the marshes. (2) *St. Elmo's Fire*: phenomenon of atmospheric electricity, manifesting itself on the masts or spars of vessels. Connected with the *Dioscuri*, Castor and Pollux (twins of Gemini), or Cabiri of Samothrace, protectors of navigation.

FIRE DIVINATION: If the objects thrown into a fire do not burn, it is a happy omen.

FISH: (1) One of the twelve signs of the Zodiac* (Pisces). (2) See Ichthyomancy, Telchines. (3) Sometimes has a phallic value in magic (the fins symbolize feminine attraction).

FIST: Closed: See Acquisitio; open: See Amissio.

FLAME: See Lampadomancy, Lych(n)omancy, Pyrology.

FLIGHT (IN THE AIR):
See Levitation, Sabbat.

FLOWER, EIGHT-PETALLED: Symbolizes in astrology the totality of the self accomplished in its works.

FLUID: Mysterious elements (whose existence is yet to be proved) which explain certain parapsychological facts. There is thought to be *fakiric.* fluid, *solar* fluid, etc. The *spiritists* made of it a 'psychic lever', calling it *perisniritic energy*. For vital fluid, *See* Magnetism, Magnale. The Count of Gasparin (1853) explained the psychophysical phenomena of *table turning* by fluid. Von Reichenbach (1845-1868) called it *'Od'*; Dr. Barety, *'radiating neuric force'* (1880); Professor Blondot, of Nancy, (1903) *'N Rays';* Dr. Kilner, of London, (1912) *'human atmosphere'* or *aura*. In telergy the 'rigid rays of fluidic threads' of Ochorowicz were spoken of, as were the 'efflorescences' of Schrenk-Notzing, and the 'psychic lever or cantilever' of Crawford. In spiritism* one speaks of *teleplasty*, of the 'extenic force or resting agent'. (Thury, of Geneva in 1857, and William Crookes in 1869). All depends on a universal fluid. *See* Ouroboros, Magnetometer (device for measuring fluid).

FLYING CARPET: One of the greatest magical beliefs of the East. The claim of being able to fly through the air is associated with *Shamanism*.

FLYING DUTCHMAN: *See* Wandering Dutchman.

FOOL: Name of the twenty-first or twenty-second major arcana of the Tarot. Shows a person walking, carrying a bag on the left and a stick on the right. A dog tears at the bottom of his trousers. Symbolizes the man who thinks he is on the path of his true destiny, when in reality he is shackled by his passions.

FORCE, NEURIC: *See* Fluid.

FOREST: Often symbolizes the unconscious, anguish.

FORTUNA MAJOR: Figure of geomancy*, symbolizes royalty, splendor, honor, victory. Affinities: sun, gold, fire. In French: great fortune; In Arabian: ingoing victory.

FORTUNA MINOR: Figure of geomancy*, symbolizing fortuitous success, worldly success, not outstanding, not always moral. Affinities: sun, fire. In French: small fortune; in Arabian: outgoing victory.

FORTUNE: *See* Acquisitio; Fortuna Major; Fortuna Minor.

FRAUD: Trickery, to act in bad faith. Deception, conscious or unconscious, used at the time of parapsychological experiences. Many of the great mediums have been caught at least once in the commission of a fraud. *See* Errors.

FROG: Less used in black magic than the toad. Symbolizes involution.

FULGURAL ART: *See* Aruspex.

FURFUR: Count of the underworld, commanding twenty-six legions. Appears as an angel, or more often, a winged deer with human arms and a flaming tail. He commands the storm, and replies only with lies, except if one succeeds in enclosing him in magic thought. He also reveals the most abstract problems.

GAIN: *See* Acquisitio.

GALLE: A priest and itinerant magician of low birth, who explored Oriental superstitions of the common Roman people. Not to be confused with the *archigalle*, official priest of the cult of the Mother of the gods.

GAMAHES: *See* Camaieu.

GANDREID: Modern Icelandic charm which gives the ability to travel through the air; on the ribs and shinbones of a horse, with a bridle of leather decorated with lunar characters.

GARLIC: In contrast to the Greeks and some ancient Asiatics, the ancient Egyptians considered garlic a sacred plant. Its curative properties, if not its scent, have long been appreciated. Rabelais notes that it has the power of counteracting the effects of *loadstone*. The magic pharmacopoeia made great use of it.

GASTROMANCY or LECANOMANCY: Divination interpreting the images formed by the refraction of light from candles across and through transparent vessels filled with clear water. *See* Hydromancy. Also practised by the interpretation of sounds made by metallic sheets or stones being thrown into a basin of water.

GAZARIENS: *See* Vaudois.

GELOSCOPY: Divination by the analysis of laughter.

GEMATRIA: Part of the Cabala dedicated to the numeric interpretation of names.

GEMINI: One of the twelve signs of the Zodiac. *See* Astrology, First Part.

GENETHLIACS: In Greek antiquity, another name for astrology. Astrologers: *genethliaucs.*

GENIE: (1) To the Ancients, signified, firstly, the principle of procreation; secondly, the family genie; and thirdly, the divine element presiding over the life of each person (a kind of guardian angel). The genie of the Roman Emperor was specially honored with the *Dea Roma.* (2) In antiquity, often synonymous with *daimon* (*See* Demon) or with the spirit and the moral action of a divinity. (3) Later, signified *sprite, gnome, sylph,* entities personifying the forces of nature. (4) In some myths, creative spirits (*Djinn* of the Arabs) or abstract qualities. As in old Oriental stories, certain fakirs and other magicians were capable of changing natural laws if they knew the genies by name. It was good to know also the 'constraining' magic formulæ.

GEOMANCY: More rarely, *geocy.* Divination interpreting the signs formed on the earth (generally dots); of Arabian origin. Also done by tracing dots on paper with a pencil, or by observing small pebbles on the sand. The practitioner: *geomancer.* Some attribute its origin to the prophet Daniel. For an explanation of its sixteen figures: *See* Acquisitio, Albus, Amissio, Caput, Cauda Draconis, Carcer, Conjunctio, Fortuna Major, Fortuna Minor, Laetitia, Populus, Puella, Puer, Rubeus, Tristitia, Via. Modern Islam practises it still in the form of the 'throwing of dots': to reply to a question the thrower lets his hand trace sixteen lines of dots which he counts in groups of four (mother-figures), further subdivided for interpretation. A geomantic *theme* comprises sixteen variable figures or *houses. See* Geomancy, First Part.

GHOUL: In Oriental superstition, a vampire which sucks the blood of living things, or who unearths bodies, during the night, to devour the hearts.

GIRL: *See* Puella.

GNOMES: Deformed dwarfs, who, according to the Jewish cabalists, guard the mines and treasures of the earth. They are jocular, sometimes generous. *See* Demons.

GNOSIS: Knowledge assuring

salvation by initiation. The faithful: *gnostics*. *Gnosticism*: system of religious philosophy claiming to assure a complete knowledge of nature and the attributes of God, thus able to give salvation and to 'conserve the major paths of wisdom'.

Gnostic cameo.

GOAT: (1) Symbolizes virility in nature. Dedicated to Dionysus-Bacchus (with the bull). Venerated in Egypt. Served as a mount for Aphrodite-Venus. Pan and the Satyrs were half man, half goat. (2) At times sacred, at times cursed: (*scapegoat* charged with the sins of the Jews; infernal goat).

GOAT, GREAT BLACK: *See* Sabbat.

GOBLIN: Sprite, elf. Sometimes torments men. Alexis-Vincent Berbiguier wrote a curious work on them in three volumes (1821). Their as-

Sabbat goat, depicted by Eliphas Levi.

sembly was previously represented as being presided over by Beelzebub. (2) Sprites of the Middle Ages in France and Germany who hid in inaccessible corners of houses. Rendered service if they were fed; otherwise they caused tedium and privation.

GOETY: Black magic, demoniac sorcery, calling on the infernal terrestrial forces in

Gothic circle of evocation, by Eliphas Levi.

opposition to *theurgy* and to the *thaumaturgy*.

GOLDEN CALF: *See* Mammon.

GOLDEN FLEECE: *See* Alchemy* (2).

GOLDEN NUMBER: Number corresponding to the 'perfect proportion'.

GOLD, POTABLE: *See* Elixir of Life.

GOLEM: Certain rabbis of Prague animated a red clay statue of a man, the *Golem,* by formulae and by writing on its forehead *Emet,* magic name of the 'Life-God'. The statue grew and did what it was commanded. It would crumble to dust if the inscription was erased (or if it was replaced by the word 'death').

GOSSIP: *See* Populus.

GRAIL: Sacred vessel sup-posedly used to serve Jesus Christ when he celebrated the Last Supper. Transported to England by Joseph of Arimathea, it became the principal object of the quest of the Knights of the Round Table in the epic period of King Arthur.

GRAPHOMANCY: Divination based on handwriting. Some speak also of *intuitive graphologue* or *psychometer* by handwriting. Not to be confused with graphology, the study of *character* from handwriting. Fairly recently Dr. Fretigny and the French Society of Psychosociology defined and stated the methodology of the 'science of writing', subdivided into ten disciplines, of which graphology is the sixth.

GREAT ART or **GREAT WORK** or **GREAT MAGISTRY:** In alchemy, transformation of metals into gold. To achieve it means 'to conquer the Golden Fleece', or 'to sit at the sumptuous table'. Unites the male element (Affinities: fire-stable-dry-active-gold-sun-sulfur) to the female element (water-volatile-damp-passive-silver-moon-mercury) with the third element, salt (or arsenic). Others speak of seven metals (represented by Apollo, Diana, Jupiter, Saturn, Mercury,

Mars, Venus), transformed by the union of the Quaternary (fire, air, water, earth), and the Ternary (sulfur, mercury, salt). Sulfur is the form or soul. Mercury or quicksilver, the material or body. Salt, the initial effluvium, is the quintessence of ether. In making the Philosopher's Stone red, the metals can be transmuted to gold (*chrysopea*). Gold is also called 'secret sulfur' and silver 'secret mercury'. In the hermetic world it occupies the center circle. Made in five stages: dissolving, purifying, sublimating, dividing, composing. Sulfur and mercury also give the material Rebis, process in colors: Black (putre-

Paradigm of the 'Great Work'.

faction), white (resurrection = silver), red (rubification = gold).

GREEN: Attributed to Venus, sinople in heraldry. Color of hope, of divine wisdom, of the revelation of love (Springtime), of gnostic initiation. Some add to it a note of misfortune.

GRIFFON: Fabulous animal, half eagle, half lion (the head is composed of features of an eagle, then a lion, with a horse's ears), called 'winged lion'. Apollo captured one in the country of the Hyperboreans, where the Griffons guarded gold against the greed of the Arimaspi, fierce, one-eyed warriors.

GRIMOIRE: Book of magic, or of magical conjuring tricks.

GRIS-GRIS: Sculptured representation of the protector

Symbolic representation of alchemic conjunction of seven metals.

chosen by primitive tribes. Carried as protection, especially against sickness. Contains mineral, vegetable or animal elements. It was hung around the neck or wrist.

GROWTH, ACCELERATED: (of plants, animals) Fakiric claim, justified by the mental fluid, fakiric or solar*. Especially the mango trick, the wheat of Osiris, Japanese flowers, etc. *See* Fluid.

GUIDE: *See* Control.

GUNA-GUNA: Black magic practised in Java.

GURU: Spiritual leader and personal teacher in India. Disciple: Chela.

GYMNOSOPHISTS or 'NAKED PHILOSOPHERS': Hindu magicians, naked (Nagas) and reputed to have great powers. One of them, Sphines, was attached to Alexander the Great's expedition.

GYROMANCY: Divination by turning about in a large circle traced on the ground and divided into quarters, each marked with a letter of the alphabet. Interpretations were made according to the letters the body covered in falling.

HABORYM or AYM: Duke of Hades, commands twenty six legions. With three heads: those of a cat, a man, and a serpent. Mounted on a viper, holding a torch; for he is a demon of fire.

HADES: Signifies, firstly, lower places (*loci inferni*), underground places where the dead stay; and secondly, the place where sinners pay for their faults. The Ancients distinguished: (1) *Erebus,* the dark region of access (they cite it as being at the edge of the ocean, under Tenarus at Cumeo, Italy, at Eleusis, Greece). Watched over by the monstrous dog *Cerberus.* (2) The *Tartarus,* fortress of the damned. (3) The *Elysian Fields* of the Blessed.

The infernal rivers were: Acheron, Cocytus, Lethe (of oblivion), Phlegethon, Styx.

The boat of the dead was guided by the ferryman, Charon. The three infernal judges were Minos, Phasamanthus, Aeacus. The god of Hades was Pluto, his wife Kore-Proserpine-Persephone.

See the famous description by Virgil, Sixth Canto of the *Aeneid*.

For the Talmudists (Jews): Gehenne. Synonymous for Pluto: in Greek Hades (place or person); in Latin: Dis, Orcus. The conductor of souls is Hermes-Mercury.

HAIR: Symbolizes instinctive forces. In many Oriental countries a lock of hair is sacrificed to the holy rivers, and the first lock of hair of a newborn baby is offered to the divinities. Superstition: young girls pull out one hair and pinch it several times with the fingernail in order to be loved. In magic, used against an enemy: *See* Spell.

HALLUCINATION: Error of the senses. Perception that the subject believes is tangible, but is, in reality, without substance. It is called *hypanogogic* by Maury if it is produced in half-sleep (pre-sleep); *hypnopompic* by Myers if it precedes waking; *veridic* if it brings exact information. It is not always easy to distinguish from a waking dream.

HAND: (1) *See* Chiromancy. (2) Since prehistoric magic, the hand has symbolized the strength and skill capable of commanding nature. On the wall of the cave at Castillo, thirteen left hands, four right: this proportion is frequently respected in magic. At the cave of Gargas, several fingers are folded.

HAND, FLUIDIC: *See* Ectoplasm, Materialization, Mummification. Eusapia Paladino claimed to produce it.

HAND, HORNED: Fingers folded, except for the index and little finger, rallying sign for the initiates, reputed to ward off the devil.

HAND OF FATMA: For the Moslems, brings good luck. It sometimes has six fingers to indicate the 'sixth sense'. Carried in a jewel, often of silver or painted red (especially on the hand).

HAND OF GLORY: In the Middle Ages, hand of hanged person cut off on the gibbet, on a Friday at midnight. Fingers folded into the palm, it undergoes a magic process of drying. A black candle is fixed to it (candle of human fat, sesame of laponia, and virgin wax, lighted at a tabernacle), of which the wick comes from the rope of the gibbet. Used to discover hidden treasures. Thieves considered it a charm, capable of producing numbness. It is also the name of Mandragora, the magic plant. It is sometimes called hand of Ibycos, from the name of an ancient Greek whose assassination by brigands was denounced by birds, cranes. It has the power of stiffening humans.

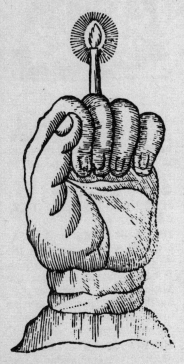

Hand of Glory.

HANGED MAN: Name of the Twelfth major arcana of the Tarot. Figure of a man hung by the left foot between two trees. Blue hair (= instinct). Symbolizes sacrifice, or rather the submission of man, giving up his strength for the sake of interior progress. *See* Ropes (2).

HARUSPEX: *See* Aruspex.

HAT: Superstition: if found on a bed, it signifies a dispute.

HATHA-YOGA: Ha = sun, Tha = moon. A form of Yoga controlling the physical body and the vitality, assuring mastery of different organs, notably the lungs in breathing (Prana).

HAUNTING: Phenomena, normally inexplicable, attached to a certain place: Poltergeists, telekinesia, apparitions, phantoms, hallucinations, etc.

HEAD: *See* Caput Draconis, Cephalomancy.

HEALER: Has the ability to cure without medicine. *See* Marcou, Mummification.

HEATHER: Superstition: briar = forecasts death.

HECATES: Giant *specters* which appeared in the mysteries of the Triple Hecate, infernal divinity and sorceress, Thraco-Greek.

HE-GOAT: Sometimes denotes the devil.

HELIOTROPE: (1) Flower,

symbolizes the sun, enthusiasm.
(2) Green precious stone,
spotted with red. The Ancients
believed that it conferred invisibility and gave the power
of *divination*.

HEPATOSCOPY: Divination
by the examination of the
livers of victims. The following
are especially examined: (a)
the lobes (disastrous if the
'head of the liver' is stunted
or absent: this was the warning
given of the deaths of Egisthe,
Cimon, Agesilas and Alexander
the Great); (b) the gall
bladder; (c) the portal vein.
See Aruspex, Extispex, Hieromancy.

HERMAPHRODITE: Bi-
sexual animal or plant. In
alchemy, watches over the
initiation, symbolizes · rebirth,
as does the rose.

HERMES TRISMEGISTUS:
Hermes-Mercury, the thrice
Great identified as the Egyptian
god Thoth, great god of magic.
Author of the *Table of Emerald,* secret hermetic magic
collection. Disciples: *hermet-
ists.* In alchemy, hermetic relationship with the Great
Work, the Philosopher's Stone.
See Kybalion. In a broad sense,
hermetism indicates the whole
set of secret doctrines.

HERMIT: Name of the ninth
major arcana of the Tarot*.
Turned towards the left, he

Hermes Trismegistus.

wears a blue cloak lined with
yellow. He signifies isolation
and the light guiding men, the
inward elevation obtained by
asceticism.

**HETEROSCOPY or
HETERO-ENDOSCOPY:**
See Autoscopy.

**HEXAGRAMME or HEXA-
GRAM:** Magic star, with the
six branches of Solomon's Seal.
Used by magicians since the
Middle Ages. Sometimes two
overlaid triangles, white and
black, symbolizing perfection.
See Pentagram.

**HIEROMANCY or HIERO-
SCOPY:** Examination of the
entrails of victims to predict

the future (especially of lambs, goats and calves).

HIPPALECTRYON: Fantastic animal, half horse, half cock. It is found especially in the Orient and on vases painted in the sixth and fifth centuries B.C.

HIPPOGRIFF: Fabulous animal, half horse, half griffon, which figures in the stories of the age of chivalry.

HIPPOMANCY: Divinatory science of the Celts, based on the study of white horses raised for this purpose.

HIPPOMANES: Love philters, comprising grasses, crushed insects, and hippomane (substance that colts have on their head at birth and which their mothers eat almost immediately). Used as an aphrodisiac. Hippomane is reduced to powder and mixed with the blood of the person who wishes to be loved.

HOBGOBLINS: Elemental and familiar spirits, often associated with fairies*. They torment girls, tease scholars and incite men to indulge in amorous frolics. Beelzebub* presides over the assembly of hobgoblins. Alexis Vincent Berbiguier* wrote at length on hobgoblins. He said they were often tormentors who could be defeated by being thrown into a bucket of water, a glass of vinegar or a fire into which a calf's heart and a dessertspoon of sulfur had been thrown. Berbiguier* was obsessed for years by hobgoblins, and he perfected a system of ensnaring them in 'bottleprisons'.

HOLLENFORT: (1) The aerial route taken by the Hollas (corruption of the name of the wife of Wotan, Holda, or Freya), designating the ride of the Valkyries. (2) In sorcery, aerial travel of witches to get to the Sabbat or *walpurgisnacht*.

HOMOSOPHY: Analogical theory of Dr. Lefebure concerning the inverse affinities (based especially on straight = masculine, curve = feminine).

HOMUNCULUS: Son of the sun and the moon conceived without sexual union, artificial man made from a base of sperm and blood by the alchemists. This creation aims at equalling God. Popularized especially by Paracelsus. Some people see it as a symbol of Mercury or a metallic embryonic sign for alchemists. The homunculus is compared to automatons* and robots, the most well-known being the Hebrew Golem (*See* Cabala). It appears that the first Golem was produced by the Rabbi Loew (16th century) and the last by the Rabbi David Jaffre, who lived in Russia about 1880.

HOROSCOPE: Point of the ecliptic which is at the horizon at the time of birth (also called *ascendant*). By extension, chart of the sky at birth, or interpretation of the state of the sky at birth.

HORSESHOE: Superstition: good luck if a used horseshoe having at least one nail is found on a path.

HOURS: Antiquity gave to the twelve hours of the day and the twelve hours of the night, attributes and personifications. In operative magic, time and the hour have great importance.

HOUSE(S): *See* Geomancy.

HOUSE, HAUNTED: House in which ghosts manifest themselves, especially after a crime. Pliny the Younger (Epist. VII, 27, 6) recounts the story of Athenodore, who 'calmed' the specters of a haunted house. *See* Poltergeist.

HOUSE OF GOD: Name of the Sixteenth major arcana of the Tarot. Represents a tower crowned by a flame coming from the sky, and from which two people are falling. Some interpret it as a divine chastising, limiting human power; others, on the contrary, as the victory of the human spirit, if it is not limited.

HYDRA: Mythical serpent with seven heads. The most famous, at Lerna, was killed by Hercules.

HYDROMANCY: (1) Divination by boiling liquids, by liquids of different colors, or by mixtures of bodies in water, etc. Practised particularly in Persia. Also called hygromancy. *See* Aeromancy, Gastromancy, Idatoscopy, Pegomancy. (2) In the temple of Aphrodite, at the source of the river Adonis in Syria, divination was practised by throwing objects in a pond. At Patras, at the temple of Demeter, the goddess rendered oracles to the sick by a mirror placed in a stream.

HYDROMEL: *See* Bell.

HYGROMANCY: *See* Hydromancy, Radiesthesia, Sorcery.

HYLOSCOPY: According to Boirac (1893) the influence of matter on man.

HYPERESTHESIA: Unusual acuteness of the senses; can provoke false telepathy. Can also be hypnotic.

HYPERNESIA: Unusual ability to recall memories. Can produce false clairvoyance and false telepathy. Can be hypnotic.

HYPNOSIS: *See* Braid, James; Ideoplasty, Passes.

Trance. A roughly similar state to that of sleep, characterized by an exaggerated suggestibility and produced artificially by the hypnotist, with or without *passes*. Term invented by Braid. One also speaks of hypnotic trances of the second *state,* of cadaveric or fakiric rigidity, of catalepsy, etc. It comprises three stages (a) somnolence; (b) hypotaxia; (c) automation or hypnotic somnambulism, which appear successively or isolated.

HYPNOTISM: Scientific and practical study of *hypnosis*. Collection of the methods which bring it about. Creator of the term, the surgeon, James Braid, of Manchester, distinguished lethargy, catalepsy, somnambulism. Azam introduced it in France. Medically, hypnotism 'renders the present time unconscious, and plunges the subject into relative un-

sciousness.' (Professor Chauchard).

HYPOTAXIA: Stage of hypnosis, having the appearance of natural sleep. Frequently accompanied by catalepsy* in the course of which the muscles become rigid and the body maintains a stiff position.

HYSTERIA: Neurosis characterized by temporary disorders of intelligence, sensitivity, movement, sometimes associated with stigmas. Charcot studied hypnotic hysteria at the Salpetriere (a Paris mental hospital). The results were contested by sceptics. Babinski calls it a 'collection of susceptible disorders able to be reproduced by suggestion, or made to disappear under the effect of suggestion or persuasion', to which he gave the name *pithiatism*. Mediums* are frequently affected by it.

IATROMANTIC: Divination based on the intestinal movements of a sick person. *See* Palmomantic.

I CHING: The Chinese *Book of Changes*, the oldest known book of divination. The eight fundamental trigrams combine to form sixty-four *koua* or hexagrams, corresponding to sixty-four possible situations met by man.

ICHTHYOMANCY: (1) Divination by examination of the heads and entrails of fish, practised especially in Greece. The fish was the secret symbol of persecuted Christians, because the Greek word *icthus* (fish) was the initials of 'Iesos Christos Theou Uios Soter'— Jesus Christ, Son of God, Savior. (2) At Hierapolis in Syria, and at Syra in Lycia, there existed, in antiquity, two oracles who interpreted the future from the lives of sacred fish.

IDATOSCOPY: Divination, a form of hydromancy*, using rainwater.

IDEOPLASTY: (1) In spiritism, the faculty of influencing matter directly by thought, and 'sculpturing' it at a distance. *See* Moulding, Telekinesis. (2) In hypnosis, according to the German Magnus Huss (1857) mimesis of hysterical people.

IGNISPICINE: Divination by fire.

ILLUMINATI, Order of the: Occult sect founded in 1776 by Weishaupt, professor at Ingolstadt. Characterized by much violence (for example, victims hanged at a 'stabbed tree').

ILLUSION: False interpretation of a normal sensation. Trick of prestidigitation.

ILLUSIONIST: *See* Prestidigitation.

IMITATION: Basis of mimetic magic, in which one imitates, for example, animals, to attribute their qualities to oneself.

IMPREGNATION: *See* Fluid, Psychometry.

IMPRESSION: *See* Psychometry.

INCANTATIONS: Formulae addressed to infernal entities, either to invoke them or to get rid of them.

INCARNATION: In spiritism, taking possession of the body of a medium in a state of trance by a spirit, reputedly from beyond. The English distinguish the control (the French call it 'guide') which directs the trance of the medium and presents to it other spirits of 'communicators', who are going to incarnate themselves temporarily. *See* Incorporation.

INCENSE: (1) Reserved for divinity, meant to have curative properties. (2) In white magic, favors the evocation of benevolent entities. (3) *See* Libanomancy.

INCORPORATION: Spirit incarnating itself in a medium. *See* Incarnation.

INCUBATION: Divinatory practice (notably in antiquity, at Epidaurus), causing the appearance of a divinity in a dream to obtain from it either a revelation of the future or a cure.

INCUBUS: A kind of spirit, masculine, malevolent, troubling the sleep of a woman by erotic dreams. *See* Succubus.

INFLUX: Occultism invokes astral, magnetic or fluidic influx, etc. Each time it cannot explain an 'influence'.

INGHILLI: Mystic sect which worships rabbits.

INITIATE: One who has undergone initiation*.

INITIATION: Tests, secret ceremonies initiating the faithful (or the initiate) to secret knowledge, and transforming his personality. *See* Spiralled Shell.

INK: A paper is blotted with ink, folded, and the future predicted from the marks.

INNOCENTS, MASSACRE OF: Symbolizes, to certain alchemists*, the metallic germs which they must dissolve.

INSENSIBILITY: Fakiric claim which allows swallow-

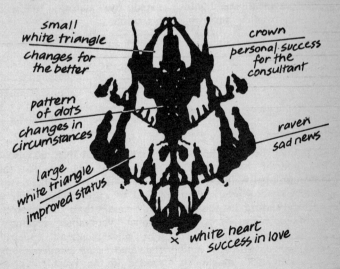

small white triangle
changes for the better

crown
personal success for the consultant

pattern of dots
changes in circumstances

raven
sad news

large white triangle
improved status

× white heart
success in love

Interpretation of an ink blot.

ing* of a sword, for example, and piercing*, without pain.

INTERCEPTERS: An anatomical arrangement in the vital organs and of which the unconscious sensitivity is comparable to that of the normal organs of the senses. Studied by Professor Bykov. R. Kherumian, who uses them in his new version of *energetic theory*.

INTERIOR THRESHOLD: *See* Caput Draconis.

INTERSIGN: Fact considered superstitiously as the announcement of an important event, called 'diosemeion' among the Ancient Greeks. The most typical was lightning, which was a favorable omen if it was on your right. Sometimes called *presentiment*. *See* Premonition

INVISIBILITY: (1) *See* Heliotrope. (2) One of the greatest magical claims. *See* Rings.

INVITED: *See* Magic Circle.

INVOCATON: *See* Evocation.

INVULNERABILITY: Claimed fakiric ability, which allows one to brave with impunity blades, nails, broken glass, fire, electric charges, and even firearms.

IRRORATION: Magic practice, claiming to relieve a sick person by watering a tree with his urine.

JACKDAW: Bird symbol of Apollo, god of the diviners*. Signifies conjugal faith, fidelity to memory (widowhood) when it is still. Hearing its song is a bad omen, especially at the beginning of an enterprise.

JAD(D)OO: African and Asiatic term for magic in general.

JADE or DIVINE STONE: Symbol of purity to the Chinese. In India, it is supposed to cure backache. It is also said that it protects against venomous creatures, and guards against epilepsy. Its value as an *amulet* is outmoded in the West.

JANIDES: Diviners, claiming

to be descended from *Janus,* who predicted the future by examining the cut skin of victims.

JAPA: Ritual Hindu formulae murmured during exercises of *Yoga,* for example.

JASMINE: *See* Capnomancy.

JAVANESE NARCOSIS: Technique of animal hypnosis by compressing the carotid artery. Used by the sorcerers of Java.

JAYET: Also called *black amber.* In Iceland it is supposed to be the best protection from witchcraft.

JET: Proves virginity. Chases away serpents and devils. Antidote: *See* Jayet.

JIVANMUKTA: One 'delivered from life', a superior *yogi* who, from his strict living, gains deliverance.

JNANA: In Sanskrit: knowledge, yoga of the powers of intelligence.

JONGLEUR: Healer and magician of Hudson Bay and Illinois.

JOY: *See* Laetitia.

JUDGMENT: Twentieth major arcana of the Tarot. Represents an angel with a trumpet, dominating two people at prayer and a third with his back turned, who is coming out of a green hole. It is interpreted as a sign of discernment, a call from the divine.

JUGGLER: First card of the Tarot representing a young man wearing a large hat, with his hair in golden ringlets, holding a yellow stick (active element of creation) in his left hand and a flesh-colored ball in his right (activity). It symbolizes the start of an enterprise, a decision to launch a project, etc.

JUSTICE: Eighth major arcana of the Tarot. It is imminent justice who reigns with scale and sword, in a red robe with a blue cloak.

KARMA: (1) Hindu doctrine of responsibility for acts which must be expiated in a cycle of rebirth (*Samsara*) to attain deliverance (*Moksha*) or Nirvana. (2) In *Yoga,* of the powers of action.

KARRA-KALF: Modern Icelandic magic. The initiate must 'clean' the devil with his tongue, who appears in the form of a new-born calf.

KELBY: Malevolent spirit of the waters who appears in the form of a horse, sometimes with a torch.

KENNE: Fabulous stone formed in the eye of a deer. Antidote.

KEPHALOMANCY or CEPHALOMANCY: Method of divination favored by the old Germans, who practised it over the baked head of an ass.

KEROTAKIS: The method of divination used by alchemists, invented by Marie la Juive (the Jewess) and which took the name of 'Marie-bath', or *Bain-Marie*.

KEY: Symbolizes the means of access to that which is hidden, temptation, liberation, wisdom. *See* Clidomancy, Clavicle.

KEY OF ST HUBERT OR ST PETER: Christian talis-mans to preserve animals from rabies.

KILCROPS: Children born of incubus and a woman. Sprenger called them 'changed children' or 'changelings'.

KNIFE: Superstition: offering a knife cuts the friendship, but this may be avoided by offering a coin to the donor to symbolize a purchase.

KNOCKING: *See* Raps, Typtology.

KRIYA: Purification, purgation, in Hindu magic and in Yoga.

KUNDALINI: Symbolically, serpent-woman coiled around the base of the backbone; Yoga, of the powers of the forces of the psychic nerves, often touched with eroticism (tantrism).

KYBALION: Collection of the seven fundamental laws attributed to Hermes Trismegistus on the 'Table of Emerald'.

LADDER: Superstition: to pass under one is bad luck.

LADYBIRD: Commonly called 'animal of the good

God", a favorable omen in superstition. Used as a talisman*.

LAETITIA: Figure of geomancy*, expressing joy, chanting. Affinities: air, Jupiter. In French: joy; in Arabian: the bearded.

LAMIA: Female demon, very beautiful, but whose lower body was that of a serpent. She enticed children so that she might kill and devour them. The Greeks and the Romans threatened naughty or disobedient children with Lamia's name, and attributed to her all the evil that befell their children. *Lamia* is analogous to the Greek *Mormo*.

LAMP: (1) *See* Lampadomancy. (2) Superstitions— extinguished suddenly: death; three lighted lamps in the same room: great misfortune.

LAMPADOMANCY: Divination by the flame of a torch or lamp, (single flame: good omen; divided: bad). Also called lychnomancy.

LARVAE: (1) For the Romans, the tragic, wandering spirits of dead men or of criminals, grimacing specters or skeletons. (2) Terrifying spirits who bring sorrow and epilepsy. Torturers of hell. (3) At present, in magic, incomplete spirits* or bungled incar-

nations*. *See* Lemures, Manes.

LAUGH: *See* Geloscopy.

LAUNDRESSES OF THE NIGHT: In Brittany, female phantoms who wash linen in isolated spots. If one sees them, it is necessary to wring out their linen, under threat of having a forced bath and a broken arm.

LAUREL: *See* Daphnephages, Daphnomancy.

LAYA: In Yoga*, of the powers of the spirit, 'fused to the universe', cosmic. For others, it encompasses all the yogas 'of the mental man'.

LEAVES: *See* Botanomancy; Sycomancy.

LEGANOMANCY: *See* Gastromancy.

LEFT: Bad omen ('sinister' means 'to do with the left side'). However, superstitions: a ringing in the left ear, someone is saying something good about you; left eyelid twitching, expectation of good news. Psychoanalysis takes note of a 'current towards the left', a symbol of the unconscious and of death.

LEMURES: Souls of the dead who come back to earth on certain days in Roman times, either by attachment to the body (Plato, *Phedon*, 81c) or to torment the living (Horace, *Odes*, 1, 28). They appeared at the *Lemuria* feasts in May, but were less frightening than the larvae and less honored than the manes*. Certain people include the vampires among them, for the lemures appeared as specters or in human form.

LEO ('THE LION'): One of the twelve signs of the Zodiac*. *See* Astrology, First Part.

LEONARD: Black goat, gigantic and foul - smelling, with three horns and a fox's ears, who presides over the Sabbat*. He is the leader of the subaltern demons and general supervisor of black magic and sorcery. The sorcerers worship him at the Sabbat, and kiss his hindquarters, which are in the form of a face holding a green candle.

LETHARGY: (1) *See* Somnolence. (2) The fakirs* call it 'burial alive' as *lethargy* or *lethargic sleep*.

LEVIATHAN: Monster spoken of in the Bible (*See* Job). Rabbinic tradition makes it an androgynous demon, which in male incarnation (Samael) is supposed to have seduced Eve; in feminine incarnation (Lilith) was supposed to have seduced Adam. It has the rank of Grand Admiral.

LEVITATION: Possibility of a person staying in the air horizontally without support. *See* Telekinesis.

LIBANOMANCY: Divination from the smoke of incense.

LIBRA: One of the twelve signs of the Zodiac*. *See* Astrology, First Part.

LIGATURE: Spell cast over one's limbs. *See* Aiguillette, Pegging, Entangle, to.

LIGHT, PARANORMAL: *See* Aura, Fluid, Luminosity.

LIGHTNING: *See* Aruspex, Bidental, Ceraunoscopy.

LINES: Term used in chiromancy* which distinguishes in the hand the line of ambition, of luck, of the heart, of the head, of life.

LITHOMANCY: Divination with the help of stones or pebbles put next to each other to form figures, or thrown on to a table.

LITTLE SABBAT: *See* Sabbat.

LITTLE WORK: Represented by the *Lunar Tree*. It is a stage of the Great Art*. In making the Philosopher's Stone* white, one can transmute metals into silver (*Argyropea*).

LITUUS: *See* Augur.

LIVER: *See* Hepatoscopy.

LOADSTONE (sometimes spelled 'Lodestone'): The sect of the Basilidians engraved on a loadstone the names of the favorable genies, and used it to make the abracax*.

Popular magic attributes miraculous properties to it: to preserve phantoms, to intensify friendship and love, to further unite married couples, to make unfaithful wives talk in their sleep. Devoted to Ares-Mars. *See* Amber.

LOSS: *See* Amissio.

LOT: (1) Destiny, luck. (2) Occult operation: claimed to be a means of knowing the future, with the help of dice thrown or dropped in an urn ('the lot has fallen', said the Greeks). We would say 'the die is cast', a *die* being one of a pair of *dice*. (3) *See* Lots, Rhapsodomancy.

LOTS: (a) Lots of apostles or saints: divination by opening the Acts of the Apostles or the scriptures by chance. The first words read gave the indication of the future. (b) Homeric or Virgilian lots: chosen by chance. (c) Prenestin lots: secret notebooks from the Temples of Preneste and Antium (Anzio). Designed by children who disclosed the future to the ancient Romans. In these temples, dice were also used for lots. *See* Cleromancy.

LOTTERY: Invented at Genoa in 1720. Claiming that the best means of ensuring that one wins is through the interpretation of a dream,

some occultists invented a code. To dream of an eagle, for example, indicates the numbers 8, 20, 46; of a woman, 4, 9, 22; of rats, 9, 40, 56.

LOUNG - GOM - PA: Practitioner of Loung-Gom, Tibetan asceticism, giving one the ability of running in a trance, without fatigue, or without nourishment. In Tibetan, Rlung (pronounced Loung): air, wind, breathing.

LOVERS, THE: Sixth major arcana of the Tarot* corresponding to the Hebrew letter *Van* and to number six. It symbolizes universal love, father of the love sentiment. Popularly one says the 'union', the upper side of the card represents a white sun, universal source, from which a lover discharges a white arrow at the central character of the three figures underneath.

LUCIDITY: More often *extra-lucidity*. It is a popular synonym for clairvoyance* and sometimes telepathy*. Goes back to the magnetizers* of the first century, as does the term clairvoyance*.

LUCIFER: The devil*. He tempts men with pride and not luxury, as Satan does.

LUCIFERIANS: Occult sect of the Middle Ages. Its members stabbed offerings in front of a statue of Lucifer.

LUCIFERISM: Adoration of Lucifer, considered as the angel of light (Lucibel), who must liberate man from the servitude of the Creator. Distinct from the more common and more vile *satanism*. In sorcery* Lucifer is also called Lucifuge Rafacale. Some make him preside in the East, associate him with Venus, call him king of hell, superior even to Satan. He is invoked especially on Mondays and thanked with a mouse.

LUCK: Favorable event; 'predisposition' to good fortune that is often deified. *See* Destiny.

LUMINOSITY: Phenomenon reputed to be produced by the 'fluid'* of mediums. In darkness, Valentine used phosphorescent oil: Craddock painted balloons, and the Thompson family phosphorescent objects.

LUNAR TREE: *See* Little Work.

LUSTRAL WATER: *See* Ablution.

LYCANTHROPY: Faculty of witches to take on the form of a wolf or another animal. Some explain it as an 'astral projection'. *See* Werewolves, Neures.

LYCH(N)OMANCY: *See* Lampadomancy.

LYNX: A sharp-eyed hunter of the cat family. The ancients attributed to it the faculty of seeing across walls (from whence comes 'Lynx-eyed'), and of producing amber and rubies with its urine.

MACUMBA: Magic dance of the South American negroes.

MAGI: For the Medes and Persians, members of the sacerdotal caste. For the Greeks and Romans, astrologer, then magician* in a broad sense, the sense that we still use.

MAGIC: Contrary to religion, which postulates humility and beseeches through prayer, magic is a technique which claims to master human beings and occult forces by the use of reputedly infallible formulae. In commanding the forces of evil, it also claims effects

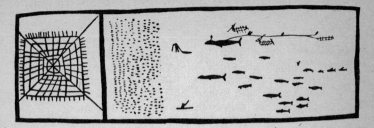

Magic drawing of the Tchouk-tchi tribe, fishermen of Oriental Siberia.

opposed, apparently at least, to natural laws. It is sub-divided into white, red and black. At lower degrees sorcery* and satanism* can be attached to it. An essential element of magic is that the formulae used shall be uttered faultlessly and word-perfect without interpolation or omission. White magic is sometimes called prestidigitation*. For red magic, *See* Red.

Magic can be divided into: (1) Contagious magic, that is, magic by direct contact or by contiguity. (2) Homeopathic magic, or magic by similitude (symbolic contact). It may also be divided into speculative magic (theoretical) and operative magic (practical). In sociology and history one must distinguish: (1) Magic associated with religion or theurgy* (if it combats it, goety* or black magic*), of which the inferior branch is sorcery. (2) A magic of pro-fessional aspect, which goes beyond religion to philosophical systems.

MAGIC, Act of: The act itself has three stages: (a) knowledge (by utilizing nature and its secrets); (b) intention (transmutation of psychic forces with a precise aim); and (c) formulae (its operation according to ritual).

The great magical circle of Agrippa.

MAGIC CIRCLE (OF PROTECTION): The magician

traces it with chalk, etc. or with his wand (some say with coal and holy water). The aim is to isolate and protect the operator, so that bad entities* cannot overcome him, except the invited demon, who is then in the power of the magician. In universal magic, the symbol of the being closed in on itself.

MAGIC DARTS: Malevolent points of lead, the length of a finger, thrown by Laplanders in the direction of an enemy.

MAGIC DECANTER: One of the most famous hydromagic* tricks. The decanter supplies various liquids at will.

MAGIC LOW: *See* Sorcery.

MAGIC SPELL: Illusion* operated by artifice. In theology and demonology, used for miracles of the devil* (the term 'miracle' being reserved for God).

MAGIC SQUARE: (1) Discovered in the sixteenth century by the Greek mathematician Manuel Moschopulos. The total of each horizontal, vertical or diagonal column is 15 (it is therefore called perfect). (*See* Diagram). There are also numerous magic squares, 16 magic numbers, and four magic stars with six

branches. (2) Whereas the *tetrahedron,* as a volume, is cosmic, the square symbolizes the universe of man. It comes from God and corresponds to Jupiter.

8	3	4
1	5	9
6	7	2

MAGICAL or MALEVOLENT ATTACK: *See* Spell.

MAGICIAN: He who produces astonishing and unexpected results by the use of magic formulae. The magician is different from the sorcerer*, who is less important an aide to the devil, specializing in evil. The Norman peasants of the seventh century distinguished the 'Great Sorcerer', or magician, from the ordinary or 'Little Sorcerer'.

MAGICIANS' DEATH PACT: Instituted by a French Count during his stay in the United States in 1842. A number of magicians were engaged, in this pact to try to manifest his existence posthumously. It is not generally known that a precedent exists: Under Louis XIV, the Marquis de Rambouillet concluded a similar pact with the Marquis de Precy, who died eight days later.

MAGNALE: According to Paracelsus, it is the attractive property of *loadstone,* considered as a universal property of nature, the 'vital fluid'*.

MAGNETISM: Comes from Magnesia, a town in Asia Minor where three Greeks discovered *loadstone*. Animal magnetism*: supposed influence of one man on another, by means of movements called passes*, by 'fluidic emanations*'. Revealed by the Viennese doctor A. Mesmer (1733-1815), from whom comes the word *mesmerism*. Great success in Paris (sulfurous currents of the Baquet healer for which Puysegur substituted a tree) from 1778 to 1788 before his expulsion. Boirac (1893) called it *psychodynamic*. In fact, the English occultist-doctor Kenelmus was perhaps its first practitioner. One speaks also of *personal magnetism* or *mineral magnetism*.

MAGNOMETER: To measure the vital force (fluid*) of the human body, the following devices were invented: *magnometer* of the Abbe Fortin, *biometer* of Dr. Baraduc, *biometer-galvanometer* of Dr. Audollent, *sthenometer* of Dr. Joire (·1904), *bioscope* of Dr. Collongues, *fluid motor* of the Count of Tromelin. The device of Puyfontaine, employed by Dr. Charcot at the Salpetriere, proved the electric nature of these influences. This did not prevent Dr. J. Wust from speaking in 1934 of *W Rays* or *magnetoids*.

MAGONIA: Mysterious country where vessels, flying on clouds, carried crops ruined by hail. See *Tempestor*.

MAGPIE: Superstition: On the ground = bad luck; in flight = luck; in a pair = marriage.

MAJOR ARCANA: *See* Tarot.

MALENGIN: Funeral object which brings misfortune.

MALPHAS: Grand president of Hades, commands forty legions. Appears as a crow. Builds impregnable citadels and overthrows enemy ramparts. Often deceives those who sacrifice to him.

MAMMON: Demon of wealth, avarice, iniquity. The Golden Calf is often connected with him, as also is Moloch*.

MANA: Term in anthropology. 'Spirit', owner of the totem*, protector of the clan which bears its name. According to Marcel Mauss, belief in a supernatural power 'spread over all the sensitive world, to which it is heterogeneous and however imminent'. More simply, occult power.

MANCIES: Divinatory techniques (from the ancient Greek *manteia*). In Homer's

Mantis, general term for diviner, is the synonym for *oionopolos*, or interpreter of messages transmitted by birds, their bearing, their flight. The *Hiereus* burned the victims, the *Thyoskoos* examined their entrails, the *Oneiropolos* interpreted dreams*. These Greek diviners were independent hereditary professionals, sedentary or itinerant.

MANDALA: In Sanskrit: circle, center. Complex drawing symbolizing the universe and the 'receptacle of the gods'. Used for meditation and magic*. The simplest is yantra*.

MANDRAGORA or MANDRAKE: Solanaceous plant with large leaves, found in Tunisia. Often used in magic during Antiquity and the Middle Ages. The Greeks called it 'herb of Circe', believing that it allowed sorcerers to change men into pigs. Its root resembles the human body. One tradition says that it grew in Paradise in the shade of the Tree of Good and Evil. Another claims that the first humans were gigantic, sensitive plants animated by the sun. Columelle named them 'half-men'. In the Middle Ages it was called 'small planted man'. (*See* Homunculus) and was confused with *maindegloire* (*See* Hand of Glory), relating it to hanged people and the search for

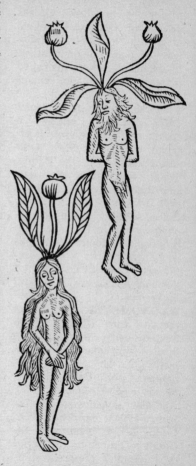

Symbolic representations of the Madragora.

hidden treasures. Some even added that it was more potent if watered by the urine of a hanged man or if born of his sperm.

The erotic, narcotic and hallucinatory properties of mandragora were widely used for philters*. In the Middle Ages it was believed that if placed in a casket with a piece of gold, it would double the number of pieces each day, and that it would open locks and predict the future.

It must not be pulled from the soil with impunity. A meticulous ritual has to be observed: a dog pulls it out by a rope, and dies from it immediately. In India, the charmers sold it for protection against snakes.

MANES: For the Romans, idolized souls of ancestors (*Di Manes*). Sometimes used broadly for all the gods of Hades as opposed to those of Heaven, or *Di Superi*. *See* Larvae, Lemures.

MANIPULATION: *See* Prestidigitation.

MANITOU, GREAT: The greatest of the Spirits of certain Indians of North America. Represented by a white eagle, 'thunder-bird' or great spirit, it is the 'father of life', sometimes called *Warianyan*. *See* Sikun, Wakan Tanka.

MANTIC: From the Greek *mantike techne* (in Latin *divinatio*). Presentiment, knowledge of future things, practised by the *mantis* or diviners. *Mantic* comes from the Greek *mania* (*furor* in Latin), sacred delirium obtained by *enthusiasm* or the presence of God in the body of the diviner. *See* Mancies.

MANTRA: Mystical sound, Hindu magical formula. A kind of Yoga* based on the powers of sound vibration.

MARCOU: Peasant expression used in France for the seventh son born of the same parents. He is usually reputed to be a healer*.

MARGARITOMANCY: Divination by a fine pearl (latin *Margarita*) closed up in a vessel, after a magical rite has 'given it life'. Popular tradition says that when shut up in this jar, it would jump when the name of a guilty person was pronounced.

MARRIAGE: Numerous superstitions: (1) Good fortune if the husband carries the bride over the threshold (survival of a primitive rite). (2) Good fortune to avoid a May marriage. (3) A piece of wedding veil under the pillow of a young girl makes her see her future in a dream. A garter of the bride brings good luck. (4) If it is raining it is a bad omen, as is crossing the path of a funeral (presages a divorce). (5) To throw rice, even some wine, on the couple assures fertility. (6) In the United States, the bride throws her bouquet behind her without looking as she leaves the church. Whoever catches it will be married within a year.

MARTINISM: Science of the 'reintegration of beings' and of the evocation of spirits*. Founded in 1754 by Martines de Pasqually. The adepts called it the 'Order of the Chosen Ones' and subdivided it into three groups, of which the highest and most secret was the Royal-Crosses. Pasqually wrote a treatise on the reintegration of beings. *The Great Orient* is derived from it. The *Martinesists* are often confused with the followers of Louis Claude de Saint-Martin (1743-1803) known as *Martinists,* and with the *Martinist Society,* founded by Papus (Dr Gerard Encausse). Louis Claude de Saint-Martin was named 'the unknown philosopher'. He attached himself to the illuminist cause of Swedenborg.

MATCH: Superstition: (1) Lighting three cigarettes with the same match brings misfortune to the last or the youngest. Dates from the Boer War.

At night an enemy sniper would have time to aim accurately and fire if a match was kept alight long enough to light three cigarettes. (2) To blow out a match for someone: a confession of love.

MATERIALIZATION: In spiritism*, paranormal formation of material objects (more rarely of the human body) by the action of spirits*. *See* Apparition, Ectoplasm, Moulding, Teleplasty.

MEDIANIMIC: *See* Mediumism.

MEDICINE MAN: *See* Shaman, Sorcerer.

MEDIUM: In the strict sense, an intermediary; in a broad sense, a person capable of understanding hidden things. In spiritism*, a human intermediary between men and spirits* who receives communications from the latter. In early occultism, a person manifesting parapsychological gifts. In parapsychology*, a gifted or sensitive person whose subconscious, separated from the conscious, is the victim of a lively imagination. There is a distinction between mediums of 'physical effects' and of 'mental or intellectual effects'. *See* Perceiver.

The first spiritist mediums were the young Katie and Margaret Fox (1847) at

Hydesville, United States. Spiritist mediums are divided into: (1) Medium of incorporation (the spirit incarnates itself in its sleeping physical envelope) or of incarnation*. (2) Medium of direct exploration, who divides himself in two, with or without hypnosis* and explores the 'forbidden ground'. (3) Medium using ectoplasm*, who is able to bring forth the tenuous material of the perispirit*. (4) Medium of aura* in whom the vital energy accumulates, permitting physical effects. *See* Raps; Table; Typtology. Allan Kardec, father of spiritism*, divides them into mediums of physical effects, sensitive mediums or those able to be impressed, auditive, speaking, seeing; healers, writers, psychographers, etc. All their phenomena are explicable by the dissociation of the personality (studies by Janet on hypnosis* and of Freud on the unconscious). Some become agitated or go into a trance.

MEDIUM, ANIMAL: Animal prodigies capable of 'divining' thought. Magnetic fly of Devant, bull medium at Delhi, telepathic bird at Agra, bird diviner at Nikko, etc. All animal mediums who have been properly investigated have been shown to have used trickery and arduous training to produce their so-called 'paranormal' effects.

MEDIUM COMMUNICATIONS: Words or texts obtained by an automatic process with the help of a medium*. *See* Spiritism.

MEDIUMISM: Collection of paranormal phenomena ascribed to the medium*. Adjective: *mediumnic* or *medianimic*.

MEETING: *See* Conjunctio.

MEMORY: *See* Cryptomnesia, Hypermnesia, Mnemotechny.

MERCURY: (1) *See* Alchemy, Great Art. (2) *See* Hermes Trismegistus. (3) The Mercurian process in astrology* is characterized by rapidity, mobility, supple adaptation, polymorphism, hermaphroditism.

METAGNOMY: Possibility of knowledge outside and beyond the usual information given by the senses and the conscious mind. Term of Emile Boirac for phenomena of clairvoyance* by opposition to diapsyche* (phenomena of telepathy*). For Dr Osty it indicated E.S.P.

METALS: In astrology* tradition attributes to metals the following affinities: Loadstone-Mars-Scorpio; Silver-Moon-Cancer; Bronze-Jupiter-Taurus; Tin-Jupiter-Sagittarius; Iron-

Alchemical dragon of Nagari symbolising mercury, necessary for transmutation.

Mars-Aries; Mercury-Mercury-Gemini, Virgo; Gold-Sun-Leo; Platinum-Uranus-Cancer; Lead-Saturn-Aquarius.

METAPOSCOPY: Technique of Jerome Cardan to interpret character and destiny from the lines* and wrinkles of the forehead. Included in physiognomy*.

METAPSYCHIC: Term pro-posed by Richet in 1905. Study of the facts reputed to be *paranormal*: objective (physical effects) or subjective (mental). Nearly synonymous with the expression 'occult sciences', without covering it entirely. Today, *parapsychology** is heard more and more, put forward by Dessois in 1889, and to be preferred to *metapsychology* (invented by Gorre in 1837). Boirac spoke of 'parapsychic phenomena' in 1893. Some reserve for it the narrow sense of spiritism* science, thus secularizing spiritism.

METAPSYCHISTS: Supporter of metapsyche.

METAVOYANCE: *See* Voyance.

METEMPSYCHOSIS: Theory according to which the dead return several times to earth, even as animals, either according to their merits or by chance. *See* Avatar, Palingenesis. Pythagoras is attributed with recognizing the soul of his dead friends, in a barking dog. He said that he, himself, was a reincarnation of Homer.

MICROMAGIC: Part of prestidigitation*. Using a trick with miniature material.

MINIATURES: *See* Micromagic.

MIRROR: (1) *See* Beryllistic, Catoptromancy, Crystallo-mancy, Enoptromancy. (2) Superstition: breaking one, accidentally or not, omen of death or seven years' bad luck. (3) Magic mirror: in China, made from a bad conductor of electricity, used to fix the will or in divination.

MISETRA: *See* Beverage of Hate.

MISTLETOE: Supposed to have the ability of curing injuries and epilepsy. Certain regions of France still call it a 'shrub of ghosts'. Superstition: brings good luck. One kisses under the mistletoe on New Year's Eve.

MITHRIDATE: Ancient name of medical opiate theriac*. Mithridates VI Eupator, King of Pontus, was mithiditized against arsenic poisoning by absorbing progressive doses of the poison. He ended up by making an electuary of fifty four substances which bears his name. The conqueror, Pompey, took the recipe to Rome in 63 B.C. Another meaning: seller of mithridate; charlatan.

MNEMOTECHNY: Tricks of prestidigitation* based on memory.

MOLOCH: God with the head of a calf. Adored by the Ammonites. Children were sacrificed to him to obtain good crops (*See* Adramelech). Demonology* made him an infernal prince, master of mothers' tears. *See* Mammon.

MOLTEN LEAD: *See* Molybdomancy.

MOLYBDOMANCY: Divination by pieces of molten lead or tin, the shapes of which are studied in a vessel of water or on a wet table. Same procedure as for *ciromancy*.

MONITION: Spontaneous E.S.P. Warning of a present event in a paranormal way; for the future one uses the term *premonition**.

MONKEY: Contrary to the West, Oriental religions and magic make it an emblem of wisdom (for example, Hanuman the 'General of Monkeys' in the Hindu epic, the *Ramayana*). Arthur Waley has

Moloch

translated a famous Chinese epic into English under the title *Monkey*.

MONSTERS: Some occultists suggest dividing them into: (1) Monsters of complex human projections (for example, Oedipus, Phaedra). (2) Monsters of classical mythology (for example, Centaurus, Sirens) or popular legends; even in these one can distinguish malformed human monsters (for example, Cyclops); half-man, half-animal monsters (for example, The Sphinx); monstrous animals (for example, Dragons, Cerberus). (3) Real monsters raised up by the demon, with or without the help of *incubus** or *succubus**.

MOON: (1) Name of the eighteenth major arcana of the Tarot. A moon with thirty varied rays and, on the inside, a profile turned towards the left, which emits nineteen tears in three colors and dominates two animals above a crab (symbol of cancer* of the Zodiac*, united with the moon). Signifies the active life of the unconscious. (2) Superstition: to see it move across a window pane: bad omen, counteracted by breaking the glass or tearing a piece of paper the same size.

MORNING: Superstition: Bad omen to see a spider in the morning, to break a shoelace in the morning or to get out of bed on the wrong side.

MORPHOLOGY: Also called *psycho-morphology* or *typo-morphology*. Study of the forms of the human body and their relationship with character and temperament. Unfortunately, complicated by excessive symbolism and multiple interpretations.

MOULDING: In spiritism* moulds obtained by the intervention of a paranormal force. *See* Ectoplasm, Materialization, Teleplasty.

MUDRA: Writing, gesture, hieratic pose (usually in Yoga) leading to the realization of a high state of consciousness.

MUMMIFICATION: (1) Paranormal intervention often ascribed to the 'fluidic hands' of a healer, who retards the normal putrefaction of an organic substance by dessication. (2) Some magnetizers claim to have magnetized and mummified: (a) Jean Puharne: a foetus, in 1934. (b) Dr Bethelot of Lausanne: pumpkins and leaves in 174 days. (c) H. Durville, of Paris: a hand of a hanged person after two months.

MUTABLE: *See* Signs.

MYOMANCY: Divination from the cries and eating

habits of rats and mice. The Smintheus, invoked in the first canto of the Iliad, would be the 'Apollo of the rats' who inflicted the plague on the Greeks.

MYSTERY: (1) In Antiquity: religion with secret ceremonies reserved for initiates*. The most important: those of Demeter at Eleusis, and of Dionysus in Orphism in Greece; those of Isis-Osiris in Egypt; those of Mithra in the Orient and the Roman Empire.

(2) In a broad sense, creation of the spirit, especially attracting the anxious, the fearful, the pseudo-occultists.

(3) Some occultists call their occult disciplines 'Great Mysteries'.

MYTH: Etymologically: fable. Psychologically, projection of an unconscious need or of a latent universal conception of people (Oedipus), of places (Olympia), of situations. (See Flood.)

NABI: See Prophet.

NADI: Symbolically in Yoga*, the veins of the body.

NAILS: Those of a coffin, stuck in a picture of the enemy, bring about his downfall. See Spells, Onychomancy.

NAME: (1) See Onomancy. (2) The name has a magical value for many people. Several ancient people believed that one could induce a divinity to act if one knew its 'real name' (Egyptian, or rabbinic tradition, for example) whence the importance of onomancy*, astrology*, etc., and the desire of certain people to hide the real name of a child (Hindus for example).

NARCOANALYSIS: Method of mental treatment by the use of shock, plunging some people with mental illness into a coma sometimes accompanied by convulsions. The therapeutic principles of states of sleep were established: (1) In 1933 at Vienna, insulin coma (hypoglycemia) of Sakel; (2) In 1935, epileptic crises started by the use of *cardiazol* by Von Meduna. (3) In 1938, *electroshock*: convulsive crisis provoked by the passage of an electric current in the brain, used by Cerletti. (4) *Narco-analysis* (Horsley proposed this term in 1936) means more specifically, states of sleep with a chemical or vegetal basis, such as those based on the drug *Peyotl* of the Mexicans.

NATAL THEME: *See* Domification.

NAULI (KRIYA): In Yoga*, violent exercise of the large muscles (called erroneously 'churning of the stomach').

NECROMANCY: Consultation of the dead to know the future. (For example, Ulysses in the *Odyssey*; the shadow of King Darius in *The Persians* of Aeschylus). Practitioner: *necromancer*, which, since the Middle Ages, has taken the more usual meaning of *sorcerer**. *See* Necyomancy. In Roman times, Thyatire or Lydia, the tomb of the priestess Ammias, replied to questions put 'of night, as of day'.

NECTAR: *See* Ambrosia.

NECYOMANCY: Older form of *necromancy*. Sometimes called *skiomancy* or consultation of the shadows, who could speak only after having drunk the blood of a freshly-killed animal.

NEGRO, GREAT: *See* Sabbat.

NEURES: The Sarmatae of Europe to whom is given the faculty of being able to change into wolves*. Herodotus spoke of them. *See* Lycanthropy.

NEURHYPNOLOGY: *See* Hypnotism.

NIGRIDO: *See* Putrefactio.

NIYAMA: The five disciplines of Yoga*. *See* Yama.

NOSE: Superstition: itching nose = sign of money, someone wants to kiss you (especially an old man).

NUMBER: *See* Arithmomancy, Arithmosophy.

NUMEROLOGY: Science of numbers. *See* Arithmomancy, Arithmosophy. Sometimes allows startling or exact speculations.

NYMPHS: (1) *See* Demons. (2) Goddesses personifying oaks (dryads) woods (hamadryads), mountains (oreads), the sea (nereids), valleys (napaeae), etc. Prophetic qualities are attributed to the daughters of Zeus. Above Platea (Greece), on Mount Citheron, existed the oracle* of the Sphragitides nymphs.

OAK: *See* Assumption of the oak; Wind.

OBERON: King of the fairies* and aerial spirits (sylphs*). Lives in India with his wife, Titania. At night they dance by the light of the moon. They flee at dawn to hide in flower beds. Shakespeare, in *A Midsummer Night's Dream,* placed them in Athens.

OBJECTROACTION: *See* Telekenesis.

OCCELLUS: *See* Paroptic, Transposition.

OCCULTISM: An ancient belief asserting that science* was unique and synthetic in origin, but it soon split up into common or *exoteric knowledge,* and *esoteric knowledge* reserved for initiates. Esoteric knowledge and its application received the name of the occult sciences.

OCCULT SCIENCES: *See* Occultism, Parapsychology.

OD: Name given by the German chemist, Baron Charles von Reichenbach, to a universal force, conductive and accumulative, manifesting itself in loadstone, crystals and animal bodies. In eight published works from 1845 to 1868 he named as odic phenomena those that derived from manifestations. Hans Driesch in his Parapsychology of 1933 revived this justly abandoned theory.

ODIC PHENOMENA: *See* Od.

OECOSOPY: In Ancient Greece, divination* based on the study of external appearances of edifices. Inherited from the Chaldeans. Xenocrates devoted a treatise to it.

OENOMANCY: Divination by wine* either by interpreting what happened while one was drinking it or by examining its reflections. The Persians often practised it.

OINTMENT of WEAPONS: Magic ointment which closed wounds when rubbed on the weapon causing the wound.

OMOPLATOSCOPY: Divination based on the examination of the shoulder-blade of a sheep or lamb which has been sacrificed and put on warm coals. The Byzantine people practised it, as did the Arabs.

OMPHALOS: Navel, center of the world; Delphi, for the Ancient Greeks (where the *omphalos,* the *ovid stone,* was supposed to be the navel of the serpent Python, killed by Apollo. *See* Pythia). Budd-Gaya (India) for the Budd-hists. At the oasis of Siwah (Egypt) a mystic omphalos was used to predict the future. Alexander the Great consulted it. It has been found at the Temple of Apollo at Claros, in Asia Minor.

OMPHALOSCOPY: Tech-nique of concentration based on contemplation of the navel (*omphalos* in Greek). Used notably by the Buddhists.

OMPHALOSEKUES: Mystic sect adoring Adam.

ONEIRISM: State of dreamer, waking or not, given value by the surrealist school; often difficult to distinguish from hallucinations*.

ONEIROCRITIC: (a) Specialist studying oneirocritics or the interpretation of dreams*. The two most famous ones of Antiquity were Aris-tander of Telmessos in Caria (who accompanied Alexander) and Artemidorus of Daldia, whose work is the basis of most of our keys to dreams*. (b) *adj.* Relating to the inter-pretation of dreams*.

ONEIROMANCIST: Special-ist in oneiromancy.

ONEIROMANCY: *See* Dreams*. Interpretation of dreams supposed to be divin-atory. The Greeks called the specialist *oneiropoios.* In the first canto of the *Iliad,* verse 63, Homer writes, 'for the dream came from Zeus'. He states that it is necessary to distinguish between truthful and untruthful dreams. The oneirocritic is also responsible for interpreting all the second-ary signs.

ONION: *See* Crommvomancy.

ONOMANCY: Sometimes called *onomomancy*: divination from proper names:. Many Ancients gave numerical values to the letters and drew omens from the total, or from the origin of the name. Besides astrological onomancy, there developed a magic onomancy based on the Cabala*. Westerners over-simplified this, saying that it was sufficient to find the secret of each name, in the following way: A = 1; B = 2; C = 3; D = 4; E = 5 etc. Jean, for example = 10 + 5 + 1 + 14 = 30 = 3 + 0 = Secret value 3. Then the symbolic value of the number 3 is consulted. Another

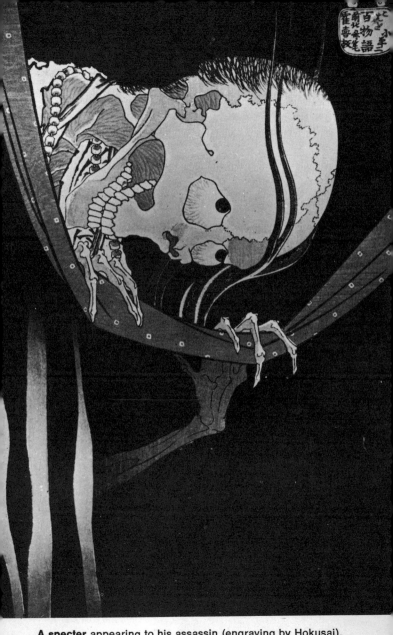

A specter appearing to his assassin (engraving by Hokusai).

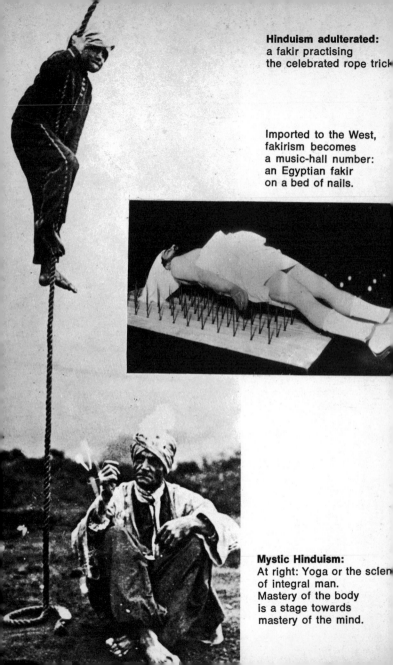

Hinduism adulterated:
a fakir practising
the celebrated rope trick

Imported to the West,
fakirism becomes
a music-hall number:
an Egyptian fakir
on a bed of nails.

Mystic Hinduism:
At right: Yoga or the science
of integral man.
Mastery of the body
is a stage towards
mastery of the mind.

Spirit photo:
above the medium,
two apparitions
of ectoplasms.
The photo or the apparition
itself reveals trickery.

Seance of magic under the Empire.

An African fortune-teller

The survival of magic:
A tradition in a village of Umbria;
in the course of a mime
acted out by the peasants,
an old lady (on the left)
symbolizing dying vegetation,
is brought back to life by a doctor
who rides on a donkey.
This rite assures the return
of fertility
and guarantees the harvest.

The Tarot,
a deck of 78 cards used
by certain fortune-tellers.
Each figure has
a divinatory meaning
which in combination
with its neighbor
reveals the fate
of the subject in question.

The Female Pope beside
The Wheel of Fortune:
future assured.

LA·ROUE·DE·FORTUNE

LA·PAPESSE

Death followed by
The Hanged Man:
death bringing disaster.

LE·PENDU

The House of God
preceding **The Moon:**
the consultant becomes
aware of his mistakes.

LA·MAISON·DIEV

LA·LUNE

The clairvoyant
(opposite page)
bent over the crystal ball,
searching the unknown.

Psychometry:
with the help of a photograph
the clairvoyant claims
to communicate with the de[...]
to find a missing person,
or to predict the future.

Radiesthesia:
the pendulum,
held over a chart
symbolizing
the different parts
of the human body,
is believed to establish
a medical diagnosis.
The consultant holds
the hand of the consultor.

current practice, anagramatic onomancy, consists of jumbling the letters of a person's name to form smaller words, supposed to be omens.

ONYCHOMANCY: Divination from fingernails and their spots. The Arabs practised it by intensive fixation on a nail coated with ink.

ONYX: Greenish marbled stone, symbol of austerity and sadness. Gives wisdom to Aquarius*.

OOMANCY: Divination by eggs*. Invented by Orpheus, according to Suidas. Formerly, according to the exterior or interior forms of the egg; in modern times (Miss Lenormand excelled in this in the nineteenth century) in examining the forms of the white of a fresh egg that is dropped gently in a glass of water. See Egg.

OPAL: Brilliantly colored stone, sometimes malevolent. Increases the fidelity of Libra and Sagittarius.

OPHIOMANCY: Divination* by serpents. Sometimes applied to newly-born children.

OPIGENES: According to Pliny the Elder, healers* of the Hellespont. They would simply touch the fangs of snakes.

ORACLES: (1) Response given by a god to the questions addressed to him. By exten-

sion, the divinity itself and its intermediaries. The great oracles of Antiquity were: (a) At Delphi (the Pythia): Apollo, following the serpent Python; (b) Dodona (leaves of oak and bronze): Jupiter-Zeus (See Wind); (c) In the oasis of Siwah, Lybia: Ammon-Zeus (oscillating boat); (d) Oracle of Branchides or Apollo Didymaeus; (e) At Cumes, near Naples (the Sibyl*); (f) At Epidaurus: god healer* Aesculapius (in a dream). See Incubation. At Siwah, as in Syria at Heliopolis (Baalbek) and at Herapolis (Bambykee), it is the statue of the god which renders the oracle by its movements.

(2) The word also indicates the diviner or his prediction. In this latter sense, etymologically, the diviner is oral; the word prophet* is used preferably for written words. Priest of Pythian Apollo, Plutarch (A.D. 85-125) has left us two treatises 'On the disappearance of the oracles', and 'On the oracles of Pythia'. See Promancy.

ORB: See Aspect.

ORTHINOMANCY: Divination practised in Greece from the cries, songs, flight and behavior of birds. The most prophetic were the eagle and the vulture of Zeus-Jupiter, the rook of Hera-Juno, the crow of Apollo, the owl of Athena-Minerva. This form of divination was supposed to have been invented by the diviner Tiresias.

OUIJA BOARD: Tablet or dial arranged usually in the form of a semi-circular alphabet, with a pointer, allowing the spiritists* to interpret the communications of the spirits.

OUROBOROS: Serpent* coiled in a circle which bites its tail. Symbolizes, for the alchemists*, the unity of matter (also, the circumference). For other occultists, it is the universal fluid* and perpetual evocation of nature. Its disciples, the Ophites (*ophis* in Greek: *serpent*). Not to be confused with the *catoblespas,* an imaginary animal so stupid that it eats its own tail. Some have replaced it by the *salamander* or the *alchemic dragon* of Nagari, with human head and feet and four tails.

The serpent Ouroboros according to a manuscript of Saint Mark.

OWL: Heard only in darkness, its cry is dreaded and considered as an omen of death. Perched on the top of a house it is a bad omen (of sterility, said Pliny the Elder). On a dovecote it is a favorable sign. The Grand Albert asserts that if one puts the heart and the right leg of an owl on a sleeping person, the person replies to all questions. Its heart, eaten in an omelet, cures drunkenness. In Ancient Greece a symbol of vigilance, bird of Athena-Minerva (*glaukopis*— with eyes of an owl). Emblem of diviners for its symbolism of clairvoyance. However, much popular magic includes it with birds of bad omen.

PACT, DIABOLICAL: Pact concluded with the devil. In exchange for one's soul, one acquires extraordinary powers for a limited period (maximum twenty years).

PACTION: Old word for pact.

PADMASANA: A physical pose adopted in certain Yoga exercises, where the legs are fixed in the 'Lotus position'.

PALINGENESIS: Return to life after apparent or real death. 'Rebirth' by initiation* or by transmigration*. *See* Avatar, Metempsychosis.

PALMING: Sleight of hand, concealing an object in the palm. 'Back and front palming' is the concealment of a card at first behind the hand when the palm is being shown, then the opposite. This pass is very difficult to do.

PALMOMANTIC: Divination based on the examination of the instinctive acts of a healthy man. *See* Iatromantic.

PANACEA: Remedy for all wrongs (universal, and there-fore superfluous). One of the dreams of the alchemists. The panacea is obtained by reducing the Philosopher's Stone to liquid. *See* Elixir of Life.

PANSOPHY: Universal philosophical knowledge.

PANTACLE: Fluid* ejector, a magic tool. The inscriptions on them are in several alphabets said to be sacred. For example, the Pectoral of the Hebrew Grand Priest and of Egyptian mummies. Not to be confused with Pentacle*. *See* Amulet (passive), Talisman (active), Gris-Gris, Phylactery, Teraph.

PARANATELLONS: Daily horoscope, universally applicable without considering the year of birth. A singularly excessive generalization.

PARANORMAL: Word invented by Whately Carington to replace *supranormal,* a term of Myers. In parapsychology, group of phenomena that classic psychology cannot at present explain. (This does not always mean that they have a marvellous or miraculous character).

PARANORMAL KNOW-LEDGE: *See* Parapsychology, E.S.P.

PARAPSYCHOLOGY: Study of the phenomena reputed to be *paranormal*. *See*. P.S.I. Faculties. Therefore, not yet understood by psychology*. Term attributed to Max Dessoir (June, 1889). One distinguishes the quantitative school (Professor Rhine and the associated theory of W. Carington) and the polypsychic trend (Professor W. Mackenzie).

PARERGON: Name given by mystic alchemists* and by the Rose-Cross to the transmutation* of metals, accessory physical work (*Parergon*) by relationship to the principal mystic work (*Ergon*): to improve oneself.

PARESTHESIA: *See* Transposition.

PAROPTIC VISION: Possibility of seeing without the help of eyes, notably by ocelli claimed to be at the ends of the fingers.

PARSLEY: Superstition: to transplant = mourning within a year. (Must sow itself.)

PASSES: (1) Gestures of the hands around the face and eyes of the subject to bring about hypnosis*. Ellivston perfected them. (2) Manipu-lations in prestidigitation*.

PATERNOSTER OF BLOOD: Rosary bead reputed to have powers against haemorrhage.

PATHOGNOMY: Study of the sign of our passions, with a view to knowing our character and, eventually, the future.

PEAK OR POINT: (1) In astrology*, point of origin of a House*, on the exterior circle of a theme*. (2) Has destructive qualities in magic.

PEARL: (1) *See* Margaritomancy. (2) Dedicated to the Moon-Phoebe (the moon Artemis-Diana had the moonstone). The occultists considered it as beneficial despite popular beliefs. Favored creative imagination, beginning of enterprises, voyages. However, the black pearl is considered fatal in India. (3) Mixed with lemon juice and pulverized, it is supposed to be a magical antidote. (4) Superstitions: blue = beneficial to souls; white = sadness (one should not offer this).

PEBBLES: *See* Lithomancy.

PEGGING: An eccentric magical operation of revenge, claiming to prevent an enemy from urinating. Works by planting a peg in a wall. Remedy: to spit on one's shoe before putting it on. If one happens to have bare feet at the time, it is best to avoid drinking anything.

PEGOMANCY: Form of hydromancy* with fountain water*.

PENTACLE: *See* Pentagram.

Pentacle of the ninth key of Basil Valentin, symbolizing the alchemic fusion of sulfur and mercury.

PENTAGRAM or PENTACLE: (1) Magic star with five points or Star of David (which is often shown with six points). Pythagorean sign of knowledge. Put on the altar in front of the magician, at the center of the triangle formed by the lamp, the center, and the sphere. (2) The pentagram of Agrippa or *flamboyant* is also used in magic.

PEOPLE: *See* Populus.

PERCEIVER: One who perceives, as opposed to *agent*: one who acts, emits. In parapsychological* tests, the subject who tries to 'divine', (cards, lots, etc.).

PEREGRINATIO: *See* Alchemy (2).

PERIS: Good genies*, fairies and sages.

PERISPIRIT: *See* Body.

PERSONALITY, SECOND: *See* Incarnation.

PETAL: *See* Phylloromancy.

PHANTOM: Materialization of the spirit of a dead person, visible but impalpable. Also called specter* or ghost. Popular tradition represents phantoms as skeletons, covered with a shroud, sometimes dragging chains, and has them dwelling in haunted castles (particularly in Scotland). They are generally uneasy souls of murdered people, or their appearance announces a future death. The Grand Albert says that not to be afraid, it is sufficient to hold some nettles and yarrow.

PHILOSOPHER'S EGG: Stone of the alchemist*. Symbolically called *chamber, pri-*

son, sepulchre or *house of the hen*. Symbol of the Creation or 'Egg of the World'. *See* Compost.

PHILOSOPHER'S STONE: Aim of alchemic research: to transmute metals into gold (*chrysopea*) or silver (*argyropea*). In the liquefaction the Elixir of Life and the Panacea* are obtained. It is called 'Fountain of Gold' or 'Wood of Life'. At the end of the Middle Ages, the following qualities were added: to command celestial powers, to make known the past and the future, to render invisible (by being held in the hand), to create perpetual movement, to resolve the squaring of the circle, to permit flying at will (by being carried in linen, on the body) and of making the *Alkahest** and the *homunculus**. Symbolically, it was called Christ, Pelican, Azoth, Crown Child, Daughter of the Great Secret, Green Lion, Serpent, Milk of the Virgin, Pontic Water, or Stone of the Sages. Appears in saline form (stone) or as potable gold* dissolving in mercurial water. *See* Compost, Projection.

PHILTER: Magic brew inspiring love, and sometimes other passions. In it were put certain herbs, frog bones, fish skeletons, nail clippings and, especially, hippomane*.

PHLOGISTON: 'Principle of fire' which makes combustible bodies burn (not fire itself), according to Stahl (1660-1734). The more rational concept of the oxidation process has replaced it in modern science.

PHOENIX: Fabulous bird of the Arabian deserts, which burned itself on a pyre and was reborn from its ashes. Egyptian authority had it come from Arabia to Egypt every 500 years to shroud the body of its father, at Heliopolis. Alchemy has taken it as a symbol of rebirth.

PHOSPHORESCENCE: *See* Luminosity.

PHOTOGRAPHY, PARANORMAL or SPIRITIST: Also called *supranormal* or *transcendental photography* or *scotophotography**. Claims to be capable of photographing the human 'fluid'* or the 'spirits'* or the 'fluidic, exterioralized double'. A long time ago, the tricks of Boguet (1875) and the 'superpositions' of the medium of D. Hope were denounced. *See* Effluviography.

PHRENOLOGY: Study of the character and intellectual ability from the formation of the skull. Founded by the

German doctor Gall (1758-1828). It is inexact and has been almost abandoned. Practitioner: *phrenologer* or *phrenologist*.

PHYLACTERY: Amulet*, talisman*. Piece of parchment, bearing a passage from the Scriptures which the Jews attached to their right arm or forehead. Often put in a small metal tube. Used the following passages from the Old Testament: *Exodus* XIII, 1-10 or 11-16; *Deuteronomy VI*, 4-9 or XI, 13-21.

PHYLLOROMANCY: Divination* from the face, then the corporal appearance. Sometimes called (and this name is probably due to the rather naive title of the work of Bartholomew Cocles) *physiogromy* or 'study of the features to deduce the character'. Launched in 1619 by Robert Fludd. Divides the head into three worlds (divine, physical, material). Developed further by Lavater, but he left out of it the study of facial expressions (it would be necessary to distinguish between voluntary and involuntary). *See* Metaposcopy.

PIGS: The sorceress, Circe, transformed Ulysses's companions into pigs (*Odyssey*).

PIN: In the Middle Ages it was said that to carry a pin which had been stuck in a shroud would prevent fear.

PISOMANCY: *See* Cleromancy.

PITHIATISM: Illness due to suggestion. *See* Hysteria.

P.K.: *See* P.S.I., Psychokinesis.

PLANETS: Astrology* attributes to them influence over our lives. Certain astrologers want to use them only on the plan of analogies*. A planet is said to be *antecedent* when it proceeds another in the course of the Zodiac*. A planet is called *burnt* when it is very close to the sun without being in conjunction with it. A *culminating planet* is that which is nearest to the middle of the sky in an astrological theme. *See* Astrology, First Part.

PLANT, COLD: *See* Waterlily.

PLANTS: *See* Fluid; Growth, Accelerated; Psychokinesis.

PLUME OF SCILLA: Cluster of feathers to adorn the head. Assures happiness to those who wear it.

PNEUMATOLOGY: Doctrine of spirits* according to Swedenborg. *See* Spiritism, First Part.

POCKETS: The fishermen of Nazare, in Portugal, do not wear pockets because they believe the devil* lives in them.

PODOMANCY: Divination*

by the feet, especially practised in China.

POINT: *See* Peak or Point.

POISON SPONGE: *See* Toad.

POLARS: Mystic sect of initiates* of Apollonian tradition, asserting itself the real Rose-Cross, submitting only to the invisible Superiors* who guide them by 'the oracle of the astral force', and waiting for the resurrection of the Count of Saint-Germain, their Messiah. Founded in Italy in 1908, under the influence of Father Julien, hermit of Rome. One of their chiefs, Zam Bothiva, has written an *Asia Mysteriosa* with telepathic* and oracular method.

POLTERGEIST: German word signifying 'noisy spirit'. Collection of objective paranormal phenomena, produced in haunted places.

POLYPSYCHIC: *See* Parapsychology.

POLYPSYCHISM: Belief in a universal soul common to all humans, or even to all beings. It is the *eggregore** of the occultists and, more or less, the *Adam Kadmon* of the Cabala.

PONTIC WATER: *See* Philosopher's Stone.

POPE: Name of the fifth major arcana of the Tarot. Throne with tiara, red cape, blue cloak. The left hand holds a triple cross. Symbolizes religion by opposition to both the initiation (second arcana or Female Pope) and abstract principles.

POPE, FEMALE: Second major arcana of the Tarot*. Blue cloak over red robe. Holds an open book. Turned towards the left. Symbolizes initiation* (opposite to Pope) or nature. Popularly, institutional and occult powers are seen in it.

POPULUS: Figure of geomancy* expressing the crowd, disorder, disordered efforts. Affinities: water, moon. In French, people; in Arabic, the meeting.

POSSESSION: State of a possessed person whose acts are directed by a demon. Combated by exorcism. Formerly, it was said that the possessed spoke in 'unknown tongues' and revealed distant things. *See* Demon, Exorcism. Certain magicians, in plunging a flexible pipe into a woman's head, claimed to 'bring up the fluid of possession'. The devil is also called *Possessor*.

POSTCOGNITION or RETROCOGNITION: Paranormal perception of past events. For the future: precognition.

POWDER: (1) Of 'perlimpinpin': charlatan remedy. According to Rivasseau, made with a skinned cat, a lizard, aspic and a toad, cooked in the embers and pulverized. (2) Of projection: capable, for the alchemists*, of transforming metals into gold. See Philosopher's Stone. (3) Of succession: powdered poison that women bought from the sorcerers of the seventeenth century to become widows. (4) Of toad. See Toad. (5) Of sympathy: remedy used by medicine and based on magnetism*.

POWER: (1) Magic power is triple: temporal, spiritual and psychic. It is symbolized by three attributes: crown (authority), throne (sovereignty), scepter (means of governing). (2) Those with supernatural powers. See Siddhi.

PRANAYAMA: In Yoga* discipline of breathing (prana), mastery of respiration. In three stages: purak(a) or aspiration, kumbhak(a) or retention of breath, rechak(a) or expiration.

PRATYAHARA: In Yoga* the abstraction of the senses.

PRECOGNITION: See Postcognition.

PREMONITION: Unexpected sensation, preceding a happening and announcing it. A certainty that something will happen without a logical reason for believing it. To be distinguished from presentiment, which is more vague; from premonitory dream*, which is confirmed, and from monition*. It is necessary to emphasize the difference between vague presentiment and premonitory certainty, or true premonition. See Intersign.

PRESAGE: Natural sign by which one divines the future. Conjecture that one draws from this. See Aruspex, Augurs, Diviners, Superstition.

PRESCIENCE: Knowledge of the future. (1) Scientifically: working hypothesis, intuition preceding reasoning. (2) In occultism, intuition in connection with voyance*.

PRESTIDIGITATION: 'Art of nimble fingers', white magic, or stage magic, producing illusions*. Includes skilful tricks based on (1) manipulation or pure skill; (2) the intervention of trickery or trick apparatus; and (3) memory (mnemotechnic)*. Practitioner: *conjuror, illusionist.*

PRODIGIES: In Greek, *terata;* in Latin, *prodigia auspicia.* Since antiquity, extraordinary signs have been considered to indicate the will of the gods. See Aruspex. The Greeks used the word *semeia* for the most ordinary signs which the Gods could interpret. The stoics were the philosophers who depended on signs from the gods. In Rome, it was for the pontiffs to decide whether the signs had significance or not, and to indicate their meaning or to refer to the Aruspex or Sybilline Books.

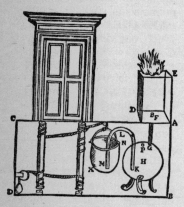

Mechanical furnace used to manufacture fake prodigies according to Heron of Alexandria.

PRODIGIOUS ARMY: According to the legends, apparition in the distance of an army, often numerous and noisy, of the souls of errant soldiers. To be distinguished from the apparition, before or after a battle, of a god, generally auspicious. (Several cases in Roman history; the Dioscuri, for example, at the battle of Regille Lake, 496 B.C.).

PROJECTION: Alchemic* operation transforming base metal into gold with the help of a piece of the Philosopher's Stone, 'projected' in the crucible.

PROJECTION OF E.S.P.: *See* Doubling.

PROMANCY: Right of consulting the oracle* before one's turn. In antiquity the Athenian ambassadors used it at Delphi.

PROPHECY: Prediction of a general order, by nature or of the future, often said to be inspired, made by a prophet* 'under the direction of God', preferably written. The most famous are: (1) The prophecies of Popes according to Saint Malachi, Primate of Iceland in 1134 (the oldest printed transcription, 1673), composed of 112 rubrics interpreted by M. Piobb; (2) The *Centuries* of Nostradamus; (3) The prophecy of St Odile; (4) The prophecy of Orval (of the French revolutionary era); (5) Those less famous, of the Monks Adson and Hermann. By extension, all predictions.

PROPHET: One who predicts by divine inspiration (as, for example, diviner*). Predicts on events of a general order (not about people). The Jews called it *Nabi*. Melampus

('Black Foot'), famous Greek diviner, was supposed to be the first mortal to whom the gods gave this gift. Endowed also with the power of a healer. Hesiod wrote his history in the form of a poem, the *Melampodia*.

PROPITIATORY: For the Hebrews, the table of gold above the arch. By extension, talisman*, protector.

PROSOPESE: For R. Sudre, all sudden change, spontaneous or provoked, of the psychological personality. He divides them into spontaneous (possession), provoked (objectivation of the types), metapsychic (incarnation, automatic writing). Partial disassociation for the actor, total for the medium*. Richet described it with the term 'objectivation of types'. *See* Doubling.

PROTECTION: Magic measure taken to preserve a being or edifice (temples especially) or an object from enterprises of the demons.

PROTEUS: Old sailor of Greek mythology capable of a thousand bodily changes. He revealed the future to those who succeeded in capturing him, but one could not do so unless he was asleep. He lived on the island of Pharos, near Egypt. In the *Odyssey*, IV, 394, Menelaus asks him for news of Ulysses.

PRUDENCE: *See* Caput Draconis.

PSEPHOMANCY: *See* Cleromancy.

PSI: Object of parapsychology*. Greek letter of which the symbol was proposed by Weiner and Thouless to designate paranormal faculties or phenomena. They distinguish *psi-gamma* or E.S.P. and *psi-kappa* or P.K. Belongs to the realm of the Unconscious. Used by Professor Rhine, of Duke University, for parapsychological faculties. *See* E.S.P., Psychokinesis.

PSYCHIC: At present, too often indicates phenomena studied by classic psychology and parapsychology. These latter should be stressed as being 'parapsychological'.

PSYCHIC LAYER: Emanations from objects which allow psychometry. They are based on a theory of *impregation*.

PSYCHIC LEVER: *See* Fluid.

PSYCHISM: All the forces which are neither material nor conscious, all the phenomena which belong neither to the physiological plan nor to clear consciousness. The occultists consider it as the 'hidden form of the vital force', therefore dynamic.

PSYCHOANALYSIS: Psychological investigation, with the object of bringing to the conscious mind repressed memories. Exploration of the Unconscious*; study of parapsychological phenomena in an 'analytical situation'. Not to be confused with *psychiatry,* which is a more general term denoting the medical-oriented study of mental illness.

PSYCHODYNAMIC: *See* Magnetism.

PSYCHOGRAPHY: *See* Automatic, Medium.

PSYCHOKINESIS or P.K. (PSI-KAPPA): Faculty that is supposed to be capable of influencing an object that is already moving. (At rest, telergy* or telekinesis*.) Term coined by Professor Rhine. *See* E.S.P.

PSYCHOMANCY: All divination* evoking souls. Numerous varieties (hypnosis*, trance*, evocation, portrait, etc.).

PSYCHOMETRY: Term devised in 1849 by the American J. Buchanan. Faculty allowing, by examining a familiar object belonging to an individual (unknown to the psychometer), a statement of the characteristics of that person, even predicting the future. (The explanation by *imprint* or *impregnation* seems gratuitous. It would be preferable to say *reading of an object.*) In classic psychology: measure of psychic phenomena.

PSYCHOPATHIC: Branch of parapsychology* comprising, according to Boira (1893), suggestion* and hypnotism*.

PSYCHOSOMATIC: What relates to the influence of the soul (psyche) on the body (soma). Certain types of 'hysterical' blindness, deafness, etc. being of mental origin, are classed as 'psychosomatic' disorders.

PUELLA: Figure of geomancy*. Symbolizes feminity, peace, solitude. Affinities: Water, Venus. In French, The Daughter; in Arabian, the hairless cheek.

PUER: Figure of geomancy*. Symbolizes virility, energy, generous violence, adultery. Affinities: Fire, Mars; in French, the boy; in Arabian, the strong.

PURIFICATION: Each action of a purification rite aims to 'make pure' or atone for a fault, mistake or crime. Sea water (or, if that is unavailable, salt-water) is required as part of the rite to purify major faults or crimes. *See* Dew.

PUTREFACTIO or NIGRIDO: First stage of alchemical* initiation*. This 'blackness' ('negro' = black) is symbolized by skeletons or crows.

Alchemical allegory of putrefaction.

PUT TO DEATH (THE KING): *See* Alchemy (2).

PYROBATY: Claiming to have invulnerability*, the fakirs* claim the ability to walk with impunity on fire or on burning coals. Frequent trickery occurs, using a protective coating based on arabic gum, egg-white, and plants.

PYROLOGY: Assembly of tricks dealing with fire.

PYROMANCY: Divination by fire. In Latin, *ignispicium*. (1) Before hieromancy* one observed the manner of burning of the legs of victims sacrificed to the gods, the state of the flames (which had to be high and clear), and the aspect of the smoke. The total combustion of an animal was called *holocaust*. At Olympia, they were boiled in a cauldron. (2) The Pythagoreans encouraged vegetable pyromancy with fumes of incense, flour of barley or laurel (daphnomancy), hair, eggs in flames (at Delphi), and laurel or eggs (at Rome).

PYROSCOPY: Modern divination by burning a document on a white porcelain plate and then reading the resultant stains. *See* Pyromancy.

QUATERNARY: *See* Alchemy; Azoth (3); Great Art.

QUEST: *See* Grail.

QUINTESSENCE: *See* Alchemy; Great Art.

PYROTECHNY: Fakiric or music-hall stunt based on tricks using fire (spitting out, swallowing, torches on the body, etc.).

PYTHIA: Priestess of Apollo, at Delphi. Legend says that Apollo, having killed the serpent Pytho(n), replaced it with a prophetess, Pythia, in the seventh or eight centuries B.C. helped by Cretans who had been converted to priests by the god. In the beginning Pythia only prophesied once a year, on the anniversary of the god at the beginning of spring; then on the 7th of each month. Eventually, except on inauspicious days, she probably rendered oracles constantly by lots (cleromancy*). Promancy* or priority of consultation was allowed, but women were prohibited. In successful times (sixth century B.C.) there were two officiating Pythias and one assistant. Before officiating, Pythia drank water from the Cassotis fountain. She officiated enthusiastically (possessed by the god Apollo) above the crevasse of the earth, astride three supports (whence the term *Delphic tripod*). Later the priests or exegetes interpreted. A copy of the oracle was kept in the Archives of Delphi (the *Zygastron*); another was given to the consultants (*Theopropes*, if mandated by a city). The ambiguity of the oracles earned Apollo the name Loxias, 'the oblique'. There was found to be trickery, and the Pythia Perialle was removed. *See* Oracle, Sibyl.

PYTHONESS: Formerly a synonym of Pythia*. Today, a woman who makes a living by predicting the future.

PYTHONS: Name sometimes given to diviners in the Middle Ages.

RABBIT: Superstition: the foot of a rabbit brings good luck, especially to the negroes of the United States.
RADIATIONS: *See* Aura; Fluid; Photography; Paranormal; Scotophotography.
RADIESTHESIA: A (healing) practice based on the supposed perception of 'electromagnetic radiations', with the help of a rod* (*See* Rhabdomancy) or a pendulum. A person acts as a witness, which serves to help the practitioner, often by 'similitude'. Used mainly for healing illness, also for finding water (*hygromancy** or divining), gold, missing persons, etc. It is important to note: (1) that specialists do not all use the same technique; (2) that the existence of these 'radiations' has never been scientifically proven; (3) that if there are

'radiations', it is difficult to understand how they can be detected on a card or a photo; and (4) that the importance of the unconscious movements of the wrist must be emphasized. *See* Water Diviner.

RAINMAKERS: Sorcerers reputed to be able to bring rain. Common formerly in China, Tibet ('weather makers'), Africa, Australia, etc.

RAIN, PRODIGIOUS: Announces great misfortune. For example, of crosses (in 1503), of blood (Lisbon, 1551), fish, etc.

RAJA: In Sanskrit, *king*. Royal yoga*, the 'most eminent' the one that surmounts all others.

RAM: (1) One of the twelve signs of the Zodiac*. Symbolizes impetuous thrust, spring blossoming, reforming action, revolutionary. (2) *See* Alchemy (2). (3) Often compared with the devil*, since the ram closely resembles the *goat* in many ways.

RAPPORT: According to E. Boirac, denotes during hypnosis* the relation of the thought of the subject with his hypnotizer. In psychoanalysis, the close relationship of the patient and the analyst.

RAPS or RAPPING: Denotes (in spiritualism*), the knocks or noises supposedly produced by the spirits. *See* Spiritualism, Typtology. Noted for the first time on a farm at Hydesville (New York State) in 1847, where the Fox family lived. The spirit declared that its name was Charles Haynes or Ryan. *See* Spiritualism, First Part.

RAT: *See* Myomancy.

RAUM: Commander of twenty infernal legions, a destructive demon identified with Alastor*.

RAYS: *See* Fluid, Magnometer.

REBIS: From the Latin *res* (thing) and *bis* (twice). Alchemical hermaphrodite* union of sulfur and mercury in the Philosopher's Egg*. *See* Great Art.

RED: (1) Color of blood, aggressiveness, fire, and love. The symbolism of the Middle Ages considered dark red as typical of the devil. This is why, besides black magic, one often speaks of *red magic* (necessarily, if it is bloody). (2) *See* Rubeus.

REDUCTION: *See* Elixir of Life; Value; Secret.

REFLEX IMMOBILIZATION: In animal hypnosis*, state of fear (cataplegy*), started either by sudden excitation or by somnolence or lethargy*, the continuation of a weak peripheral excitation, prolonged or uniform. In this hypnotic state, animals can move their limbs, which is impossible for cataplegics*.

REGURGITATOR: *See* Swallowing.

REINCARNATION: Doctrine associated with *Karma,* professing that the spirit* comes back to earth in another form, even as an animal (that usually means a degradation, a chastisement). *See* Avatar, Metempsychosis, Palingenesis.

REMATERIALIZATION: Reappearance of an object that has been made to disappear or, according to the fakirs*, 'reduced to nothing'.

RES-PA: *See* Tou-Mo.

RESTING AGENT: *See* Fluid.

RESURRECTION, FAKIRIC: Return to life of a fakir*, after an immersion or burial. Some of the 'illuminated' (Blacaman, Petrovitch, and Pascal de Champaubert) neglected to revive themselves! (2) Fakiric pretense of being able to revive a dead bird, thanks to 'solar fluid' (the trick consists in the substitution of a live bird).

RETROCOGNITION: *See* Postcognition.

RETROGRADATION: In astrology*, backward movement effected by a planet. Often a bad omen.

RETROSCOPY: Name given by some to clairvoyance of the past.

REUNION: *See* Conjunctio; Populus.

REVERSED (THE): *See* Tristitia.

RHABDIC FORCE: Force which manifests itself in the rod*. *See* Radiesthesia.

RHABDOMANCY: Divination with the aid of a rod* (ancestor of the pendulum) or with the aid of rods thrown into a bowl (according to the figures formed) or thrown into lots (according to the secret characters set down). The divining rod was used from the fifteenth century to discover metallic ores. *The Baton Universel* (also the title of a work of Le Noyer, 1674) is reputed to discover everything. *See* Radiesthesia.

RHAPSODOMANCY: Divination*, which was practised until the beginning of the Christian era, by opening at random a book of peoms and interpreting the verse thus chosen. The Middle Ages sometimes called it 'Lots of saints' by practising it with the Bible.

RIGHT (Right-hand side): Good omen generally. Superstition: ringing in the right ear = someone saying something bad about you.

RINGS: (1) *See* Dactyliomancy. (2) *Solomon's ring,* which gave to the wearer absolute power over all nature and the ability to make himself invisible. Also called *Bedouh.* (3) *Gyges's ring*: from the name of the pastor who became king of Lydia (Asia Minor) thanks to a ring found on a gigantic body buried in the earth, and which could render things invisible. Story told by Plato and Cicero. (4) *Ring of Samothrace*: covered with magic characters, containing grasses and small stones coming from certain constellations. (5) *Traveller's ring*: a magic ring which allowed one to walk indefinitely without becoming tired. (6) *Chinese magic rings*: a group of six or nine large metallic rings allowing amazing results by manipulation. (7) *Superstitions*: on the surface of a cup of coffee, a ring signifies money or good weather; a smoke ring from a cigarette signifies a kiss. (8) *Dschoudar's ring*: magic ring from *The Thousand and One Nights,* 606th night and those that followed.

RITUAL: (1) Assembly of conditions in which certain ceremonies (circumstances of time, place, costume, movements, words, etc.) must be carried out with meticulous care and without deviation from the traditional order. Development of these operations. Collective, then individualized, the essence of the rites preserves a precise ritual which becomes more and more abstract. Often, at this stage, it is degraded. (2) Manual describing the rites.

RITUAL MURDER: Human sacrifice with a magic aim (for example, the heart of the victim is taken out). A soldier of Cortez counted 136,000 skulls in the Great Temple of Mexico, all victims of ritual sacrifice.

ROAD: *See* Way.

ROBOT: *See* Androids.

ROC BIRD: Fabulous giant bird.

ROCOT: *See* Kilcrops.

ROD: (1) See Radiesthesia, Rhabdomancy. (2) In the sixteenth century, a divining rod which reputedly found gold or hidden treasure. (3) Magic Wand, usually belonging to fairies or magicians; that of Moses, which was changed into a serpent; that of Circe changed Ulysses' companions into pigs. Must be of hazel wood, and cut with a new knife. *See* Caduceus. (4) Sidereal Rod, a tablet covered with cabalistic characters, used by astrologers. The rod is thought by many to be a symbol of the phallus.

ROPES: In several maritime countries, magicians sell ropes with three knots, a 'rope of the winds'; undoing one of them obtains a moderate wind; two, a violent wind; three, a tempest. (2) Formerly the rope of a hanged person was supposed to bring luck and get rid of toothache and migraine. (3) Hindu rope: *See* Fakirism, First Part.

ROPE-TRICK: English name of the famous Hindu trick with the rope, described elsewhere.

ROSE: Often represented in alchemy*, the final purification of the mind, the rebirth. Above all, an example of an object which can be brought back to life.

ROSE-CROSS: Twelfth century movement of Raymond VI, Count of Toulouse, and that of the fifteenth century of a more or less mythical character, Christian Rosen-Kreuz (†1484). Expanded in the eighteenth century, when it was full of symbolism, psychism and alchemy*. Symbolized by a circle containing a cross. In 1888, two brotherhoods were established in Paris. (1) Stanislas de Guaita created the Cabalistic Order of the Rose-Cross, admitting notably the utility of Evil. (2) Sar Peladan founded the 'Aesthetic Rose-Cross of the Temple and the Grail, and, with Elemir Bourges and the Count of Rochefoucauld, launched the Rose-Cross salons. Besides humanitarian ends, the first object was to reveal the esotericism of Christian theology, the second to prepare the reign

'Specter of the Rose' obtained by an alchemical process of the Abbot of Valmont.

of the Holy Ghost. The society was reconstituted in 1907 in the United States. The Danish astrologer Max Heindel, claiming to have been contacted by the 'Invisible Unincarnate Superiors*' or 'Elder Brothers', founded a Temple of the Rose-Cross in 1920, at Los Angeles. Mrs. May Banks-Stacey was the first Grand Master, claiming to hold manuscripts of the

Rose-Cross Emblem.

first American Rose-Cross (sixteenth century, Philadelphia). Members: Rosicrucians.

ROUND or CIRCLE: (1) Of fairies*, legend places them in a glade. (2) Of sorcerers*. *See* Sabbat.

RUBEUS: Figure of geomancy* symbolizing fire, passion, war, virility, blood. Affinities: Fire, Mars. In English, red.

RUBIFICATION: *See* Alchemy.

RUBY: One of the rarest of the precious stones. Occultism dedicates the ruby to Mars and claims it is excellent for fortifying the heart, blood, brain, genital organs and gallbladder. Protects against plague, serpents, spiders and poisons. Cures trouble in the left ear. Favors effort, contest, courage. Symbolizes faith and glory. Stone of Leo the Lion.

SABAISM: Attendance at the sabbat*.

SABBAT or SABBATH: (1) Sacred day of rest for the Jews, the seventh day, Saturday, called *Sabado* in Spanish, *Sabbato* in Italian, *Soubbota* in Russian.

(2) In magic* a nocturnal meeting of sorcerers* and

witches* arriving on brooms, or on a goat* by air one Saturday evening (sometimes a Wednesday or a Friday). The devil* presided, in the appearance of Leonard or the Great Black Goat or Great Negro, three-horned and eight feet high (sometimes accompanied by a 'Queen of the Sabbat' and a witch). The chosen location was wild and desert country, often the neighborhood of a marsh and subsequently nothing would ever grow there again. The witches' brooms were smeared with the fat of a child and the witches straddled them crying *Emen-Hetan,* leaving through the chimney, carrying a stolen child, who would be consecrated to the devil Leonard and his lieutenant. The children who were not fit for sorcery were cut up and cooked for the banquet. Leonard lit up the assembly with his middle horn and homage was rendered to him by embracing his hindquarters, which were in the form of a mask or a human face. The banquet and orgies followed (dancing in a circle, back to back). The meeting was a caricature of social customs and religion. Toads*, dressed in velvet, played a prominent part. Thousands of descriptions of these scenes have been given. The cock's crow made the participants disappear after they had smeared themselves with Leonard's excrements. From the ninth century, sorcerers met at Brocken, in Germany, at the tomb of St. Walburge at Eichstadt, on the May 1, hence the name, Night of Walpurgis, or *Walpurgisnacht.* In the sixteenth century sabbats were held everywhere. There were little sabbats at which the devil was not present

Setting out for the Sabbat.

and which prepared for the great sabbats.

SAGITTARIUS: One of the twelve signs of the Zodiac*. *See* Astrology, First Part,

SAINTS, LOTS OF: *See* Rhapsodomancy.

SALAMANDER: (1) In magic, spirits of fire. *See* Demons (3). (2) Salamander-men: fakirs specialized in exercises with fire.

Ouroboros the Serpent transformed by the alchemists into a salamander.

SALIENS: In the Middle Ages, their dances and movements gave indications of the future.

SALT: (1) *See* Alomancy. (2) *See* Alchemy. (3) Superstitions: (a) to spill it == misfortune; (b) to mix it with pepper == quarrel; (c) to pass it brings misfortune to the last one; (d) dish too salted ==

amorous cook; (e) to buy salt on January 1st and carry it with a clove of garlic, in a sachet, avoids illnesses.

SAMADHI: Deep Yoga* concentration, resulting in blissful union with the Divine. Yoga of the powers of ecstasy (more accurately of *enstasis*) giving mastery of Self. Active enstasis* (third stage of samyama).

SAMYAMA: The three stages or angas* of the intellectual technique of Yoga: (1) *dharana*, (2) *dhyana*, (3) *samadhi*.

SAPPHIRE: Blue precious stone, dedicated to Jupiter. Especially when dark and set in bronze it protects the liver, lungs and the arteries; cures sore eyes; dispels worries.

SARDON: *See* Adramelech.

SATAN: *See* Devil, The; Lucifer.

SATANISM: *See* Luciferism.

SATTVA: The vegetarian diet of sorcerers* and Hindu 'holy men'.

SAUCER: Sometimes used in spiritualism* in place of the ouija* board or table-turning*. On a marble stand, where *yes* and *no* and the twenty six letters of the alphabet are traced on a dial, the saucer, moved by one finger of each participant, indicates the responses.

SAWN WOMAN: (1) On stage, famous trick of magician entertainers. (2) At Perugia (Umbria), annual magic rite, miming the 'sawing of the old masked woman', taken for an oak (nature that dies).

SCIOMANCY: See Necyomancy.

SCOLDER: See Tristitia.

SCORPIO: One of the twelve signs of the Zodiac. See Astrology, First Part.

SCOTOGRAPHY: Name given by certain spirits* to the 'thought photography' of some mediums*.

SCOTOPHOTOGRAPHY: See Photography, Paranormal; Scotography.

SCOX or CHAX: Duke of Hades, commands thirty legions. Appears as a stork. False story-teller, unless one succeeds in enclosing him in a magic triangle, and thief, especially of silver and horses. Indicates hidden treasure, which gift Asmodeus also had.

SECOND STATE: See Catalepsy, Trance.

SECRET OF SECRETS: See Clavicle.

SEMEIA: See Prodigies.

SENSE: (1) See Hyperesthesia. (2) Sixth sense: See E.S.P. (3) Seventh sense: See Aithesis.

SENSITIVE: See Medium.

SEPARATION: In astrology* means that two neighboring planets in a theme* are in the process of moving away from each other.

SEPHIROTH: The ten attributes manifesting the unique and inconceivable God of the Jewish Cabala*. Grouped in a 'Tree' each of them also corresponds to a planet, a part of the body, etc.

Perspective representation of the sephirotic tree.

SEPULCHER: See Philosopher's Egg.

SERPENT: (1) See Ophiomancy; Ouroboros; Telchines. (2) In magic, often symbolizes the forces of the Earth, sexuality, both constructive and destructive. (3) For certain alchemists*, the crucified or slaughtered serpent represents the original force which engendered the Great Work*. It

The crucified serpent.

Bird-spirits who assist the Shamans.

was inspired by the 'bronze serpent' of Moses.

SHABD: Kind of Yoga* based on 'mystical sounds'.

SHADOWS: *See* Necyomancy.

SHAKTI: Energy goddess of Hinduism. Yoga of the energetic forces of nature.

SHAMAN: Great sorcerer of primitive tribes. Sometimes called *medicine man. See* First Part.

SHAMANISM: Sorcery, especially of Central Asia, practising ecstasy*. By extension, all techniques of ecstasy of primitive tribes.

SHAMELESS: *See* Amissio.

SHINING CHILD: One of the rare apparitions that is not unlucky. Appeared, since 1820, at each important stage in the career of the Irish Marquis of Londonderry.

SHOCK IN RETURN: In black magic, the fact that spells can return and act against the operator.

SHOE: Superstition: on the table, heralds departure or misfortune.

SIBYL: Among the Ancients, women predicting the future. The most famous were the Erythraean, the Cumaean, the Samean, the Cuman and the Tiburtine. One of them helped Aeneas descend to hell: (Virgil, *Aeneid,* VI). The earliest, Herophile, prophesied at Delphi, on a rock, before the first Pythias*. By extension, divineress (for the masculine: See Bacide). There were about a dozen operating simultaneously in the Roman era. Sibylline: See Cassandra; Pythia. According to the legend, the Cumaean Sibyl sold books of oracles (the Sibylline books) which the Senate consulted at the Capitol on important matters.

SIDDHI: In Sanskrit: the miraculous powers possessed by the most eminent ascetics and yogis* (called siddha).

SIDEROMANCY: Divination interpreting the movements of pieces of straw thrown in an odd number on to a fire. (In Greek: *sideros*.)

SIDETABLE: In prestidigitation*, device allowing the adroit removal of an object without the audience noticing.

SIÈVE: See Coscinomancy.

SIGN: (1) All that 'signifies', indicates something, especially secretly. Contrary to symbol*, it can be chosen arbitrarily or accidentally. See Prodigies. (2) See Zodiac, Astrology, (table). Fixed signs: Leo, Scorpio, Taurus, Aquarius. Cardinal or. mobile signs: Libra, Aries, Cancer, Capricorn. Mutable or cadent signs: Gemini, Pisces, Sagittarius, Virgo.

SIGNS, CELESTIAL: Comets, meteors, etc. to which a value of prediction is attributed. *The Gazette of Nuremburg* was doubtless the first to call attention to what we call flying saucers (14 April 1561).

SIGNATURE: (1) Assembly of signs by which an object, a plant, or a being manifests its virtues (more or less magical). (2) In *Astrology** planetary signature has a meaning close to the planetary term, dominant.

SIKUN: Occult power, good or bad, with the American Indians. If *Skan*, the Heavens or the Force Which Judges, declares its holder fallen after his life, he becomes typically bad, and is ranged among the inexplicable, mischievous forces.

SILVER: Notable in the symbolic opposition: gold-masculine-sun-day-fire-warmth-fecundation; and silver-feminine-moon-night-water-cold-fecundity. Largely used in alchemy. See Great Art.

SKELETON: See Putrefactio.

SKIN: See Janides.

SKULL: Possesses a magic value for most beliefs, especially those of primitive people.

SLATES: Used in prestidigitation* and often falsely, in spiritism* (direct writing).

SLEEP: See Lethargy.

SLIP, TO: With cards, to slip the card secretly on top of the lower part of a cut deck.

SMOKE: *See* Capnomancy, Libanomancy.

SNEEZING: First sign of life from a man created by Epimetheus, and animated by fire stolen from the gods by his brother, Prometheus. Popular belief says it is bad in the morning, good in the afternoon. Trace of magic in 'Bless You' or 'God bless You', which some say after a person has sneezed.

SOAP: Superstition: in Italy, to pass it by the hand heralds a dispute.

SOLAR TREE: *See* Great Art.

SOLOMON'S SEAL: Star with six branches or star-shaped hexagram*. This figure, probably of Jewish origin, forms an image of the world. One of its two interlaced triangles symbolizes white, the world or macrocosm, and the other, black, man or microcosm. A static value, con-

trary to the swastika*, which symbolizes dynamism and active creation.

SOMNAMBULISM: Automatic movements occurring during provoked sleep (magnetic* somnambulism by hypnotism*) or natural sleep (ideo-somnambulism, or ordinary somnambulism or vigilambulism). Reference is sometimes made to the subject of 'division into two'. In somnambulism or hypnotic automatism*, the third stage of hypnosis*, all sensorial and motor reactions of the subject are inhibited, amnesia takes over and the suggestive post-hypnotic realization (execution of an order after waking) becomes possible. The Marquis de Puysegur discovered provoked somnambulism in 1784.

SOMNOLENCE: One of the three phases of hypnosis*. It is improperly called lethargy*. The subject gives the impression of needing sleep and imagines that he can no longer carry out the movements that his hypnotizer declares are impossible for him.

SORCERER, SORCERESS: *See* Magician, Sabbat, Sorcery. It seems that Jules Michelet was right to say 'for one sorcerer, ten thousand sorceresses'. Generally sorcerers have a physical defect and are aged. In his *Discours des Sorciers* (Paris, 1605), the judge Henri Boguet said that one recognized them by the broken cross which they carried, by marks in their hair, by the change into a wolf and spitting on the ground when forced to adjure the devil. Among primitives, the sorcerer is sometimes called a medicine man. *See* Shaman. Sorceresses are often represented with a black cat, a yellow dog, an owl, or a toad, astride their broom or a goat. Their arsenal includes a cauldron, a spindle, a wolf-skin, a book of spells, and philters*. They attend sabbats*, make spells, cut up children, etc.

SORCERY: Popular deviation of magic*; is in strict opposition to religion. Part of magic concerning sorcerers and witches and their practices is based on a pact with the devil. By its 'little recipes' and its cruelty, it is opposed to magic, a more organized knowledge than some students of the occult sciences have considered. Christianity confused them in its condemnation. Sorcery, according to J. Palou, is especially due to wretchedness. The most famous cases were those of Joan of Arc, Urbain Grandier, the Marshal of Ancre. Many tribunals did not admit accusation of sorcery after 1672, but there was one last trial in France in 1731 (the Jesuit Gerard).

SPACE: In occultism, one plans according to space affinities: North = water; North-east = mountains; East =

lightning; South-east = winds; South = fine; South-west = earth; West = clouds; North-west = air.

SPARROWHAWK: In Egypt sorcerers used to eat the hearts of these birds. Messenger of spells and charms, it is supposed to be influenced by spirits.

SPECTER: *See* Phantom; Mistletoe (shrub of specters); Haunting.

SPELL: Usually a verbal formula which allows the inflicting of harm by magic. Legends speak of witchcraft*, of the folklore of charms*, demonology, of illusions. Currently one speaks of spells. *See* Shock in Return; Envoutement. Collin de Plancy, in his *Infernal Dictionary* of 1818, distinguished seven categories: to inspire a criminal passion, to inspire hate or envy, to cast ligatures, illness, death, madness, and to impoverish.

SPIDER: With the cat and the octopus, the spider is the usual omen of anguish. Most people are familar with formulae like 'spider in the morning, chagrin; spider at midday, pleasure or profit; spider in the afternoon, a present; spider in the evening, hope'. If it spun its web on the statues of gods or on military standards, it was a disastrous omen for the ancients. To squash it is favorable. Its web is used for preventing wounds becoming infected. Certain primitive sorcerers carried spider webs with them.

SPINNING: In prestidigitation*, pretending that one takes the card on the top of the pack, when one really takes the card below it.

SPIRALLED SHELL: Often the symbol of initiation.

SPIRE: In occultism, symbolizes evolution.

SPIRIT CABINET: Four upright posts and some curtains, reputed to isolate the spiritualistic medium.

SPIRIT, GREAT: *See* Manitou.

SPIRITISM: Doctrine believing in the possibility of the souls of the dead coming to communicate with the living, normally by the intervention of a medium*. Launched by Swedenborg, revised in 1847 in the United States by the two young daughters of the Fox family. Codified, in 1848, by Andrew Jackson Davies in his work, *Relations with Spirits*. Propagated in France by Hippolyte Denizard Rivail, called Allan Kardec (*The Book of Spirits* and *The Book of Mediums*), with ten moral laws. Many spiritists* accept reincarnation*, but always in

human form. It is said that they go on a pilgrimage to caress the marble bust of Kardec, on his gravestone in the cemetery of Pere-Lachaise. Cao-dai* is a very curious Oriental variant. Other variants from the West: Antoinism*, Martinism*. The recorded 'communications' have a surprising intellectual poverty. *See* Body; Medium; Raps; Saucer; Spirit Cabinet; Table.

SPIRITISTS: Participants in spiritism*. *See* Medium. For several occultists, the father of spiritism was Emmanuel Swedenborg of Stockholm (1688-1772).

SPIRITS: Genies* or demons. More specifically, the immortal soul of dead people, manifesting itself or not. Kardec divides them into: imperfect, good, pure. *See* Body; Elementals; Entity; Sparrowhawk; Spiritism.

SPIRITUAL GOLD: *See* Alchemy.

SPIRITUALISM: The whole philosophical or religious system, based on spirituality, in other words, admitting the existence of the spirit. Opposed to materialism. Not to be confused with spiritism*, which is, however, a *spiritualist doctrine*. Spiritualism can be subdivided into relative (the spirit prevails over matter) and into absolute (matter only exists as a consequence of the spirit).

SPIRITUAL PILGRIM: Name given sometimes to the astrologer in the eighteenth century.

SPONTANEOUS GERMINATION: *See* Growth, Accelerated.

S.P.R.: Abbreviation of the Society for Psychical Research founded in 1882, in London, on the initiative of Professor William Barrett of Dublin and of J. Romanes. Made a particular study of telepathy*. Its documents were cautiously studied by Edmund Gurney (from 1886), then less cautiously by Frederick Myers (died in 1901).

SPRITE: Goblin, familiar and teasing demon. *See* Goblin.

STAR: (1) Name of the seventeenth major Arcana of the Tarot*. Represents a person emptying a red pitcher from each hand. Overhung by eight stars, sign of destiny, of the Collective Unconscious. (2) Superstition: a falling star grants a wish formulated during its passing.

STATURE: Tall stature characterizes magicians* in representations, notably on prehistoric rock paintings in the south of Africa.

STOLAS: Grand Prince of Hell, commanding twenty-six legions. Appeared either as a crowned owl with very long feet, or a man teaching astrology* and the value of plants and precious stones.

STOLEN CHILDREN: In the Middle Ages it was believed that children were stolen, either by the fairies* who wanted to substitute them with little monsters, or by the witches* for the sacrifices of the sabbat or to dedicate them to the devil. This could be avoided by tracing a cross on the door and on the cradle by putting a piece of iron near the child, or leaving a light burning.

STONES: (1) *See* Lithomancy, Gastromancy. (2) Toadstone. *See* Toad. (3) Of a hyena: biliary stones of this animal are supposed, if placed under the tongue, to give divinatory powers. (4) Of reconciliation: *See* Diamond. (5) Divine: *See* Jade. (6) Moonstone: dedicated to Diana-Artemis. Favors cellular drainage, passive sensibility, poetic imagination, memory, solitude. *See* Pearl. (7) Eagle Stone: *See* Aetite. (8) *See* Alectorius.

STRAMONIUM: Variety of tobacco used in magic.

STRENGTH: Eleventh *lame* of the Tarot representing a character dressed in blue, with red cape, patting a seated lion. Symbolizes detachment in action, self-control, active dominance over the animal sphere.

STRIGE: Nocturnal vampire*.

STRONG, THE: See Puer.

SUBJECT: See Medium.

SUBLIMINAL: That which is not noticed by the conscious mind. In spiritism*, the subliminal Ego denotes the psychic substance to which we return after death.

SUCCESSION: See Powder.

SUCCUBUS: In the strict sense, apparition* of a nightmare, limited to sleep. In a broad sense, incarnate demon, as a seductive woman to tempt man and to be united with him in his sleep. Rabbinical tradition regarding fallen angels; thus Lilith would have tempted Adam before he knew Eve. See Incubus.

SUGGESTION: According to Pierre Janet, provocation of the acting out of an impulse involving a non-deliberate act. Contrary to hypnosis* it can be collective. If it applies to oneself it is called auto-suggestion.

SULFUR: In alchemy*, the volatile principle, fire-sulfur. Represented in cryptography by an equilateral triangle standing on its base. See Alchemy.

SUMMING UP THE ODDS: See Geomancy, First Part.

SUN: Name of the nineteenth major Arcana of the Tarot*. Represents the sun dominating two children in front of a wall. Expresses the fraternal age, solar harmony. In depth psychology, symbol of the father and of conscience.

SUPERIOR UNKNOWN or ELDER BROTHERS: Mysterious people or entities* (?) from whom the Rosicrucians* (notably Max Heindel), and the society Astrum Argentinum* of Aleister Crowley (See First Part, Biographies) claim to have received advice.

SUPERSTITION: Belief or practice creating obligations, fears and reliances not founded on reason. Deviation of religious sentiment. Superstitions can be classed according to their nature, their origin (religious, social prohibition, etc.), and their object.

SUPPORT: Anything that serves to support, naturally or artificially, a meditation, a clairvoyance*, spell*, etc. The photograph which acts as a double for the living being is of great value in this domain.

SUPRANORMAL: See Paranormal.

SUSPENSION OF VITAL FUNCTIONS: Fakiric* pretense asserting the power to control or suspend the circulation, respiration, alimentation at will. See Fasting. It permitted fakiric burial or immersion alive.

SWALLOWING: Fakirs swallow needles, broken glass, nails, etc. without pain. Numerous tricks. It is necessary to distinguish them from the regurgitators, who swallow different objects, hold them in the stomach, and bring them up again. Much fraud occurs in this connection.

SWASTIKA: Religious symbol of India and China, consisting of a gammadion cross with six equal arms turned towards the right. *See* Solomon's Seal.

SIBYLLINE BOOKS: Books, according to Roman tradition, supposedly by the Cumaean Sibyl*, given to King Tarquin. Put in the temple of Jupiter, burnt, then reconstituted. Interpreted by two, then ten, later fifteen specialists. Consulted especially in cases of marvels.

SYCOMANCY: Divination with the help of fig tree leaves stirred in the night by the wind. At Dodona, the oracle of Zeus sometimes replied by rustling the leaves of oak trees. *See* Wind.

SYLPH: Aerial sprite in Celtic and Germanic countries in the Middle Ages. *See* Demons (3); Elf.

SYLPHIDS: *See* Fairy.

SYMBOL: In occultism, all that evokes an object, a being, an abstraction, by virtue of relations and natural or created affinities. *See* Sign. The science of symbols is called *symbology*. Symbolic thought is that form of thought which passes from one notion to the other by analogy. To group several of these thoughts constitutes an analogical chain.

T: In Greek, tau. Letter of great value in magic. At the beginning of some magical ceremonies, one pronounces the oration of thirty-three *tau* or ceremonial oration of the demiurge*.

TABLE: (1) *See* Emerald; Hermes; Trismegistus. (2) Table turning: table used in spiritualism to communicate with the spirits*. The ideal table is a light stand, on three feet. On it is made a chain of hands in order to warm it. The table then knocks under the effect of the spirits (usual code*: one knock = *yes*, two = *no*). (3) Flying table (Mongols and the Tibetans): served to catch thieves.

TABLE, WARM THE: In spiritism*, preparing the table for the coming of the spirits.

TABOO: Polynesian religious institution forbidding the touching of a thing or a being, because of its sacred character.

TABULA SMARAGDINA: *See* Emerald.

TALISMAN: From the Greek *telesma*, rite. Object marked with cabalistic signs which brings good luck, or which

Arabian talisman.

communicates a supernatural power, resulting in an operation by the spirit. It is only useful for a specific goal. Protector, mostly active. *See* Amulet, Pantacle. Common talismans: a piece of rope from a hanging, horse-shoe, cricket, elephant hair, four-leaf clover, lizard's tail, St Christopher's medal, etc.

TAPAS: For the Hindu, internal warmth, asceticism.

TARANTULA: *See* Elixir of Life.

TARANTULA SPELL: Persons said to have been bitten by a tarantula* claim to be possessed*. Several cases have occurred in the south of Italy.

TAROT: Symbolic book or *Book of Thoth*, of the Bohemians* or Tziganes. *See* Hermes. It has 22 major and 56 minor cards*, in the packs for divination. The figures of these seem to have been drawn in the fifteenth century and are believed to illustrate the alchemical Great Work*.

TAURUS: One of the twelve signs of the Zodiac*. *See* Astrology, First Part.

TEETH: (1) Of wolf: attributes of witches*. Children were formerly made to carry them so they would not be afraid. (2) Of the dead: used in black magic against certain spells and to unknot the *aiguil-*

*lette**. (3) Of a horse: to carry one in a pocket protected against toothache (superstition). (4) Luck: to have the incisors taken out brought good luck. Since prehistory, necklaces of teeth have been used in magic.

TELCHINES: Legendary genies* or 'children of the sea' (another tradition makes them three blacksmiths, genies of fire) who live mainly in Crete, Rhodes and Cyprus. Gifted with marvellous powers, they command the atmospheric elements and may be metamorphosed at will, notably as serpents* and fish*. They often are harmful.

TELEKINESIS or TELERGY: According to Myers, a material force intervening in the telepathic* act. In general, the possibility of lifting or moving objects at a distance, without direct or indirect contact. *See* Levitation. To be distinguished from *psychokinesis* or *P.K.*

TELEPATHY: Word created by Myers, who defined it as a communication of impressions from one mind to another without recognized sensorial means. Parapsychology prefers to regard it as an inexplicable coincidence between the psychophysiological states of two people. *See* Clairvoyance. In a broad sense, unusual form of sensibility at a distance, extrasensorial. In a strict sense, possibility of transmitting thoughts to others, or of reading from near or far (telepathic broadcasting or receiving). It is practically always due to trickery. It is more currently called transmission of thought*. It is said to be *composite* when it is not pure (mixed with clairvoyance, for example); *psychometric* if it pursues a goal of psychometry*; *triangular* if it is produced between three people, of whom one is often a medium*. Adjective and noun: *telepath*.

TELEPLASTY: Faculty of spirits* of the dead or of some living mediums imparting at a distance an imprint on a waxen or plastic material. *See* Fluid.

TELEPSYCHY: (1) Knowing at a distance. Sometimes confused with telepathy*. (2) Some occultists use it in the sense of suggestion* of acts, without employing verbal instructions.

TELERGY: *See* Telekinesis.

TELESMA: *See* Emerald; Talisman.

TELESTHESIS: Name sometimes given to clairvoyance*. Word created by Myers. *See* Cryptesthesia.

TELESUGGESTION: Suggestion* which the Swedish doctor, Jon Bjorken, states is possible at a distance.

TEMPERANCE: Name of the fourteenth major arcana of the Tarot*. A kind of winged angel, dressed in red and blue, with blue hair, exchanging the liquid of two pots. Symbolizes dynamic balance, vital energy in transmutation.

TEMPESTOR: Sorcerer* stirring up tempests. *See* Magonia.

TEMPLARS: Order of the Knights Templars founded by St Bernard, Hugh of Payens and eight other French knights in 1118. Along with their Christian cult they worshipped an idol, Baphomet*. They were accused of flouting the crucifix and of practising Sabbats* in their chapel of Laon (Aisne). They were condemned by Pope Clement V in 1369.

TEPHROMANCY: Divination by questions written on a board sprinkled with ashes and then exposed to the wind.

TERAPH or TERAPHIM: (1) According to the scriptures, pantacle* of divination and of magical protection, often in human or animal form. (2) Occultism considered some teraphim like automatic idols, possessing souls. In the Middle Ages, the head of the assassinated eldest son,

opened and rubbed with oil and ammonia, a gold coin under the tongue, was thought to predict the future. Gilles de Rais was accused of these practices. The Baphomet* of the Templars* was also said to be a teraph.

A magician consulting an Egyptian teraphim.

TERMS: *See* Decan.

TERNARY: *See* Great Art.

THAUMATURGY: Workers of miracles (but of divine plan, therefore opposed to black magic, goety*, or diabolic plan). Thaumaturgy is therefore a 'white magic'. *See* Theurgy.

THEME OF CONCEPTION: Certain astrologers* in determining the future of the consultant, prefer to use a theme based on the time of conception rather than the usual one of the time of birth. The time is either specified, where possible, by those interested, or fixed arbitrarily by tracing back 273 days from the birth.

THEOMANCY: In the sixteenth century denoted the four kinds of oracular divination*.

THEOPROPES: *See* Pythia.

THEOSOPHY: Religious doctrine whose object was unity with divinity. The Theosophical Society, founded in New York in 1875 and at Mount Adyar, near Madras (Madame Blavatsky, Col. Olcott, then Annie Besant and Leadbeater) extols a kind of syncretism. After Madame Blavatsky's death in 1891 a split occurred in the movement, leading to the formation of a separate organization in the United States under the leadership of William P. Judge. Along with a pacifist and generous morality, it spreads a few fakiric insanities. Practitioner: *Theosophist*. In France Gerard Encausse, known as *Papus*, founded a group for theosophical propaganda known under the name of *Isis*.

THERIAC: (1) Opiate medicament, formerly called mithridate*. (2) The most famous pharmaceutico - magical mixture, called *electraury**, probably invented by Andromaeus, doctor to the emperor Nero, and vulgarized by Galen. It comprised seventy-four substances, among which dried roses, bithune, apoponax, some honey of Hymettus, some wine from Palermo and especially some viper flesh. The preparation lasted four months. It kept its properties from thirty to sixty years and was usable five or seven years after its making. Reputed to be a supreme antidote against all illnesses. *See* Panacea.

THEURGY: Kind of magic* which calls on the forces of nature or on celestial powers. Opposed to goety*. Practitioner: *theurgist*. *See* Thaumaturgy.

THIRTEEN: Offen brings bad luck (thirteen guests at the table, etc.). In the Tarot*, the thirteenth card signifies rebirth, whence perhaps comes the fact that some consider thirteen brings good luck.

THORYBISM: *See* Poltergeist.

THOUGHT: *See* Scotography.

THOUGHT FORMS: *See* Egregore. The theosophists* distinguish its quality (determining its color), its nature (form), its precision (clarity of contours).

THOUGHT READING: Popular synonym for clairvoyance*, telepathy*.

THRIES: Special dice used in Ancient Greece (Delphi,

Skiron, Byra) for divination*. Thought to have been created by Athena.

THUMB: Inserted between the other fingers: magic symbol of the creative act.

TIBET: Like India, a land where the supernatural is seriously studied. State Buddhism, of a Tantric variety, has been practised there for centuries, but has recently been driven out by the Chinese communists.

TIBETAN SUSPENSION: Trick of the fakirs* consisting of placing themselves, with arms and feet swinging and the throat bare, on the blade of a sword.

TOAD: (1) Dedicated to Saturn, it is the auxiliary of the witches of the Sabbat*. They are clothed in scarlet silk, with a cloak of green or black velvet. The devil baptizes them during the Sabbat. They wear a bell around their necks and a small bell on their right leg. (2) The toadstone, which conjuring books* say is found in the heads of toads, was the antidote for poisons and changed color in the presence of a toxic substance. The powder from toads is used copiously in philters and in the 'poison sponge'. To make *toffana,* one of the two poisons of the Borgias, a toad is stuffed with amanite, hemlock, and foxglove, then its body is 'dis-

Tibeto-Mongolian dance celebrating triumph over the demons.

tilled'. In country areas the toad is used as a protection against hypnotism* or as a basis for spells* and the knotting of the aiguillette*. In the seventeenth century the doctor Van Helmont asserted that a toad, carried alive in a box of horn, guarded against plague.

(4) Certain alchemists represent a woman giving the breast to a toad who offered her a man, for the toad symbolizes masculine energies.

TOBACCO: *See* Stramonium.

TOPAZ: A clear or straw-colored stone which, in occultism, corresponds to the Sun-Apollo and to the alloys of gold. Governs the right eye, the heart and the balance of arterial circulation. Gives confidence and prestige. Often protects marriage, love. Favorable to Cancer, Gemini, Pisces, Scorpio.

TOTEM: Any animal worshipped, especially by the North American Indians, as an ancestor of the race. It is taboo*. The tribe immolates it to secure its virtues. The totem pole is an isolated pole representing the animal totems.

TOTEMISM: Religion venerating a totem (animal or, less usually, vegetable).

TOU-MO: In Tibetan: *Gtu-Mo*. Art of warming oneself naked in the snow. Practised by the ascetics. 'Clothed in cotton' or Res-pa, disciples of the master Milarepa (eleventh century).

TOWN: *See* Alchemy (1).

TRANCE: In occultism, state where activity and thought are divorced from the self. Synonyms: hypnotic* state or mediumnic* or 'second'. In parapsychology*, unconscious state during which a paranormal activity may be manifested.

TRANSFER: (1) In spiritism, *see* Rapport. (2) In psychology, fact of bringing back to someone his former thoughts or the traits of another.

TRANSFIXION: Fakiric* performance in which the great specialist was Minn Dajo, a Dutchman.

TRANSMIGRATION (OF SOULS): Passage from one existence to another. *See* Avatar.

TRANSMISSION OF THOUGHT: *See* Telepathy.

TRANSMUTATION: *See* Alchemy.

TRANSPIERCE: *See* Transfixion.

TRANSPORT: Name sometimes given to the theft of the witches.* *See* Sabbat.

TRANSPOSITION: Faculty by which mediums* perceive, other than by normal action of the senses [for example, to see with the tips of the fingers (*paroptic vision*) due to the *ocellus*.]

TREASURE: *See* Draconite.

TREE: (1) In mythology and magic represents the changing force rising from the earth (tree of life), vegetative life, the unconscious. Symbolizes *synthesis* followed by *analysis* (genealogical tree, trees of Sephiroths*, etc.). (2) Widely used in magic in country areas. *See* Assumption of The Oak. (3) *See* Magnetism, Sephiroth.

TRES-BAS: *See* Devil.

TRIANGLE: With many occultists it is the ternary stage, adding the notion of time (fatality) to the binary stage (attack and defence). As an ideogram, it symbolizes divinity, the dialectic. Certain literary esoterists specify: equilateral == absolute; isosceles == static; scalene == dynamic; rectangle == harmony. Pointed upwards it symbolizes fire; downwards, rain.

TRICKERY: *See* Fraud.

TRIDENT: A horseshoe found in the street, advocated by Paracelsus as a protection against impotence. Instrument of numerous magicians and Hindu and Tibetan ascetics. Neptune, the Roman sea god, is often represented as carrying a trident.

The magical trident of Paracelsus reconstructed by Eliphas Levi.

TRILL, DEVIL'S: Violin melody which Tartini, violin virtuoso of the eighteenth century, claimed to have heard in a dream and wrote on awakening.

TRINITY: Masculine. The quaternity adds the feminine principle as a supplement.

TRISTITIA: Figure of geomancy*, symbolizing restriction, depression, scruples, failure, anxiety, despair. Affinities: Earth, Saturn. In French: Tristesse; in Arabic: the reversed.

TUB OF MESMER: *See* Magnetism, Tree (3).

TURN AROUND: *See* Gyromancy.

TURQUOISE: Mottled blue precious stone used as a talisman* especially in central Asia. For seamen: symbol of earth, courage, hope. Protects the nostrils, the cerebellum, the sympathetic nerve. Dispels nasal trouble and sore eyes*. A contradictory stone, as it assures both the success of amorous men and the virtue of young girls. Suits those born under the sign of Taurus.

TURTLEDOVE: Symbolizes conjugal fidelity and chaste widowhood.

TYPOLOGY: Science studying human types according to their constitution and temperament (*typomorphology* of temperaments) or according to their character. Many occultists use this science when speaking of planetary types.

TYPTOLOGY: Study of paranormal noises (raps*). In spiritism*, method of attracting the communications from beyond given in the form of 'knocks' or 'raps'.

TYROMANCY: Divination based on cheese.

TZIGANES: *See* Tarot.

UKOBACH: Demon who maintains the infernal cauldrons. Often called the inventor of fireworks.

UMBRELLA: Superstition: to receive one signifies one's departure; to open one in a house means bad luck.

UNCONSCIOUS: Not possessing characteristics of consciousness, that submerged part of the human mind not ordinarily in evidence.

UNDINES: *See* Demons (3).

UNICORN: (1) 'Pure' animal, fabulous white creature,

reigning over the forests. Like a horse with a horn in the middle of its forehead. Lets itself be approached only by a young virgin. Unmerciful to hunters. (2) In alchemy*, symbolizes the creative or destructive power; or eagle, lion, mercury.

UNION OF OPPOSITES: *See* Alchemy (1).

UNIVERSAL SOLVENT: *See* Alkahest.

URANUS: This word, which denotes a planet, analogically defines a process. The Uranian process, or characteristic of Uranus, is explained as a gradual change which suddenly manifests itself.

VALKYRIES: *See* Hollenfurt.

VALUE, SECRET: It is the sum of the figures which constitute a number. The conversion to this secret value is made in different ways. *See* Numerology, Onomancy.

VAMPIRE: (1) *See* Lemures, Ghouls. Different from *werewolf**. (2) Popular imagination supposes that a dead sorcerer comes from the grave at night to suck the blood of the living, preferably of young girls.

VASES: The divinatory practice of three vases (earth, copper, glass) brings knowledge of the past, present and

future, when performed on a solitary hill.

VATICINATE, TO: From the Latin *vates,* divine, inspired. To predict the future, to act as a diviner.

VAUDOIS or GAZARIANS: Disciples of Pierre Valdo. In the fifteenth century refugee sorcerers* in the Alps and Upper Alps. By extension, *vauderie*: reunion of sorcerers. One of the most famous is that of Arras (1459-61).

VENEFICE: Evil spell, usually by 'poisoning'. Poisoning by witchcraft*.

VENUS: This term, which denotes a planet, analogically defines a process. (1) The Venusian characteristics of

Venus are seen as beauty, charm, sweetness, harmony, femininity. (2) Black Venus or Nocturnal Venus, idol (in the form of a black stone) of the Mother of the Gods of Ancient Asia Minor, has been likened to Lilith, woman of Samael or of Satan*. As such, Venus has been associated with Lucifer.

VERB: In magic, the correct word is all-powerful, and over-comes the forces that one wishes to annex.

VERBENA: (1) Plant which, infused, held in the hand or used as a perfume, is believed to develop the gift of clair-voyance*. (2) In the sixteenth century the Neapolitan Pipemo claimed that whoever eats it cannot effect coitus for seven days.

VERGRABEN DER KRANKHEIT: Burial of an illness. Popular German magic believes that if a magician buries an illness with his hand (previously rubbed with a moleskin) he frees the patient of it. *See* Assumption of the Oak.

VIA: Figure of geomancy* symbolizing interminable slow-ness, wandering, in-stability, contrariety. In English: *road;* in Arabic: *the way.*

VICTORY: *See* Fortuna Major; Fortuna Minor.

VIGILAMBULISM: *See* Som-nambulism.

VIOLET: Color of semi-mourning in popular tradition.

VIPER: *See* Theriac.

VIRGIN: *See* Puella.

VIRGO: One of the twelve signs of the zodiac*. *See* Astrology, First Part.

VISIONS: (1) *See* Apparition. (2) At Lebadea in ancient Boeotia, from the sixth cen-tury B.C., the oracle of the cave of the hero Trophonius was rendered by visions and subterranean voices. The con-sultant was at times insulted or put to sleep.

VOODOO: Secret religion im-ported by the slaves of Guinea and of Dahomey to Haiti and Brazil. The mysteries have two main rites: (1) The *radas* or 'royal rite of the sun' (snake) and the *petro,* which gives magical virtues. The frenetic crises are called *ioa*: the devo-tees dance at night to the sound of drums, with sacrifices of fowls. To reach the para-dise of Ife the initiated must 'cross the sea' with sacrifices of white animals (mutton, pigeons, hens). There are also funeral rites: the master of the burial grounds, Baron Samedi, can revive *zombies*. Haiti officially recognized voodoo in 1945. The *Canombles* con-

freres of Brazil practised analogous rites.

VOYANCE: Faculty, process and result of being able to 'see' what is hidden to read the future. The terms aithesis*, clairvoyance, lucidity* or extra-lucidity, are preferable. The simplest form of clairvoyance is *spontaneous telepathy*. The subject is complex and difficult to define; the word is inadequate because (1) it is not a matter of *seeing*, but of a 'special faculty', and (2) it denotes at the same time the cause, state, faculty, process and result. Therefore is at least necessary to call it the 'faculty of' clairvoyance, 'process of' clairvoyance, etc.

Among the clairvoyances with rational support* are psychometry* (personal object), rhabdomancy* (rod) and radiesthesia* (pendulum), as well as those of the coffee mark, mirrors, crystal balls, cards, etc. There is also a clairvoyance by intervention of the spirits* (*See* Medium*) or 'radiations'. Occultism claims that clairvoyance is hereditary and is indicated in the hand* (chiromantic signs). It is a means of knowledge, not of sensibility, but sometimes takes the form of sensation, whence comes the difficulty in eliminating conscious attention, which disturbs it (the support*, or hypnosis*, can help here).

VULNERARY OINTMENT: According to Paracelsus, magic ointment which cured wounds from a distance.

WAKAN TANKA: With the American Indians, it is the Great Mystery, the non-personified cosmic force. *See* Manitou, Great; Sikun.

WAKINYAN: *See* Manitou, Great.

WANDERING DUTCH-MAN: Dutch phantom vessel. Its appearance near the Cape of Good Hope was a very bad omen. It travelled with all sails set.

WANDERING JEW: The cobbler, Ahasuerus. Having denied Christ, like Judas, he was condemned to wander without rest. He sought in vain for death.

WATER: Symbolizing purity, receptiveness, femininity. Water is often used in magic. *See* Dew, Gastromancy, Hydromancy, Idatoscopy, Pegomancy, Rhabdomancy, Water Diviner.

WATER DIVINER: Radiesthesist* specialized in the search for water*. It comes in two categories: (1) Pure or without a support, that is, one 'senses' the water without any aid; (2) With support, that is, using a rod* (preferably of hazel, in the form of a V), or two metallic stems, two bobbins, etc. or pendulum* (metal, wood, agate, etc.). The dowser holds a branch of the V in each hand, the horizontal point outwards. *See* Hydromancy, Rhabdomancy.

WATER DIVINING: *See* Radiesthesia.

WATERLILY: Plant, also called 'cold plant', because it was used in the philters to calm amorous passions. It would be, in effect, an *anaphrodisiac*.

WAXY POSITION: *See* Catalepsy.

WAY: (1) Humid, dry, royal. (2) *See* Via. (3) Way of point: in geomancy*, expresses the filiation between the Judge and two (bicephal) or four (quadricephal) Mothers or Daughters, as well as the different factors intervening for the question asked. In the negative, one says that it 'does not pass'. *See* Geomancy, First Part.

WEREWOLVES: Humans transformed into wolves. *See* Lycanthropy, Neures.

WHEAT OF OSIRIS: *See* Growth, Accelerated.

WHEEL OF FORTUNE: Name of the tenth major arcana of the Tarot*. Represents a wheel on a pivot, topped by a sword-carrying sphinx. Variable interpretation. One generally concludes that destiny and liberty are not opposed.

WHITE: (1) *See* Albus. (2) Color of light, purity, of benevolent divinities; in astrology* of silver, of the moon, of creative forces of the night. (3) *See* Magic. (4) Egg white: *See* Oomancy.

WHITE HORSE: Superstition: good omen, especially in pairs. Black = death. *See* Hippomancy.

WHITE LADY: Fairy*, generally benevolent.

WILLING GAME: *See* Cumberlandism.

WIND: (1) Is connected with Gemini*. (2) At Dodona, in ancient Epirus, the oracle of

Zeus was considered the oldest in Greece. Zeus, associated with Earth-Dione, rendered his oracles by the wind rustling in an oak tree or through plates of bronze. Priestesses, the Pleiades, interpreted the signs of the oak. Priests, who lay on the ground and never washed their feet, interpreted the sounds of the bronze; the poet Callimachus called them 'the servants of the basin which was never silent'. To replace the suspended bronze basins, which were damaged by the effects of the wind, the Corfunas offered two columns, one with a bronze child holding a whip with three chains, the other a basin which the chains would knock. (3) *See* Sycomancy.

WINE: (1) *See* Oenomancy. (2) Superstitions: (a) spilt on the tablecloth = good luck if one wets the forehead with it; a champagne cork brings luck.

WITCHCRAFT: Means of harming, spell of sorcery, prediction of the future.

WITNESS: *See* Radiesthesia.

WOLVES: (1) *See* Lycanthropy, neures. (2) Werewolves, wolves from which it is necessary to shield oneself; men or women who have been metamorphosed, or have metamorphosed themselves, into wolves. The Roman authors spoke of them. (Virgil, *Buc.*, 8, 97; Apuleius *Met.* 11, 22; Petronius, 62). When they become human again, they keep any injuries they received as wolves.

WOOD: Superstition: to touch living wood prevents bad luck.

WOOD OF LIFE: Name sometimes given to the Philosopher's Stone*.

WORDS: *See* Cledomancy.

WORK: *See* Parergon.

WORLD: Name of the twenty-first major arcana of the Tarot*. Naked person, dancing in the center of a three-colored crown. In the four corners, an angel in a blue cloak, a yellow eagle with blue wings, a yellow lion, a horse (the only one of the four without a halo). Signifies spiritual illumination or final harmony.

XENOGLOSSIA: In spiritism*, comprehension of a language unknown to the medium (reading, speaking, writing).

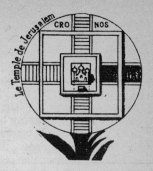

YAKIN: One of the two columns of the Temple of Solomon*, in magic. It is masculine and symbolizes the generative attribute. It is red (intelligence, vigor, glory) and corresponds to the sun. *See* Bo'az.

YAMA: The five masteries of Yoga*, one of which is fasting (Upasana). *See* Niyama.

YAN GAN-Y-TAN: Kind of demon of Finistere which moves about in the night. To encounter it is a bad omen. Emaciated, with pointed ears, he ceaselessly turns the five fingers of his shining right hand.

YANTRA: The simplest of the Mandala*, often nine triangles in a square. Kind of yoga* 'of the powers of geometrical forms'. Also, a Yogic dance.

YAWNING: Considered by some to be dangerous, as it 'permits demons to enter'.

YLIASTER: According to Paracelsus, supreme undifferentiated cosmic unity. First matter of all things. Would be polarized into negative-feminine (Cagaster) and positive-masculine, which together engender the *Chaos* or *Ideos*. The primitive matter (*Hyle*) is decomposed into three sources (sulfur, mercury, salt), the union of which produces corporeal matter (*Yliadus*) with its four elements (*Tetrasomia*). *See* Great Art.

YOGA: Philosophical system of India, elaborating a doctrine 'enstasis of the soul', or technique by which the soul is enlightened and mastered after the subduing of the body. Practitioner: Yogi(n). Subdivided into: Bhakti*, Hatha*, Jnana*, Karma*, Kundalini*, Laya*, Mantra*, Raja*, Samadhi*, Shabd*, Shakti*, Yantra*. *See* also Anga; Asana; Chakra; Dhyana; Guru; Mandala; Nadi; Niyama; Pranayama; Siddhi; Yama.

ZARBIES: Instruments of torture used by the Herbetian dervishes of Albania.

ZODIAC: Zone of the celestial sphere which comprises the planets known of old, and which the sun appears to travel through in the space of a year. It is divided into twelve equal parts (or signs of the Zodiac), which have the names of the nearest constellations, starting from the equinox of spring. *See* Astrology, First Part, and the table of Planetary Signs*. It is necessary to distinguish (1) The real Zodiac, where the constellations have an important variable; (2) The astro-

Signs	*Corresponding Divinities in Antiquity*
ARIES	Athena - Minerva
TAURUS	Aphrodite - Venus
GEMINI	Apollo
CANCER	Hermes - Mercury
LEO	Zeus - Jupiter
VIRGO	Demeter - Ceres
LIBRA	Hephaestus - Vulcan
SCORPIO	Ares - Mars
SAGITTARIUS	Artemis - Diana
CAPRICORN	Hestia - Vesta
AQUARIUS	Hera - Juno
PISCES	Poseidon - Neptune

logical Zodiac divided into twelve equal parts or signs or *dodecatemories*, each occupying thirty degrees of the arc. The Zodiac represents a process of evolution of the universe. This development commenced with the uncontrollable bursting of Aries* to evolve to Pisces*. The signs of the Zodiac are listed on the previous page.

ZOHAR: *The Book of Splendor,* principal work of the Jewish Cabala.

ZOMBIES: Denotes the 'living dead' of Haiti. In the tradition of the Creoles of the Antilles, the sorcerers would revive dead people to work in their gardens (whence the name *Zombie garden*) or to accomplish a mission. *See* Voodoo.

ZOOMORPHISM: (1) Form of religion or magic representing divinities and demons in animal form. Example: in Pharaonic Egypt. (2) *See* Fairy.

The magical head of Zohar.

ZODIACAL AFFINITIES

Signs of Zodiac	Characters	Affinities	Colors	Animals	Metals	Minerals	Plants	Part of the Body	Planets
Libra	Serene justice; harmony; religious; courteous; problems of the other; revelation.	Warmth; air; dampness; autumn; day; sterility.	Delicate.	Snake.	Copper.	Diamond; marble; quartz.	Olive tree.	Kidneys; internal; genital organs.	Diurnal domicile of Venus. Saturn is exalted here, Mars is in exile and the sun in descent.
Aries	Sudden blossoming; impetuous, even revolutionary; initiative.	Fire; masculine; north; Mars; red; rapidity; pioneer.	Red.	Ram.	Iron.	Amethyst; wax; pyrites; desert sand; sulfur; red stones.	Primrose.	Head; brain.	Domicile of Mars and of Pluto. Sun here is in ascendent, Venus in exile, Saturn in descent.
Cancer	Silence; hidden strength; invisible influences; maturation and putrefaction; unfrequented tracks.	Summer; water; humidity; femininity.	Matt or opalescent white.	Crab; octopus.	Silver; platinum.	Lime; pearls; white; delicate stones.	Lily of the valley; carnation.	Stomach; breast; gestation.	Domicile of the Moon. Jupiter is in ascendent, Saturn in exile, Mars in descent.

Signs of Zodiac	Characters	Affinities	Colors	Animals	Metals	Minerals	Plants	Part of the Body	Planets
Capricorn	Abstraction; solitude; rigor; mature principles; absolute.	Cold; earth; night; dry; mountain; sterility; material weakness; systematic.		Spider.	Dross of lead.	Ashes; coal; onyx; black minerals; mountain rocks.	Flax; lilac.	Bones; knees.	Nocturnal domicile of Saturn; Mars is in ascendent, Moon in exile, Jupiter in descent.
Gemini	Dualism (opposition or synthesis); psychic intelligence; intuition.	Air; warmth; spring; masculinity; positive.	Many-colored or streaked.	Hare.	Mercury.	Beryl; garnet; opal.		Chest; nerves; hands; respiration; arms.	Diurnal domicile of Mercury; Jupiter in exile.
Leo	Radiance; nobility; pomp; generosity; honor; pride; despotism.	Warmth; fire; dryness; sterility; masculine; positive king.	Golden yellow.	Lion.	Gold.	Chrysolite; hyacinth; ruby.	Sunflower.	Heart; back; spinal marrow.	Domicile of Sun; Saturn in exile.

Sign								
Pisces	Water; humidity; night; cold; silence; sleep.	Sweetness; collective psychism; permeability; misfortune; pain; sadness (hospital of the Zodiac).	Whale.	Tin.	Coral; sea sand; pumice; sea rocks.	Saracen.	Feet; peritoneum.	Diurnal domicile of Neptune; nocturnal of Jupiter; Venus in ascendent; Mercury in exile and in descent.
Sagittarius	Fire; warmth; dryness; masculinity; positive; beauty; autumn.	Overture; facility; synthesis; defiance; independence; risk; joyful.	Horse; wild boar.	Tin.	Carbuncle; turquoise.	Cherry tree.	Thighs; hips; liver.	Diurnal domicile of Jupiter; Mercury in exile.
Scorpio	Cold; humidity; night; obedience.	Roundabout way; secret; curiosity; research; critical; auto-destruction; obstinacy; occult strength and fertility; fermentation; indiscipline; death; anxiety.	Reptiles; scorpion.	Iron; platinum.	Loadstone; Arti-haematite; topaz.	Artichoke; belladonna.	External; genital organs; bladder; sinus.	Nocturnal domicile of Mars; Venus and Proserpine are in exile; Moon in descent.

Signs of Zodiac	Characters	Affinities	Colors	Animals	Metals	Minerals	Plants	Part of the Body	Planets
Taurus	Fertility; instinctive, self-willed power; solidity; matter; avarice.	Earth; cold; night; spring; fertility.	White; green.	Bull.	Bronze; brass.	Alabaster; agate; white coral; emerald.	Almond tree.	Neck; larynx; endocrine system; ears.	Domicile of Proserpine and nocturnal of Venus; Moon in ascendent; Mars in exile.
Aquarius	Humanity; universality; current; collectivity; briskness.	Air; warmth; masculinity; positive; violence; winter; danger.			Lead.	Black pearl; sapphire.	Snake-weed.	Legs; ankles; blood circulation.	Domicile of Saturn and of Uranus; Sun in exile.
Virgo	Instinctive; hidden life; secret; multiplicity.	Cold; night; earth; dryness; sterility; vitality; femininity.		Goose; bear.	Mercury.	Jasper; silex.	Wood.	Intestines; gall-bladder; abdomen; assimilation.	Domicile of Mercury; Jupiter and Neptune are in exile; Venus in descent.

PLANETARY TYPOLOGY

TYPES	Affinity System Glandular-Type	Morphological Characteristics	Physiological Characteristics	Psychological Characteristics	Astrological Attributes	Astrological Affinity (Zodiac)
JUPITERIAN	Hypersurrenal, apopleptic.	Wide forehead, auburn hair, early baldness, clear eyes, short nose, full mouth, sturdy body, gestures a little clumsy.	Solidity, resistance and absorption, plumpness, hypertension, fragile liver.	Social, good, generous, just, sensual, methodical, organizer, taste for honor, expansion, brightness.	Warmth, dryness, masculinity, order, balance, cohesion.	Sagittarius Pisces
LUNAR	Hypothyroideal, nutritive.	Well-rounded, soft, thick hair, short nose, broad—often fat.	Favorable, chronic debility.	Imagination and memory for details, dreamer, subordinate, passivity.	Cold, dampness, femininity, negativity.	Cancer
MARTIAN	Hyperhypo-physical, inflammatory.	Low forehead, short hair, nose broad at base, thin mouth, square chin, solid, angular, medium stature.	Congestive, blood, brutal, early impotence, kidney and eye trouble.	Impulsive, choleric, undisciplined, intellectually limited, military excellence, brutal but courageous, conquest, sadism.	Warmth, dryness, fire, masculinity, materialist.	Aries Scorpio

TYPES	Affinity System Glandular-Type	Morphological Characteristics	Physiological Characteristics	Psychological Characteristics	Astrological Attributes	Astrological Affinity (Zodiac)
URANIAN	Spasmodic.	Singularization.	Mutation, independence.	Original, changing, rebellious.	Originality.	Aquarius
MERCURIAN	Unstable, thyroideal, neural.	Dull complexion, pointed chin, thin nose, oval face, bulging forehead, agile, fine bones, adroit.	Strong nervous, neuro-arthritis troubles.	Curiosity, ingenuity, good orator, diplomatic, even 'arranger', mobility, polymorphous, movement, adaption.	Mobility, infiltration, hermaphroditism, polymorphism.	Gemini Virgo
SATURNIAN	Hyposurrenal, depressive, atonic.	Bony, big eyes, sad, thin, tall, not very muscular.	Prematurely old, eats much without gaining weight, subject to broken bones.	Distrust, pessimism, solitary and anxious, systematic mind, undistinguished, collector, inhibition.	Preservation, usury, tightness, cold, dryness, earth.	Capricorn

TYPES	Affinity System Glandular-Type	Morphological Characteristics	Physiological Characteristics	Psychological Characteristics	Astrological Attributes	Astrological Affinity (Zodiac)
SOLAR	Hyperthyroidism, Energetic.	Long curly hair, broad forehead, wide-eyed, fine nose, defined mouth, elegance, balance, long muscles, fine bones.	Assimilates with easy effort, not continuous, fragility, lung, heart, especially respiratory.	Facility, harmony, much influence and enthusiasm, curious, generous, artistic, brilliant, completeness, maturity, individualization.	Radiating, harmony, power, warm, dry, masculine, positive.	Leo
PLUTONIAN	Impulsive.	Vivacity.	Gruffness, destruction.	Explosive character, aggressive, sadistic.	Violence.	
VENUSIAN	Hypolypophysary, sympathetic.	Gracious, thick hair, supple, wide eyes, fine nose, plump, small mouth, dimples, good proportions, beautiful legs.	Fragility of ligaments, often stout.	Feminine, greedy, sensual, gay, seductive, not very intellectual, attraction, beauty.	Harmony, sweetness, seduction, intimacy, warmth, dampness, femininity, passivity.	Taurus Libra
NEPTUNIAN	Comatic.	Assimilation.	Integration.	Collectivization.	Fluidity.	

GEOMANTIC AFFINITIES

Figures	Zodiac	Planets	Elements	Metals	Gems	Colors	Perfumes	Senses	Body Organ	Day	Weather	Duration
Acquisitio	Pisces	Jupiter	Air	Tin	Amethyst	Purple	Sandal-wood	Smell	Liver, ovaries	Thurs	Fine	Year
Albus	Libra	Venus	Water	Copper	Coral	White	Rose	Touch	Veins, glands	Fri	Salubrious	Month
Amissio	Gemini	Mercury	Air	Mercury	Beryl	Azure blue	Myrtle	Perception	Peripheral nervous system	Wed	Dry	Hour
Caput draconis	Ascending knot	Lunar	Air	Brass	Cornelian, turquoise	Yellow	Cloves	Smell	Cerebellum	Thurs	Salubrious	Year
Cauda draconis	Descending knot	Lunar	Earth	Cast Iron	Haematite obsidian	Brown	Aloes	Hearing	Sympathetic nerve	Sat	Unhealthy	Year
Carcer	Capricorn	Saturn	Earth	Lead	Jasper	Black	Myrrh	Hearing	Skin, bone, spleen	Sat	Somber, frost	Several years
Conjunctio	Virgo	Mercury	Mercury	Mercury	Emerald opal	Rainbow colored	Ambergris	Perception	Intestine innervation	Wed	Cloudy, variable	Hour
Fortuna major	Leo	Sun	Fire	Fine gold	Amber diamond	Yellow gold	Incense	Sight	Right eye	Sun	Warm, dry	Year

GEOMANTIC AFFINITIES

Figures	Zodiac	Planets	Elements	Metals	Gems	Colors	Perfumes	Senses	Body Organ	Day	Weather	Duration
Fortuna minor	Leo'	Sun	Fire	Gold alloy	Topaz chrysolite	Yellow orange	Benzoin	Sight	Right eye	Sun	Warm, dry	Year
Laetitia	Sagittarius	Jupiter	Air	Bronze	Sapphire	Violet	Cinnamon	Smell	Arteries, liver, lungs	Thurs	Fine, light wind	Year
Populus	Cancer	Moon	Water	Fine silver	Pearl	Silver white	Iris	Sight	Left eye, stomach	Mon	Very rainy	Month
Puella	Taurus	Venus	Earth	Copper	Emerald	Green	Lavender	Touch	Throat, sexual glands	Fri	Warm, humid	Month
Puer	Scorpio	Mars	Fire	Iron	Garnet	Bright yellow	Muse	Taste	External genital organs	Tues	Warm, dry	Month
Rubeus	Aries	Mars	Fire	Steel	Ruby	Red	Carnation	Taste	Head, blood	Tues	Stormy	Month
Tristitia	Aquarius	Saturn	Earth	Lead	Jet	Jet black	Galbanum	Hearing	Endocrine glands	Sat	Cold, dry, dark	Several years
Via	Cancer	Moon	Water	Silver alloy	Moonstone	Broken white	Camphor	Sight	Stomach, left eye	Mon	Humid	Month

BIBLIOGRAPHY

General Works
de Plancy, C.: *Dictionnaire Infernal,* Paris, 1862.
Barret and Besterman: *The Divining Rod,* Methuen, London, 1926.
Fielding, J.: *Strange Superstitions and Magical Practices,* Philadelphia, 1945.

Alchemy
Jung, C. G.: *Psychology and Alchemy,* Zurich, 1944.

Astrology
Hutin, S.: *Astrology—Science or Superstition?,* Bay Books, Sydney, 1972.

Shamanism
de Martino, E.: *Magic—Primitive & Modern,* Bay Books, Sydney, 1972.

Devil and Sorcery
Tondriau & Villeneuve: *A Dictionary of Devils & Demons,* Bay Books, Sydney, 1972.

Hypnotism and Suggestion
Chauchard, P.: *Hypnosis and Suggestion,* Paris, 1951.
Rhodes, R. H.: *Curative Hypnosis,* Elek Books, London, 1954.

Magic
de Martino, E.: *Magic—Primitive & Modern,* Bay Books, Sydney, 1972.
Levi, E.: *Transcendental Magic,* Rider, London, 1968.

Mancies
Real, P.: *Interpret Your Dreams,* Flash Books, 1968.

Parapsychology
West, Dr. D. J.: *Guide to Parapsychological Tests,* 1953.

Spiritualism and Metapsychics
Carington and Fodor: *Poltergeists Down the Centuries,* Rider, London, 1953.
Thurston, H.: *Ghosts and Poltergeists,* Burn Oats, London, 1954.
Tondriau and Real: *Yoga,* Flash Books, 1962.